From the same author

From the Moment We Met:
The Astrology of Adult Relationships

Relationship astrology – synastry – is not just an exploration
of compatibility and possibility; it calls us to honour the
mystery and soul of our attachments – not for what we want
them to be, but for how they truly are. *From the Moment
We Met* offers a guide through the labyrinth of astrological
symbols and images towards a clearer understanding and
acceptance of your adult relationships.

The Family Legacy:
Astrological Imprints on Life, Love & Relationships

Images of the soul of a family are encoded into the symbols
of the horoscope, therefore each individual's natal horoscope
is systemic – its multidimensional symbols revealing the
family system through time. *The Family Legacy* invites
you to deepen your understanding of your place in the
family portrait by participating with the evocative symbols
embedded in your horoscope.

Vocation:
The Astrology of Career, Creativity and Calling

Your vocation is soulful; a deeply felt longing to be of
service, to follow your passion and to live a meaningful
life. Astrology is an ideal career counsellor, as it maps out
the paths and patterns of your vocation. Using astrological
symbols and images, *Vocation: the Astrology of Career,
Creativity and Calling* is your guide to participating in a
more fulfilling career and lifestyle.

ISBN: 978-0-9944880-5-3

First edition published 2019 by Astro*Synthesis
PO Box 111
Stanley, Tasmania 7331
Australia
www.astrosynthesis.com.au

The author can be reached at: brian@astrosynthesis.com.au

Charts calculated using Solar Fire software
Cover Designer: Cat Keane
Proof-reader: Jane Struthers
Project Manager and Layout: Frank C. Clifford

Cover Image: *Night* by Edward Robert Hughes (1851–1914). While his painting *Night With Her Train of Stars* is better known, this image spoke to me, as if it were a personification of the *anima* of the night sky. Night is the theatre where the symbols of the horoscope emerge from backstage to become animated and evocative images – ones that find their voice through the artistry of astrology.

Use of lines from *Renascence* by Edna St. Vincent Millay
courtesy of Holly Peppe, Literary Executor, Millay Society (Millay.org).
All other poems cited are in the public domain.

SOUL, SYMBOL and IMAGINATION

The Artistry of Astrology

BRIAN CLARK

Astro*Synthesis

Acknowledgements

Astrology A Cosmic Science was the first book I read that introduced me to a soulful way of thinking about the artistry of astrology. It was 1972 and it was the 'spiritual' connection that spoke most clearly to me, but its author Isabel Hickey also spoke eloquently about soul and the magnitude of horoscope symbols. I was blessed to cross paths with Issie, as she was affectionately known, and her Star Rovers. Thank you Issie for opening the gate onto a magical pathway.

Our worldwide astrological family overflows with grace, warmth, humour, creativity, talent and wisdom and I thank each of you who have contributed to my way of thinking about the art of astrology and the many who have kindheartedly welcomed me into your community. At home in Australia I have been supported by colleagues, students and clients and their kindness, generosity and acknowledgment has infinitely enriched my life in ways I could never have imagined.

Thank you Narelle for your sponsorship of our Sydney Soul Seminars which helped me focus my gaze; Tom and Geoffrey for your soulful guidance, and Team Frank – Jane, Cat and Frank – for putting it all together.

Without Suzanne, Cameron, Melissa, Michaela, Lexi, Christina, Trinity, Alexandra, Lachlan and Glennys, my soul would never have sung.

And to you, the reader. May astrology touch your soul with its rich imagination and depth of insight,

Brian Clark
July 2019
Stanley, Tasmania

TABLE OF CONTENTS

Renascence

The world stands out on either side
No wider than the heart is wide;
Above the world is stretched the sky,—
No higher than the soul is high.

The heart can push the sea and land
Farther away on either hand;
The soul can split the sky in two,
And let the face of God shine through.

But East and West will pinch the heart
That cannot keep them pushed apart;
And he whose soul is flat—the sky
Will cave in on him by and by[1]

Edna St Vincent Millay
'Renascence'

– PREFACE –
THE FINE ART OF ASTROLOGY

I remember clearly my first 'professional' astrological consultations over forty years ago; *professional*, because I began advertising my services as an astrological practitioner and charging fees. I remember too the immense responsibility and apprehension I felt. At the time, there was very little literature or conversation about astrological consulting; therefore, each consultation became a hands-on learning experience. I was not aware that astrology would become my life profession, but as I look back over these years I can see how my vocational journey opened out onto an expansive, unique and enriching field.

Clients from all walks of life and differing social, religious and ethnic backgrounds made appointments. With every client, I felt as if I was starting the astrological experiment all over again. I imagined my consulting room as both a sacred and a private space, closed off from the outer world during the ninety minutes that the client/s and I engaged in the consultation process. For the first few years of practice, my consulting room was in my house and the time I spent cleaning and rearranging both the house and the room felt as if I was tilling the ground in preparation for the consultation. This awareness of organizing the space to welcome the client always remained, as the ritual of preparing is an integral part of the consulting process. It was as if I was inviting not only the client into the space, but the gods as well. When I finally had my own dedicated consulting room, I intentionally chose the pictures, décor, statues and sculptures. At the time I was unaware that this was my attempt to create a psychic space where the unconscious could be present in a safe environment without judgement.

What was shared and revealed in these astrological sessions was often so intimate and private that an intense relationship was forged with the client in that moment. I never knew into what territory the consultation would lead us. While the horoscope offered clues as to the matters we might discuss, as much as possible I let the client lead the journey until the symbols of the horoscope began to speak. At the beginning of my practice I was unaware that the symbols could speak, since I was so focused on how to interpret them. Equipped with an armada of techniques, I was conscientious and mindful of how I might explain these images without the astrological jargon that meant so much to me but was a foreign language to the client. I discovered it was not the explanation, but the engagement with the client, being fully present and participating in the moment with the symbols, that really mattered.

As a novice I was trained to see the astrological symbols through descriptive and often prescriptive eyes, feeling pressure to delineate what I saw. Often an image would arrive unbidden or I would sense something beyond the traditional meaning of the astrological symbol. Over time I began to recognize how the presence of and participation with the symbol could open up the conversation and transport us to a place beyond my knowledge and sometimes beyond the client's. The symbol was contained through its astrological correspondences. As the symbols began to reveal themselves in this way, I was led beyond the realm of my training and understanding. Astrology opened up other worlds to me.

Astrology called me. From my mid teens I had always been fascinated with other dimensions of reality, but in these early days my vocabulary was not diverse enough to describe what I meant by this. I recognized another world that was spiritual, not material. When applying the methods and techniques of astrology, I felt as if I was researching my life purpose, discovering unidentified characteristics in myself and others, questioning the authenticity of my beliefs and values. It was a study unlike anything else I had done before, as it encouraged self-reflection and examination. It invited my full participation, not just my intellect.

Later I found words like *Self, individuation* and *heroic journey* which were somewhat descriptive of the process, but words were never enough. It was the personal stories of my clients and the myths of our human collective that brought astrology to light. Conversations with my clients and their horoscopes led me into areas of life I had not yet encountered, nor quite understood. Therefore, counselling training became imperative to improve my ability to sit with the client through their pain, suffering, tears, betrayals, losses, confusion, despair, traumas and, at times, triumphs. I also sought out a sympathetic psychologist for supervision in order to talk about some of the processes taking place with me when I was engaged with clients. I sat in a psychic development circle, attended a regular dream group, studied Jungian psychology and went back to university to complete a Masters in Classics and Archaeology. There was always more to learn about astrology, as new developments were always taking place. But, as a practitioner of the art of astrology, I knew I needed to supplement my astrological learning with psychologically sound counselling practices and other philosophical worldviews to help me serve both astrology and the client.

As I reflect on my vocational journey, I see that astrology engages us in two dimensions of being: the rational and the imaginal, and that its symbols mediate the space between these worlds. The astrological symbols are portals to ways of knowing Life. As a practice which involves the archetypal world of ideas, images and symbols, it places the practitioner between the event and the experience, as the one who can see through the literal to the symbolic. Therefore, astrology is so much more than a predictive and prescriptive typology: it is a soulful and evocative practice. While my clients were often seeking answers and solutions to problems, I recognized that connecting with meaning and insight around their predicament seemed to be more valuable than a concrete answer. That was what drew them to my consulting room: not the problem, nor the answer, but the chance to engage in another way to understand what was happening to them. Paradoxically, in not knowing the answers or how the astrological images might manifest in the future, I could hear the symbols speak. Rather than trying to find them, they found me. It was the symbols that led me and the client to explore more fully and deeply the geography of the soul. For me it was, and still is, a magical practice.

Relocating to north-west Tasmania in 2014 heralded a slower pace of life and work. Astrology had been my vocation for over forty years and my full-time career for over thirty. Though we might change our profession, retire from our work or start a new occupation, vocation is intimately part of who we are. While the rhythm of my work altered, my vocation did not change; but now I had more time to contemplate my astrological life. Early one morning, during this period, I awoke with a table of contents from a book inscribed in my mind's eye. I recognized that the list of chapters I saw was a way of organizing my thoughts, experiences and reflections. I recorded the table of contents as I saw it, and that morning, five years ago, I began writing what you are reading now.

This book is reflective in nature. It is not a 'how to' book, nor a book of 'techniques'. What I hope it is, is a book of questions about the fine art of astrology and what happens when engaging in its mystery. If you are a student or practitioner of astrology, you have already encountered its magic. Although it has not always been an easy task, I have tried to be true to my experience as an astrologer to present my ways of thinking about the process of astrological consultation and connection. My reflections are notes to myself about this paradoxical non-linear world, which parallels the literality of the horoscope. In the following pages I look at the art of astrology through different lenses to amplify my experiences. In trying to conceptualize my own understanding, I have drawn on the wonderful ideas of many others who have explored similar otherworldly terrains from which astrology originates. Carl Jung's and James Hillman's psychological explorations are highly resonant for me, as the archetypal topography they charted is akin to the psychic landscapes I encountered in my astrological consultations and work. Thomas Moore's writing on attending to the soul in our everyday lives has been enormously enriching and inspiring. Poets, especially the Romantic poets, stir my passion for romancing imagination, and I have gratefully borrowed some of their verse. My astrological community has a host of articulate symbolic thinkers who have enriched and inspired my understanding: Liz Greene and Geoffrey Cornelius are two such contemporary perceptive astrologers whose work I greatly admire.

Describing the art is difficult. Astrology has an elusive quality and is hard to pin down. As it is complicated, if not impossible, to articulate, I often reach for others' ideas or explanations to relieve my uncertainty when struggling to express my understanding. I have tried to be true to my own experiences, not to intellectualize or moralize, but I cannot guarantee that I have always been successful. My task was to try to find my voice. What a difficult task, as often there are no words for the insightful encounter with psyche; attempts to speak about this often flatten the soulful experience. So much remains contained in the privacy, intimacy and mystery of the astrological symbols.

Astrology can be engaged in intellectually without psyche. It can be studied from the perspective of its rich cultural history, its development of theory and techniques or its mathematical symmetry. It is exceptional in charting the natural cycles of time both personally and collectively. As part of our culture and history, it is scholastically valued through the translations of its ancient texts and its affiliation and enmeshment with other forms of divination, healing, magic practices and mystery rites. But when psyche is engaged in astrological practice, something stirs, as if the soul has been heard and valued. What arises is not easily explicable. Its symbols are not causal; its revelations are not quantifiable. I can testify to the profundity of the art, but I cannot explain it. What happens in an astrological consultation belongs in that moment, sealed by psyche in its timeless vessel. So much remains in the intimacy and privacy of the consultation. Therefore, while case studies are valuable for teaching and verifying techniques, they cannot do justice to the soul, as it defies explanation and exposition. I have tried to offer some examples, not to validate astrology but to acknowledge its mystery.

Through the course of this book I endeavour to amplify the experience of soul or the psychic encounter in astrological practice through various lenses such as imagination, time, symbol, metaphor, night, creativity, symptom, fate, death, myth, vocation, place and dream: ways that soul breaches the surface of the horoscope. How can we begin to explore a more soulful application of astrology without conceptualizing or defining soul, but by acknowledging its mystery and ambiguity in astrological work? My hope is that I can draw on my experiences without too much explanation or rationalization so that a connection to soul in your astrological work can be acknowledged and valued in your own way.

Hence I begin with the question of soul, as for me it is at the heart of astrology.

– PROLOGUE –
CONSIDERING SOUL

Our birth is but a sleep and a forgetting:
The Soul that rises with us, our life's Star,
Hath had elsewhere its setting,
And cometh from afar[2]

William Wordsworth,
'Ode on Intimations of Mortality from
Recollections of Early Childhood'

The question of soul – *our life's Star* – is fundamental to astrological practice and tradition. Each horoscope is an invitation to consider the gods that live through us and the archetypal powers that pave our path of life. However we consider soul, whether it is thought of as psyche, our inner life or perhaps the true or divine self, to an astrologer the symbols of the horoscope are keys that potentially unlock gates into its otherworldly realm. We may conceive of this double or secondary world as imaginary, psychic or spiritual; yet no matter how we conceptualize this place, this is where we encounter the sacred shards of soul.

Reflections on soul and its relationship to the horoscope vary considerably throughout astrological tradition depending on the epoch, the practitioner, their spiritual beliefs and philosophical orientation. Even though soul is ambiguous, defies description and is open to interpretation and imagination, it is the essence of astrological ritual. This question of soul is the heartbeat of astrology. Soul's early roots were associated with the breath of life in the body.

Yet soul conveys something more than just breath – it is what gives life its depth, meaning and substance. Soul resonates with the inner life, embracing our private and spiritual self-essence, creative expression, even the vocation we are meant to follow. As an image of the life breath, soul authenticates the natal horoscope, which could be likened to a lifelong meditation on the first breath of life. The horoscope is akin to soul.

Symbols are the language of the soul. Through the auspices of astrological images and symbols, the practice of horoscopy kindles the connection to our essential nature. Horoscope symbols stimulate contemplation about living a heartfelt life and inspire revelations about our inner world and spiritual character. It is as if the symbols animate the horoscope, opening a new dimension that allows a deeper, unseen meaning to emerge. Like the soul itself, the horoscope spans two worlds: the incarnate and the heavenly; it can exist in the past, the present or the future while still remaining timeless. To imagine and work with the symbols of the horoscope as a way to affirm and animate this life force *ensouls* the practice of astrology.[3] I imagine the horoscope to be like a vivid dream: the dream of one's life. And, like a dream, it calls us to participate in a conversation with our soul whatever we might imagine that to be.

With no context or ways of thinking about soul, astrological practice can drift on a sea of ungrounded impressions and intuitions. When astrological practice succumbs to a mechanistic model, symbols become rationalized as the expression of a cosmic order; no longer symptoms of the soul, but causal signs. Without the inquiry into soul, astrological symbols remain fixed in literality, facts rather than images, interpretations rather than revelations. Without the depth that soul engages us in, astrology becomes a static form rather than a dynamic process. Engaged with soul, countless impressions are summoned up that are difficult, at times impossible, to articulate; yet this is the nature of soul.

Through time soul has accounted for the amorphous, yet eternal, aspect of the self that is freed from the body at death, a divine essence that needs to be saved from sin, even the 'wow' factor in a piece of uplifting music. Food, cities and buildings have been described as having soul. It is not material, but can be sensual and deeply felt; therefore its nature is of two worlds. Evocative, soul conjures up a collection of ideas, images, beliefs and feelings; but one thing seems common, which is that soul appears unworldly and eternal. It is an invisible quality that breathes life into the life, a smouldering ember that becomes a passionate flame. Soul cannot be manufactured or commoditized, but is present in an ephemeral thought, a profound experience, in reflective and timeless moments or in feeling the anguish of being human. Words such as alive, appetite, breath, character, chi, consciousness, essence, force, ghost, heart, inner life, mind, morality, spirit, virtue, vocation, warmth and wisdom[4] suggest its presence.

Our 'life's Star' has been likened to an acorn and a seed, linked with our destiny and our purpose, guided by a *daimon*, a genius or a guardian angel. The enduring heavens, full of images, also evoke these mysteries of soul, destiny, fate and calling. Astrology's skyscape is and always has been a living museum for the stories of the soul.

Philosophically, soul has been a prime consideration. Over time soul has become annexed to religious doctrines, philosophical theories and New Age concepts, becoming entangled with notions of morality and spirituality, which exploit the concept of soul. Its commercialization institutionalizes its mysteries and abandons soul to a product. When randomly used, the word is no longer imaginative, but glib and ordinary. Or sometimes, as Adolf Guggenbühl-Craig expresses, the usage can be 'embarrassing'.

> Now 'soul' is a difficult term to use. Some psychologists avoid it, trying to create a psychology without soul. Others replace the religious-sounding 'soul' with the more neutral 'psyche'. I am all for employing the word 'soul', yet, when used too often, it sounds pompous or sentimental. There is no way out: if you don't use the word 'soul' you avoid the basic issue of psychology; use it too often and it becomes embarrassing.[5]

Similarly for astrologers, 'there is no way out'. No matter how we conceive of it, soul is at the heart of astrological handiwork. It is always there, beyond the interpretations, the astrological analysis and theorizing. As a consulting astrologer I deeply felt I needed my own way of thinking about soul; therefore I followed some threads through time to help me feel comfortable with this question of soul.

From an ancient perspective, soul was the life energy that entered the body at birth and left at death. It was the essence of life, the breath, carried on the wind or borne lightly on the wings of a butterfly. The word 'soul' first enters western literature in the Homeric epic *The Iliad* around the 8th century BCE. By the Classical period, three centuries later, soul had undergone a significant semantic amplification cultivated through the philosophy of Plato, Aristotle and the Stoics. Through subsequent periods soul remained a perpetual focal point of inquiry for all philosophers. The doctrines of subsequent practices like theosophy, anthroposophy and psychology continually redeveloped the understanding of soul. Similarly, astrology was not immune to the changing conceptualizations of soul.

In Greek, the closest word to the English soul is *psyche*; in Latin, *anima*.[6] 'Psyche' characterizes a mix of indefinable ideas such as soul, mind and spirit derived from the Greek *psychein*, to breathe or blow, continuing the tradition of linking soul and breath.[7] *Psyche*, as an animating spirit or soul, entered the English language by the mid 17th century. By the early 20th century it was associated with the amalgam of thoughts, emotions and behaviours[8] or *psychology*, which suggests the study of the human soul. A *psychologist* implies a student of the soul; hence to me astrologers, in the spirit of the word, are in essence psychologists.[9] From antiquity to modernity, soul remained a fluid and indeterminable idea, best amplified and imagined like a symbol itself.

Psyche incarnated late into Greek myth. While important concepts, virtues, qualities and feelings like Justice, Peace, Health, Love and Retribution were personified as goddesses or heroines, Soul/Psyche was not embodied by the early Greeks, even though by the Classical period soul had become aligned with the image of a butterfly. In representations of her creation, Athena places a butterfly on the head of Prometheus as an image of ensouling the first man. I find it curious that the notion of soul, so important to poets and philosophers, does not anthropomorphize until later antiquity. In the 2nd century CE, Psyche became immortalized as the partner of Amor (Eros) through the pen of the Latin writer Apuleius in his unusual novel *The Golden Ass*. This pairing of Soul and Eros is not only a much loved story of a heroine overcoming the odds to find love, but is both allegory and myth.

Eros is Psyche's soulmate. Unlike Psyche, Eros incarnated early in Greek myth, being one of the five primal deities that emerged out of Chaos, the gaping void and womb of creation. As a primal force of creation, Eros is many things. Essentially he humanizes the desire for life and union; no wonder Psyche and Eros are united, as the theme of life and soul is fundamental and universal.

A millennium before the old woman told the tale of Psyche and Eros in *The Golden Ass*, the Greeks had already developed a notion of psyche, evident in *The Iliad*. Psyche left the body on death and became a shade, the ghost-like mirror image or *eidolon* of the person while alive. The legacy from the Homeric period was that the soul could still be imagined after death. Thereafter the notion that psyche was the life essence of an individual and connected to life in all its forms became established. Soul needed to be lived. It was seen as separate to the body; hence Hippocratic medicine differentiated between the illnesses of the body and those of the soul.

In early epics, qualities like courage and passion were assigned to the soul. Playwrights from the 5th century BCE referred to the soul's desire, pleasures, emotions and virtues, aligning the soul with morality.[10] Plato reshaped the ideas he inherited on soul, endowing it with wits and aligning it with an intelligible life form. His discourses characterize mental and psychological aspects belonging to the soul, not the body – soulful ideas that continue to echo through our modern discourses.

And so the philosophical enquiry throughout antiquity about whether the soul is separate from the body, whether it leaves, returns, even reincarnates, continued. During creative transitions, such as the Renaissance, the question of soul was philosophically renewed, finding an expression through other mediums including painting and prose. The Romantic period also brought the soulful dimension of purity, beauty and suffering to life through the imagery and words of poets like John Keats.

Soul-making

In a letter, John Keats reminded his brother of Psyche's late incarnation: 'the goddess was never worshipped or sacrificed to with any of the ancient fervour – and perhaps never thought of in the old religion: I am more orthodox than to let a heathen Goddess be so neglected.'[11] As a Romantic poet, Keats could not neglect Psyche, not just because she was the embodiment of beauty, but because her suffering through her trials of life was 'soul-making'.

Keats's interest in Psyche's anguish inspired him to reflect on the world as the 'vale of soul-making'.[12] A few days before he copied his *Ode to Psyche* in his journal, he wrote to his brother:

I say 'Soul-making'... Do you not see how necessary a World
of Pains and troubles is to school an Intelligence and make
it a Soul. A Place where the heart must feel and suffer in a
thousand diverse ways![13]

His words resonated through me when I read them for the first time.
Keats accentuates the poles of beauty and suffering as layers of the
soul, but he also locates the incarnate and worldly experience as
being where soul is crafted. Keats's 'World of Pains' was the 'vale
of soul-making', the place where a meaningful relationship between
the suffering and trials of the body in the world and the beauty of
the soul could be felt. Like Apuleius, Keats is struck by Psyche's
trials which were 'soul-making', an active process of working with
soul. The ancients knew the act of ensouling, but now Keats gives
us a new verb for it: 'soul-making'.

The majority of my clients come for an astrological consultation
to contextualize and understand their suffering; therefore I found
Keats's image of our worldly trials as the 'vale of soul-making' not
only inspiring but enormously helpful. I applied this image to the
horoscope, which for me is an imaginative map of this vale. Keats
helped me see that active participation and work with the symbols
of the horoscope is in itself soul-making. I recognized in myself, as
well as many of my students and clients, how the images evoked by
the horoscope offer ways to participate with our trials and pains, not
from an analytic or causal perspective, but from a soulful one. The
horoscope infuses the mundane world with meaning and connection
through the medium of its symbols and images.

Reflecting on Soul
Inspired by Keats, James Hillman began his manuscript *Re-
Visioning Psychology* with: 'This book is about *soul-making*'.[14] In
his efforts to realign soul with psychology, Hillman introduced an
archetypal psychology that addressed life as *psychological* in its
authentic sense: that is, the study of the soul and its connection
to life. Similarly, astrological intelligence can be aligned with the
process of soul-making, as it orders and makes meaning of our
worldly trials through the study of the starry heavens.

Hillman's early reflections identified four aspects of the soul. For
me his delineation of the soul as the unknown component which

engenders meaning, turns events into experiences, is communicated in love and has a religious concern, is a wonderfully succinct beginning to reflect on soul and the horoscope. In *Re-Visioning Psychology* Hillman added 'three necessary modifications'. He suggested that soul is the deepening of events into experiences, its religious concern derives from its special *relation with death* and that soul is the imaginative possibilities in our nature.[15]

Twenty-one years after the publication of *Re-Visioning Psychology*, Hillman published *The Soul's Code*, a more contemporary contemplation on the essence of soul reaching back to Plato's Myth of Er to draw inspiration for amplifying soul's companions of calling, fate, *daimon* and necessity. Hillman used the 'acorn theory', which suggests that 'each person bears a uniqueness that asks it be lived and that is already present before it can be lived'.[16] Astrologers were already familiar with this thought, as it is central to the system of astrology, as well as the idea underpinning Dane Rudhyar's conceptualization of a transpersonal astrology. The horoscope is a time-honoured tradition that has continuously embraced Hillman's 'acorn theory'. As the spokesperson for realigning soul with psychology, Hillman leaves a legacy of how contemporary astrologers might consider soul.

Hillman suggests that soul is not a concept but a symbol that resists definition in the same way as all symbols.[17] Symbols convey meaning beyond the limit of any definition that we could give them. In the same way, soul defies a limited view or fixed definition and perhaps is better described in the ancient way as fluid, porous, flighty and permeable.[18] Soul is a perspective, a way of seeing or thinking, a symbol rather than a fixed point of view or belief. And, like the horoscope, the soul offers us its riddles to be divined.

Ironically, what is so deeply personal, so interior to my being, so private and so soulful, cannot be said to be mine, as soul is not ruled by my personality nor managed by my will. While there are many traditions and ways to view the soul in relationship to body and even spirit, it is never aligned with self-image or ego. As the early Greeks suggested, soul is ethereal and relatively autonomous.[19] Hence, for a consulting astrologer, some of the deepest and most profound work with our clients and our students remains private and sacred. Astrological expertise belongs to the soul, not the personality.

On Psyche's Wings

Psyche is the root for many of our modern words which refer to this human fusion of thoughts, spirituality and desires. For instance, *psychosomatic* aligns body and soul, addressing the interface between the two; *psychopathology* refers to the suffering of the soul while *psychosis* proposes the idiosyncrasies of the soul. In a technological world that no longer has ways of thinking about soul, Psyche's words become diagnostic and clinical, ailments to be fixed or medicated, rather than essential aspects of our nature.

Soul defies description, let alone translation. As psychoanalysis was establishing itself, seeking respect as a systematic and orderly discipline, it seemed necessary to distance itself from the mystifying and unstructured 'soul' which had become patented by religious institutions. The objective-sounding 'psyche' aroused less scepticism.

Psychoanalysts were keen to align their discipline with medicine and science rather than religion and faith; hence, delineating psychic disorder rather than soul trauma became more acceptable. Soul remained a symbol of the night while psyche became its daytime counterpart.

As an overarching symbol, soul is unbound by human prescription, defying categorization and conclusion. Carl Jung experienced the split between the established scientific and scholarly avenues with his own imaginative and instinctive experience of soul/psyche. Jung's conversations with his soul, precognitive visions, automatic writing, inner voices and creative imagination gave form to many of his original psychological ideas.[20] But in a world that valued literality and scientific proof, these sources could not be easily footnoted, nor acknowledged.

Astrologers too experience the pressure to be literal, predictive and certain; however, the horoscope invokes the symbolic and non-rational world where images, feelings, voices and sensations are the medium for clarity and insight. Practitioners are susceptible to falling into the gap between the factual and the imaginative, as astrological techniques are guides to a symbolic way of knowing. Without awareness, astrological techniques are championed as the reason for the successful judgement, rather than the key that unlocks the portal of imagination. This was why meditation on the soul became a valuable companion to my astrological practice, as it assisted me to understand another world not bound by physical, literal or rational parameters.

Acknowledging soul as a symbol that operates autonomously, outside the boundary of coherent thought and beyond scientific statutes, frees our capacity to see through the material to a soulful world where life has meaning and purpose. I feel that ensouling our everyday life is the essence of astrological work. To return to Hillman:

> By *soul* I mean, first of all, a perspective rather than a substance, a viewpoint towards things rather than a thing itself. This perspective is reflective; it mediates events and makes differences between ourselves and everything that happens.[21]

Horoscope symbols awaken images previously unknown to us. Like a dream, these images arrive unbidden, not while asleep but while being reflective and engaged in contemplating the symbols of the horoscope. In its capacity to mediate and link the inner world with the outer one, the astrological images of the horoscope assist in ensouling our world by rendering the trials of life meaningful, connective and coherent.

Soul is reflective, subjective and inward, offering meaning to worldly experiences so I can be involved with them, not just experience them as random, fated and/or disconnected. For me, soul is the capacity to symbolize an event or experience so that it might be felt, embodied and remembered, reminding me of the authenticity of all feeling, the eternity of all attachments and the sacredness of all life. In contemporary thinking soul is the uplifting 'X factor' that brings a piece of music alive, renders a poem inspiring, enlivens a theatrical performance or makes work meaningful. Soul animates the mundane world through creativity and connection, encouraging participation in and with the world. Having this appreciation of soul brings the horoscope and its connections to the outer world to life.

Objects become ensouled when they deepen our experience of being alive, strike a profound chord, stir a mysterious yearning or hold memory. Possessions that have soul are not manufactured or mass-produced. They might be uniquely crafted or creatively nurtured; a treasured gift, invested with care and attention or an *objet d'art* which has an embedded integrity. Soul has been systematically separated from most contemporary creative endeavours through mass production and economic rationalism. Our plastic, fast-food, self-service, New Age, pre-fabricated, digital world has left us bereft; as the title of one of Carl Jung's books suggests, we are modern man in search of a soul.[22] Similarly, astrology can be disconnected from soul when theory, academic proficiency, technical superiority, prediction and literality obscure the heartfelt inquiry that the horoscope invites.

I think of soul as an attitude. Foremost it respects life in all its manifestations, inner and outer. By nature it is paradoxical; it is eternal yet it is known only in the present. Soul is both incarnate and ephemeral. It is awakened through the beauty and suffering of the outer world, yet is invisible in itself. It deepens the quality of life; it stimulates and enchants. It is sacred. Soul is mystery. Yet, ironically, openness to its ambiguity and symbols leads us to a resonant knowing. I bring this attitude to mind when preparing a horoscope, remembering that soul is found in the mystery and not in clarity.

At the end of a recent consultation a regular client expressed her gratitude for our sessions and how meaningful they had been to her. She had done this before but this time I felt moved to ask her what her experience was, what was of meaning to her. She spoke eloquently about feeling authenticated and understood, 'as if my soul had been embraced by the cosmos'. She shared how important the night sky was to her as a child and that our consultations provided a space where she could reconnect to it in an imaginative way through the medium of the horoscope's symbols. She felt seen and acknowledged by the starry heavens, which she described as a feeling of being cared for and embraced by forces much larger than herself.[23] Jean is both an imaginative and practical individual, and like many she values the imaginative art of astrology, as its symbolic process inspires a soulful reconnection to the night sky. Like many others, Jean cannot explain through facts or evidence what she values about our appointments; it is through the heart that she demonstrates her appreciation.

Jean's imagination is the vital aspect of the process that allows her to engage with the horoscope. Through her imaginative faculties and willingness to participate with the astrological symbols, a door opens up onto the landscape of her soul.

IMAGINATION

So hopeless is the world without;
The world within I doubly prize;
Thy world, where guile, and hate, and doubt,
And cold suspicion never rise;
Where thou, and I, and Liberty,
Have undisputed sovereignty.

What matters it, that, all around,
Danger, and guilt, and darkness lie,
If but within our bosom's bound
We hold a bright, untroubled sky,
Warm with ten thousand mingled rays
Of suns that know no winter days?[24]

Emily Jane Brontë,
'To Imagination'

Imagination is often perceived as a whimsical pastime or an empty notion, belittled as 'fanciful' or dismissed quickly with a turn of phrase like 'my imagination is playing tricks on me'. To Emily Brontë, imagination was her *daimon*, her guide to a private world she particularly valued, uncontaminated by pollutants from the outer world. Imagination allowed her to see through to a more soulful realm, an inner site canopied under an 'untroubled sky'. This other world, by whatever names we might call it, has always been part of the human experience, never questioned by mystics, poets, artists or children.

For artists, including astrological artists, imagination is another way of knowing and perceiving. It is a means of seeing through the literal world. Many artists consider imagination to be a divine or inspired aspect of being human. This sentiment can be unsettling to many, especially if there is no framework within the culture to appreciate imagination. In contemporary western culture, what is not factual, proven, statistically verified or scientifically established is often deemed doubtful, far-fetched, a fantasy or false memory, banished to a wasteland with little credence or respect.

The faculty of imagination resides in a different hemisphere to the objectivity of logic. Often spontaneous and uninhibited, imagination perceives objects, experiences and ideas through symbols, images, associations, correspondences and metaphors. It is a subjective skill. As a result a society with little context for imagination or introspection is poorly equipped to understand, let alone appreciate, the profundity of imaginative handiwork like astrology, a prime example of disenfranchised imagination in my culture.

Creativity and artistry are often the exceptions to the appreciation of imagination, perhaps because something tangible or sensual is produced. Artistic expressions of imagination are housed in galleries and museums throughout the world. In these modern-day sanctuaries devoted to the Muses, imagination can be consistently appreciated and valued. But Urania, the Muse of Astrology, does not seem to fare as well as her sisters; perhaps her origins are too deeply entrenched in a destined and causal world.

Dane Rudhyar, a seminal voice in 20th-century astrology, was also a musician and painter. He compared astrological practice with artistic ability,[25] echoing earlier voices that had also valued astrology as an imaginative art.[26] He encouraged a symbolic deliberation on astrological signatures that liberated astrology from being merely observed from a rational and predictive perspective. Rudhyar felt that astrologers had sold out to science and literalism 'in order to gain some kind of recognition and respectability'.[27] But, in a modern world that values technical expertise over imagination, shaking off astrology's affiliation with 'literalism' for a new home in the Faculty of Arts would never be easy.

Astrology's Imagination

Astrology addresses the psychic dimension of personal experiences through analogies between cosmos and human experience, archetypal imagery, cyclic time, symbolic language and correspondences to ancient deities. It opens the doors of perception onto other ways of perceiving the world. Astrological images assist us to pre-tend and pre-view the world we inhabit. Because of its creative and symbolic language, astrology invites reflection on profound aspects of the human experience, which can acknowledge and confirm deep-seated and intimate feelings. Its affinity with cycles, the eternal return, time and timelessness, along with space and place, invite contemplation on the soul's odyssey.

The panoramic vault of the night sky, illuminated by the lamps of the planets and stars, rouses the faculty of imagination and it is the cosmological marriage of astronomical knowledge with the imagination that is the art of astrology. Astrology is an informed imagination; yet the vast majority of literature concentrates on the techniques and historical application of astrology. The role of imagination in astrology can be easily overlooked, due in part to the continued attempt to validate its systems from a purely causal approach. The intricacy involved in articulating the imaginative process is so very individual and private, which perhaps is why very little has been written on the process of imagination in astrology. Being ephemeral in nature, the imaginative process eludes us when we try to articulate it.

Interpreting the horoscope is like active imagination informed by symbols, signatures, images and traditions of horoscopy. When we engage with psyche's symbolic process, the sacred features underpinning our outer experiences can be deeply sensed and felt. Astrological imagination is not unbound, nor intuitively uninhibited, but held and safeguarded by the logic of the art.[28]

Like dreams, astrology resonates with the language of images, symbols, metaphors, riddles. But, unlike dreams, it does not arise solely out of one person's unconscious. It is a story from the collective imagination and tells its tale through the mystery of each individual's birth. As both a learned and imaginative discipline, astrology engages with personal and collective symbols that facilitate an ability to see through literal events and chronological time into memories, feelings and experiences obscured by rational intelligence. Astrology, as a servant of the imagination, is a vehicle for consciousness and a response to the soul's call for deeper meaning. Hence, our first calling to astrology is often a spiritual attempt to find connection to something beyond literal awareness. Carl Jung called imagination 'the mother of human consciousness',[29] as it nurtured our earliest efforts to be mindful of the soul before the advent of literacy and philosophy. Dialects of the imagination, such as myth, allegories, rituals, icons, signs and metaphors, are the agents of astrological revelation. The art of astrology engages us in an 'imaginative consciousness'.[30]

Imagination is neither fantasy nor intuition, although they are often confused because of their similarity. Memory and hallucination are also close allies but, again, subtly different. My experience has led me to value imagination as the faculty inspired by the symbols and signatures of the horoscope, which reveal meanings beyond my tangible, tactile perceptions and intellectual ideas and concepts. Sometimes this mode of knowing forms a picture: at times it is a moving image, at others it is like a photograph. Occasionally it is as if I hear an inner voice reading a script or it is as if someone is telling me a story, as thoughts move though me. All the while there is an observing part of me that is focused on listening and connecting the images and impressions into a coherent storyline. I know colleagues who experience this differently, like a form of astrological transference. One man feels it very viscerally, such as a pressure on the back of his neck, a sore shoulder, heartburn or a pressure on his arm. Another colleague has described her imaginative process as feeling, as her states can range from boredom to being overwhelmed, saddened or angry when engaging with a client and their horoscope. Others use the word 'intuitive' as a way of expressing how their imagination is accessed through a flash of inspiration or a vivid picture. It is as if there is a sudden engagement, as though one is being captured by the symbol. And all this seems to occur in a second. I have come to accept that there are many modalities of imagination. In a way they are elemental since imagination is an innate aspect of being human. I often wonder if each individual may have their own unique access to imagination through a specific astrological element or the alchemy of their unique temperament.

Imagination for an artist or poet guides their brush or pen. Images surface from a creative wellspring onto the canvas or paper, not cogently constructed, but arising from an amalgam of artistry and creativity. The rational plays a major role in their training and preparatory work, but it is imagination that guides the strokes of their brush or pen. Imagination for an astrologer arises from the sweeping symmetry of the heavens. Trained in the astronomy and harmony of the celestial spheres, imagination guides the astrologer to arrange their insights and forecasts through the cycles and symbols they are reading in the horoscope. Imagination is a form of vision that permits us to see through the material, to read what is not there, what is invisible. Like an X-ray it assists in seeing beneath the situation at hand.

The act of horoscopic interpretation is firmly rooted in astronomical premises, but its art is born from engaging with images that arise through the symbols, then considering and evaluating them in the context of the presenting client or situation. As the capacity to perceive what is not wholly present, imagination validates the presence of absence, inspires us to solve problems, to have theories, to produce, invent and play, but it also allows us to conceive of fictional worlds, create supernatural beings and dream of the structure of the cosmos. Imagination is cognitive flexibility and connectivity, as it brings unrelated ideas together and sees associations which have not been noticed before; an act that disturbs the dominance of the rational mind and the sanctuary of certainty and familiarity.

A horoscope can also be read directly from a theoretical and/or technical standpoint. Without the spice of imagination, the reading may still be informative and interesting, but is unlikely to pierce the mystery or evoke an intimacy that is possible beyond the pattern of the horoscope. Astrology speaks the language of the soul through its heavenly images.

Stories from the Imagination

There are many ways to imagine a horoscope. I have mentioned how I envisage it as the dream of one's life. Another way I imagine the horoscope is as the storybook of the soul. Like all fictional narratives it has the potential to awaken the imagination, to stir the soul and inspire me to reflect and remember.

If the horoscope is the narrative and the soul is its author, I, the astrologer, become its reader. The storybook is programmed in the code of the soul through the night sky's symmetry and symbols; therefore, as the reader I have to be both skilled and unknowing of the symbolic arrangements in the particular horoscope. Adept enough to be able to recognize the archetypal landscape and province of the symbol, technically proficient to gauge the archetypal condition, yet sufficiently open to allow what the symbol suggests to its author. Through poetry, metaphors, time frames, associations and correspondences I amplify the horoscopic symbols so the imagination of the client can stir memory, connection, empathy, insight and meaning, which feed back into our consultation. Astrological imagination brings disparate sensations, experiences and times of life together in a coherent pattern that offers a soulful way of thinking.

Reading a horoscope is complex, as the consultation creates an intimate and private space. Therefore I try to be as open and vulnerable as I can to what presents itself during the session. When called to interpret a horoscope, I am drawn away from my own experience to engage in relationship, not only with the person whose chart is before me, but with the soul of this person as well: their ideals, their morals, their beliefs, their experiences. Yet in the intimacy of the encounter my own feelings, memories and experiences are stirred, both by my imaginative response to the horoscope and by the client/other who is sharing their story with me.

I am also reliant on their participation and imagination to assist in connecting and linking the images that arise from the reading into a consistent pattern. In reading the narrative I become involved and intimate with the horoscope and its author, the soul. When I connect with the horoscope as the story of the soul I enter a realm outside my personality, which invites empathy, non-judgement, consideration and kindness. When the world beyond the factual and the literal is evoked, boundaries soften, a veil lifts and the spiritual, psychic, otherworldly realm becomes more accessible. It is as if astrological imagination evokes the stories of the soul, making them accessible and available to the self.

Another way I imagine the horoscope is as a wise counsellor and witness, which inspires me to contemplate my own and my clients' struggles. Its symbols help me to imagine the consequence of my actions and confront me with the ethical and moral aspects of any situation. Symbolic arrangements in the chart encourage me to see different ways of action through a playful encounter with the signs and images. They also support me to ask 'What if?' broadening my worldview from a fearful and self-limiting position to a more soulful and expansive one. The gift of imagination is that it offers hope and the possibility of improvement. At other times, specific and pragmatic counsel is revealed through the marriage of my astrological training with my imagination.

Imagination is fictional by nature; therefore to demonstrate it through a case study or chart example seems paradoxical. Horoscope case studies are excellent learning tools, but are often devoid of the imaginative story that underpins the attempt to demonstrate an interpretive version of a particular technique. Imagination may be better revealed by telling a story that brings the narrative of the horoscope into play. I also imagine astrology as storytelling, as if the horoscope were a moderator between the worlds of soul and literality. Each encounter with a client and their horoscope can be a moving and soulful exploration. However, this is never guaranteed, as it is dependent on the receptivity and participation of the client, as well as my own openness. The astrological consultation takes place in this field of relationship created by both the client's and the astrologer's personal and collective unconscious.

Ruth had barely sat down when she burst into tears. I pushed the box of tissues that are permanently on my consulting table closer towards her. She took one, looked down and said, 'I'm sorry'. I poured her a glass of water and waited a moment before I asked what she was sorry for. 'I have been a mess lately' she replied, 'crying all the time and I don't know why.'

That was not surprising to me: her Moon in Gemini in the 12th house was being aspected by Neptune on its passage through Pisces. This was one of the major transits in her chart at the time. An image arose in me of her standing on an isolated island with floodwaters rising around her. The image accompanied a feeling of being alone, trapped, helpless. Another image arose of her standing on a beach with wild waves crashing on the shore. When my imagination is stirred I know the consultation has begun for me. I wondered if aloneness and helplessness were the feelings that had brought her to the consultation. Or perhaps an inner tsunami was unsettling her, but where should I begin? How might I engage with her?

I felt confident that it had not been the first time these feelings had arisen. As I had been drawn to the Neptune transit of the Moon, I stayed with this image. Ruth was 51, so I thought I could begin by exploring the timeline of the transit, as it would have been astrologically significant about 41 years ago, when Neptune was in

Sagittarius transiting in opposition to her Moon. Neptune's cycle is 165 years, so 41 years represents a quarter of the cycle. There were other times in the Neptune–Moon cycle I could have chosen, but I instinctively chose this time. I felt strongly about this, so it was as if I were following an imaginative trail through Ruth's horoscope. I asked her: 'What can you remember around the age of 10?'

She seemed upset. 'Why are you asking?' I tried to explain that I was trying to find a way to begin to understand the feelings that might be speaking through her tears. 'But what does being 10 have to do with anything?' Ruth was puzzled, and so was I, so I explained that I was drawing on an image in her chart that linked these times together and wondered if there was a connection and, if so, perhaps we could unravel that. If not, we could try another door.

Ruth grabbed another tissue, wiped away more tears and told me that when she was 10 her sister drowned. Many other symbols in her chart were resonant with this image of loss and suffering. My task was to reflect back a meaningful way to think about all of this. Astrological techniques and psychological theory can open windows to the soul, but it is imagination that can breathe new life into the wounds that encase it. 'Where were you when this happened?' I asked.

'I was there,' she sobbed. She began to remember the flood of feeling: panic, loss, guilt, helplessness, as she stood on the shore watching her sister being swept away by a forceful wave that had suddenly appeared. Then she felt all her feelings freeze in the aftermath of the search for her sister, the mangled body, the parents' grief, the fatal silence. She did the best she could to return to life.

Ruth had come for the consultation because her daughter was leaving to work overseas for at least a year. She would be alone. Her husband had left after 10 years of marriage, another period of loss and helplessness, resonant with the psychic watermark outlined by the trauma of her 10-year old self. Ruth had then raised Jenny, her only child, on her own. Her initial reason to come for an appointment was to see if the chart could offer any insight into what she might do to fill the space created by her daughter's absence. She had no idea she would burst into tears as she sat in my consulting room chair. But now a series of losses had been strung together that helped her recognize patterns in time when she had felt alone and helpless.

Feeling adrift, at sea, tearful, she recognized her apologetic surrender to the force of her feelings, which at times were overwhelming. She likened them to the wave that took her sister. She recognized that she disconnected from these feelings by freezing them, leaving her in the cold, yet there they were in her unbidden floods of tears. Her next question was forceful: 'How do you think I could work with this pattern?' I felt permission to be able to address the symbol as if it were freed for that moment from the fear of loss. We returned to the present. From there we focused on the horoscope, imagining ways to participate with the overwhelming feelings in a personal way, to find the genuine sense of aloneness that her 12th house Moon needed. My technical understanding of the horoscope was my guide and container to explore the images in a hopeful and soulful way.

The sheer presence of a horoscope invites the imagination to play, for no matter the expectation or conscious agenda, the reality is that neither client nor astrologer knows where the symbols will lead. To the uninitiated the horoscope is a chart of squiggles and glyphs. To the astrologer it is a map of revelatory symbols; either way, it evokes an imaginal space. Therefore in an astrological consultation, no matter the intention or contract, there is a psychic reality that encloses both the astrologer and the client. And the shared psychic space that is created invites the client and the astrologer to imagine and participate in a meaningful discovery of the horoscope.

In this imaginal space I experience connections beyond explanation, what we might call synchronicity; sometimes spontaneous insights, which some may call intuition. For instance, why did I choose the time when Ruth was 10, when I could have chosen another transit to the Moon or another time in the Neptune cycle? Certainly my imagination was informed by the archetypal imagery of Neptune and its cycle as well as the 12th house Gemini Moon, hence the waves, the flooding, the helplessness; but how these images would give meaning to Ruth's life events and felt experience was a mystery. However we conceive of it, engagement with the horoscope invokes distinctive intervals where sensual and physical boundaries become porous, where a participation mystique can take place on levels beyond a rational paradigm.

As the reader of the horoscope I am not immune to becoming involved; at times, I am torn away from my observing and analytical perspective and also affected by the atmosphere of the in-between space. At these times my own memories and wounds are opened. Ruth did not know that my best friend had drowned when I was 19 years old, and when she described her terror-filled feelings on the day her sister drowned, I held tightly onto my memories of that Labour Day weekend when David drowned. Nor did Ruth know we shared the same Ascendant–Descendant degree, an astrological image that expressed a mutually sympathetic viewpoint on life. I now recognize that these synchronies are part of the topography of an astrological consultation. I have also learnt to contain my feelings and responses in service to the client.

While I feel it to be of great value to try and conceptualize imagination, as an astrologer I find it difficult to be succinct or specific about it, since it is a process always in flux. Imagination allows us to amplify the symbols which open up universal and collective correlations in a particularly individualistic way, dependent on the signatures of the horoscope. As we begin to discuss these associations in the consultation, a relational dialogue develops that can engage us both in a potentially transformative process, offering both a profound, often sacred acceptance of the Self.

And that cannot be delineated, nor factually proven, but it is experienced. This is our apprenticeship.

1

SYMBOL

The soul moves among symbols and unfolds in symbols.[31]

W. B. Yeats

As astrologers we participate with symbols every time we engage with a horoscope. Every horoscope invites us to inhabit its symbolic world that values the sacred and the mysterious. Symbols are not fixed in time, but free to move between the past and future. Besides being fluid, they are also limitless and timeless.

Entangled in workaday responsibilities and domestic tasks, we can easily lose touch with a symbolic life. Yeats wisely said, 'One is furthest from symbols when one is busy doing this or that.'[32] Yet symbols are all around, even in the midst of our everyday jobs and mundane tasks. They are always present if we are receptive, always there to reconnect us to the imaginative life. Astrologers are also susceptible to losing contact with the symbolic process, as we are constantly called upon to problem-solve, predict and be definitive about the meaning of an astrological symbol. When predictive and factual, astrology becomes landlocked in materiality, isolated from the divine that symbols evoke. When we move towards literality, we move away from the symbol's connective and revelatory power.

A horoscope contains a remarkable arrangement of symbols that invite us to be imaginative, open to an alternative reality and another way of knowing. Since horoscope symbols evoke a psychic response when we engage with them, these reactions can be complex, complicated and confusing, not only for us, but for those we read for. Therefore I would like to amplify some ideas about symbols as a prelude to focusing on astrological symbols.[33]

Symbols evoke what cannot be characterized through thoughts or rational explanations. While they are often indefinable, symbols are the agents for what is nameless, ambassadors for what is unidentified. Therefore the intellect can find great significance in symbols, as they add value to what cannot be conveyed through a philosophical or conceptual framework. A symbol is uncommitted in that it does not stand for something specific, but directs us beyond itself to a meaning or revelation, giving form to feelings and inner truths. Having a poetic, ironic and ambiguous quality, the symbol of birth might suggest death; perhaps excrement might indicate gold.[34] Being illogical, mysterious and contradictory, symbols are naturally paradoxical. As the symbolic process is amoral and non-judgemental, it invites repressed, unknown and neglected aspects of the self to be pictured and considered without the threat of negative responses.

Symbolic language and images are used by all religions in an effort to honour the realm of the divine or what lies beyond the scope of human comprehension. Symbolism enriches our myths, stories, poems, novels, films and dreams. Symbols are the poetry of the soul and, as Paul Tillich suggests, open the gates of the soul:

> Every symbol opens up a level of reality for which non-symbolic speaking is inadequate … But in order to do this, something else must be opened up – namely, levels of the soul, levels of our interior reality. And they must correspond with the levels in exterior reality which is opened by a symbol … So every symbol has two edges. It opens up reality and it opens up the soul.[35]

The language of astrology is an intricate symbolic language which bridges the literal world with the world of soul. To invest the literal world with meaning we need both symbols and imagination to bring both worlds together.

The word 'symbol' has evolved in meaning from the early Greek *symbolon* which combines the prefix *sym*, meaning 'together', with *bol*, meaning 'to throw'. Hence the idea of a symbol was 'to throw things together', referring to what is brought or cast together. Symbols were seen as tokens or permits, outward signs pointing to something else. Symbols connect visible reality to what cannot be seen, bringing things together to reveal what is invisible or unknown.

Symbols have manifold associations and numerous possible meanings. For instance, a snake might suggest a phallic symbol to a

Freudian, a deeper layer of unconscious material for a Jungian, fear to someone who has no experience of snakes, transformation to a therapist or a matriarchal icon to an archaeologist. In religion and myth the serpent is a potent figure, whether it reveals itself in the Garden of Eden, in a dream in the temple of Asclepius, in Medusa's hair or on Athena's aegis. Astrological symbols are underpinned by a potent amalgam of heavenly and mythic information and images. A plethora of astrological literature attests to the various ways astrological symbols can be portrayed and interpreted. When these symbols are described objectively, as if read from a textbook or dictionary, they may open up the literal reality, but not the soul. And without the stirring of the soul, symbols lose their numinous nature.

Symbols have always existed. Underpinning the astrological symbol is a divinity, an archetypal essence; yet however we might name it, the energy reveals itself through the symbol when we consciously cooperate with its evocation. Astrological symbols cover the broad spectrum from the astral to the physical, linking and uniting the soul with the material world.

Astrological Symbols
As an astrological practitioner I do not have to know what a particular symbol may mean to the client. What I do need to know are the astrological traditions and meanings of this symbol, my own experiences with the symbol and skills to articulate this in the best way I can. My task is to illuminate the symbol adequately so the client resonates with the symbol within themselves. As the client begins to amplify this symbol in the context of their lives I begin to hear what it means to them. If I try to define the symbol in the context of their lives my focus narrows onto a literal landscape, whereas when I open up the symbol and invite participation with the symbolic process I begin to hear how this finds expression in their world. If I only equate an astrological image with a literal manifestation, I perpetuate a causal world which keeps me bound on a mortal grid without the life-sustaining nutrients of the soul.

Students who joined our classes at the Chiron Centre after being taught by other teachers would sometimes become agitated when they were confronted with the proposal that symbols did not have fixed meanings, nor came with a fact sheet of keywords that nearly fitted a situation. Astrological symbols are contained by tradition and technique, but not confined to a methodology of manifestation.

Carl Jung stressed that symbols are living things and remain alive as long as they are 'pregnant with meaning'. Living symbols are those that we participate with, reflect upon and are mindful of. It is as if symbols are the energetic characterizations of unconscious contents which facilitate recognition of unknown parts of the Self. By connecting to our symbolic life we begin to understand deeper and concealed aspects of ourselves. But Jung also warned about symbols losing energy and dying. When a symbol is no longer meaningful and revelatory by nature, its meaning is no longer evocative or consequential:

> The symbol is alive only so long as it is pregnant with meaning. But once its meaning has been born out of it, once that expression is found which formulates the thing sought, expected, or divined even better than the hitherto accepted symbol, then the symbol is *dead*, i.e. it possesses only an historical significance.[36]

Yet we continue to call it a symbol even when its meaning and energy have gone. For instance, many Christian symbols such as the cross, or Christ's birth and the gifts of the Wise Men, are now lifeless, as their vibrant symbolism has been killed off through dogma and commerce. Interpretation also contributes to the death of a symbol. When the reading of a symbol creates interpretations, it inhibits the energetic power of the symbol to inspire meaning and revelation. When institutions and conventions consciously ascribe a permanent meaning to a symbol it is at risk of becoming a sign, merely a pointer to that tradition, belief or doctrine. It is as if the symbol is dead inside but still lives on outside as a sign.

Astrological symbols are universal and have a myriad of rich associations. Many of the symbols are resonant with archetypal images and myths, and when we engage with these symbols something beyond our logical and sensual perceptions is revealed, a world often described as divine or magical. Astrological symbols have been imbued with techniques, methods and dogma for over two millennia; therefore these symbols have rich layers of meaning.

When they inspire us to participate with the authenticity they reveal, the symbol touches the soul.

My experience is that symbols live when we free ourselves from their prescribed interpretations and engage with the authenticity of their images. Dane Rudhyar said, 'The practice of transpersonal astrology is extremely difficult, because one has to see through what is considered the usual meaning of every factor being studied'.[37] Being true to the symbol and oneself in the moment, not the dogma or theory, encourages the ability to find meaning beyond the everyday reality of facts, information and logic. This way of seeing is focused through symbol, not a code of belief.

In our astrological learning we may be easily disconnected from the symbol by interpretive information. When astrological students first encounter astrology, the symbols are often highly evocative and revelatory, as they are experienced openly and subjectively. They have not yet been yoked to representing a some-thing. Learning the tradition of calculations, rulerships, considerations, associations, meanings and interpretations can dull the life of the astrological symbol. The energy of the symbol is still there, but it becomes objectified through analytical knowledge when linked with an explanation. Symbolic systems demand participation in their mysteries, not an objective view. Objectification conceives informational systems, which in themselves are helpful, but their language is no longer symbolic. Becoming skilled at the traditions, techniques and systems of astrology is an essential prerequisite to its practice. The art of astrology is not detached; it is participatory, allowing the symbol to reveal itself, held in the sanctity of the moment.

We need astrological theory and insight to engage with the symbol. But we also need to suspend our rote interpretations to understand the symbol. This process allows re-engagement with the life of the symbol and its capacity to assist us to see through to a meaningful situation. Symbols contain potent meanings, but they are not accessed through the intellect. It is the fluidity of imagination and intuition that help the symbol reveal itself. Astrological language is full of interpretive meanings which are easily forgotten, but once a symbol reveals its meaning it is remembered effortlessly. Students have often been astonished at how I remember a symbol in their chart. It is never through memorizing their horoscope but because the symbol has revealed itself in conversation or during class participation and continues to live.

I always encourage advanced students and astrological practitioners to return to the beginning of their astrological journey, when the terrain was novel and uncomplicated, when we knew nothing, yet were open to and in awe of astrology's mysteries and revelations. For me, many personal experiences of stepping across the astrological portal into another way of seeing the world spring to mind. Most were ordinary experiences that confirmed to me that astrology constellated something beyond rational thought that was revealing and extraordinary, like these two simple examples from the very early stages of my astrological career.

It was 1978 and I was just beginning to teach classes and sponsor workshops. I would get my pamphlets and brochures reproduced at the local print shop. One day the printer engaged me in a conversation about astrology and agreed that there must be something to it; for instance, he wondered if there was a pattern to the times when his printing machines broke down or jobs were done incorrectly. Of course he asked my opinion on this and I obliged. I mentioned the sub-cycle of Mercury retrograde three times a year for three weeks and I offered to flag these dates on his calendar for the next year, suggesting that these might be opportune times to service and repair the machines, reschedule the backlog and attend to re-visioning the next four months of work. We spoke about the inherent wisdom of moving forward, regrouping, and then moving forward again. I do not recall any direct feedback about whether his printing machines were more efficient, but I do remember he told me that since our discussion he was less anxious about getting everything done immediately! He was heartened by the rhythms of Mercury, who he now imagined watched over his business. As a printer he was inspired that there could be a patron of, and a pattern to, the process of printing. As he was very appreciative, he would not take any payment for the next few jobs I had printed.

Ironically, forty years later the Internet is awash with Mercury retrograde warnings and instructions. Sometimes, it feels as if the symbol is no longer there – just a matter of fact!

The second instance was with a psychotherapist I had met during a training seminar. At this point I was already seeing clients. He was aware I was an astrologer and, being open to astrological symbols and images, he was interested in my opinion about a difficult client he saw twice and sometimes three times a week. He explained that the client was difficult to 'pry open', unable to free-associate, hesitant at sharing his dreams and was a concrete thinker. Were there any times I could think of that might be more favourable to him being open to imaginative explorations? Consulting the client's chart or having a conversation about him I felt was unethical; therefore I wondered about the technique of the void-of-course Moon. During this time the Moon is symbolically released from aspect or definition, perhaps more liberated to free-associate or be unbound. I thought this was an appropriate symbol for both the client and psychotherapist. The psychotherapist was open and thought it would be a great experiment. The void-of-course Moon can last anything from a few minutes to many hours, even at times two days when all the planets have a low zodiacal degree. I listed the dates for him for the next six months, explaining that many of these times would fall out of office hours, but if it were possible why not make an effort to schedule the client at these times. He agreed. When we met a few months later he thanked me, not because the client had been perceptibly more open during the two occasions that the appointments converged, but because of the permission to feel part of something larger and to respect this mystery. The astrological symbol honoured something greater than his psychotherapeutic techniques. In these simple ways astrology connects us once again to an imaginal and symbolic way of thinking, and in doing so reconnects us to soul-making.

Both instances were before the widespread use of computers, the Internet, social media, blogging and webinars. As I reflect back I recognize the naiveté and how little I knew. Yet not knowing does not prohibit the pattern, the cycle or the symbol. Ironically it is often knowing, expert and scholarly opinions and rationalizations that harness the symbol. Before knowing, there is engagement and participation with the symbol. Today we can ask the great god Google[38] about Mercury retrograde and over a million and a half results are available, some of which are fascinating commentaries on its cycle, its influence, its pattern and its celestial symmetry, including endless advice and warnings for the next period. And there are even more results for the void-of-course Moon, along with specialist opinions and anecdotes. But the symbol has become buried beneath the rubble of beliefs, comments, case histories and judgements. In this way, symbols become prescriptive and informative, no longer engaging us in the mystery.

Signs and Symbols
Jung's view was that we should distinguish between a symbol and a sign. When an expression represents something known, this is a sign, not a symbol.[39] This is an important distinction in astrological practice. A symbol is an indefinite expression with many meanings, pointing to something not easily defined and therefore not fully known. But a sign always has a fixed meaning because it is a conventional abbreviation for, or a commonly accepted indication of, something known. For instance, a Yield sign informs the motorist of a necessary behaviour. A zodiac sign can be both a sign and a symbol. When Aries is used to acknowledge precise characteristics such as initiative or courage, it is a sign; however, if it is used to evoke feelings, images and memories then it is a symbol. Dane Rudhyar defined a sign as follows:

> Anything that conveys definite information to someone can be called a sign if it deals with a fact or series of facts belonging to the level of reality that the person being informed can perceive, comprehend and become actually related to.[40]

This need to differentiate between signs and symbols in an astrological context is vital for knowing our place in working with astrology.[41] As a sign language, astrology can give information about character, personality and timing. The recipient is then left to use this information in their own way. This implies that the client is passive and need not be present or interactive with the astrologer, as the horoscope is read in a literal fashion. However, without a participatory and engaging interaction with the client, their personal connection to the symbol is left unexplored.

Similarly with psychology and medicine, two different streams exist. In psychology Cognitive Behaviour Therapy is sign language, whereas Depth Psychotherapy engages in a symbolic system. Allopathic medicine uses signs of the body in treatment, whereas alternative medicine can use the symptoms as symbols of the soul. Branches such as financial astrology use the signs; archetypal or transpersonal astrology endeavours to use symbols. Even when engaging with a symbol an astrologer can remain objective and uninvolved by conceptualizing and intellectualizing the symbol. Depth Psychotherapy, complementary medicine and archetypal astrology are also prone to being engulfed by the prevailing *mythos* of literalism.

Being Involved with the Symbol
In other words, how can we engage with the symbols of astrology if we continue to codify and present them as straightforward and objective, as if each transit of Uranus is a psychological separation or a Neptune–Mercury aspect manifests as the dubious trickster or that Pluto in the 7th is an encounter with a demonic other. No doubt these are subjectively verifiable, but does this approach keep the symbols alive?

Foremost is the imagination, the essential faculty that unhinges the doors of perception. Imagination is a type of disciplined consciousness that is not empirically determined nor focused on the literal world. It inspires perception beyond the ego and permits an experience of something deeper and more meaningful. Secondly, we must recognize that the symbolic process is participatory. Astrological techniques lead us to the archetypal territory, but it is our imagination that makes contact with the symbol, facilitating our intuition and feeling responses to be midwives to the process of revelation. Listening and engaging are crucial aspects of the participatory process, as is the appreciation of the illogical nature of the psyche. Working with symbols we learn to value their inconsistencies and contradictions. To be involved is to also 'stick to the image',[42] not reduce it to a concept, nor dart off to another part of the chart that reiterates the theme, but to continue to hear its metaphorical essence and deepen our participation with it. As we deepen our involvement with the symbol, analogies arise which open up meaning. Carl Jung was fond of saying *image is psyche*; the more we stay with the image the more we participate with psyche.

To participate with astrological symbols it is of great importance to recognize their archetypal dimension. For instance, the planets are profound personifications of archetypes that are placed in a unique way in the horoscope and in varying degrees of relationship with the other planets. Being archetypal symbols, planets are metaphors and best expressed through image.

Astrology's archetypal nature allows the astrologer to imagine the nature of the soul. It also allows an organization of various behaviours, feelings and experiences through a planet's archetypal essence. Astrological knowledge differentiates the archetypal nuances and allows a more specific and multi-dimensional representation of the image. Symbols begin to find meaning when the astrologer utilizes archetypal resonances and organizes these through their own understanding and imagination. Astrological training helps to differentiate and deepen the archetypal images, but it is the individual's participation, imagination and engagement with the symbols that constellates awareness.

An experience with an early client showed me the mystifying nature of being involved with symbol and psyche. Sharon was 28 when she came for the consultation. My early experiences are still alive in me, as they were profoundly instructive in the period before I had any formal counselling training, deeper psychological insight or theoretical models to work with. It seems the psyche is not that interested in theories and training; it responds when we are engaged with symbols, not concepts. In fact, sometimes my lack of training allowed me to be more forthright.

Sharon was 'happily married' but with a Neptune–Mars conjunction on her Descendant I did wonder what might have been left out of her assessment. With Uranus on the IC opposite the Sun, and a Moon in Aquarius opposite Pluto, there was a lot to discuss about her family of origin. It was talking about family that shifted the focus of our consultation. Sharon shared that she wanted a family, but had been unable to fall pregnant. She and her husband had been trying for years; perhaps this was what was missing in the relationship that I had sensed earlier? Certainly I was aware of the ambivalence of the Moon in Aquarius opposite Pluto, but both were square to Venus in Scorpio perched on the cusp of her 8th house. The T-square evoked powerful images for me. I tried my best to articulate this dynamic but I lacked cohesive language to express the intensity I felt. Over the jumble of words I was using, such as 'passion', 'secrets', 'danger', 'disconnection', I heard loud piercing sobs. I waited until she was ready to speak. It seemed like forever.

She blurted it out; something she said she had never told anyone. At fifteen she had been gang-raped by three boys. I did not know how to respond: what to say or do. It was as if what happened next was wiped off the record, as I have no recall, nor do my notes reveal much. We both knew something had happened, but I did not know what that was.

Nearly three weeks later Sharon phoned me to thank me for the consultation and how liberating it had been, as she was able to share this with her husband and walk again through the trauma, which seemed to change the way she felt in herself. She then said 'I have something to tell you'. It was something I could not even have imagined, but when she told me I was awestruck. 'I'm pregnant,' she cried. And so did I.

Sharon would have already conceived when she came for the consultation. It must have been the 'right' time for her to be open. Uranus was beginning to transit the T-square while the North Node in the 5th house was ending its passage across this dynamic aspect. Somehow the astrology of the moment did not need to be named, as the process that the symbols revealed was beyond this transitory arrangement. Many more times throughout my career I was witness to the profound and autonomous nature of symbols, which would feel reduced if I tried to explain or clarify them.

I was grateful that I had been both a participant and a witness to the process, recognizing how much of the process was beyond my own understanding. I could recognize how I cooperated in creating a space for something to happen – and, as mentioned previously, this necessity to create a soulful space for something to happen has always stayed with me.

I also reflected on how Sharon must have trusted in something in that moment to reveal her secret. Whatever it was, I sensed it was the recognition of her own power that her horoscope could clearly reveal and I could hold for a moment. I too have Venus in Scorpio square Pluto and in that moment I was also called on to use its containment and empowerment in service. From that day in August 1980 I began to be comfortable with the mysteries that are part of astrological work, not needing to identify or conceptualize them, but to accept them as part of the terrain that astrological symbols excavate.

2

TIME

Time is
Too Slow for those who Wait,
Too Swift for those who Fear,
Too Long for those who Grieve,
Too Short for those who Rejoice,
But for those who Love,
Time is not.[43]

Henry van Dyke,
'Time Is'

Time tells fascinating stories of births and endings, of pasts and futures, of fictions and fantasies. It is highly sentimental, poignant and expectant. Being so emotionally charged and mysterious, time touches the chords of our soul. Yet we can never really know time. It remains a mystery, inaccessible through the senses. We cannot touch, taste, feel, smell or hear time; we can wonder and think about time, but it defies our sensibilities. Contemplating time is like a meditation on life, a record of having existed. Whether mystic or pragmatic, time is unfathomable.

With history and memory we compose a continuous narrative of our personal and collective experiences through time. This is where astrological intelligence is of great value, as it embodies the paradoxes of time through its many timepieces, aligning the qualities of any moment with the heavens. Astrology sees through chronological time into mythic time, offering images and symbols to help us participate in time. Astrology is horological, a natural treatise on time, and each horoscope is a testament to the poly-dimensional experience of time. As a timepiece, astrology utilizes the observable and measurable cyclic motion of planets and stars to symbolize and imagine time.

A horoscope ensouls time, animated with the spirit and nature of each moment. The word 'horoscope' is derived from the Greek *hora*, meaning 'hour', and *skopein*, 'to look at'; therefore horoscopes are like snapshots of moments in time. Mythologically, *hora* references the Horai, the trinity of goddesses whose collective name refers to the seasons and the eternal ordered round of time. Individually the Horai were known as Dike, Eirene and Eunomia or Justice, Peace and Order, and together they represented the hours, the dance of the seasons and the passing of time. The Horai were goddesses of the seasons, who oversaw the turning of the heavenly wheel through the phases of the year. They were daughters of two orderly and methodical gods, Zeus and Themis,[44] so the hours are instinctually ordered through the passages and returns of the seasons. Each horoscope or horary chart invokes these earlier custodians of the seasons, along with the virtues of justice, peace and order that underscore time.

The Horai were also the sisters of another trinity of goddesses known as the Moirai, or the Fates. As weavers of time, each sister had a particular role in the assigning of the earthly lot: Clotho spun the thread, Lachesis measured the length and Atropos cut the cord. The length of the cord that was spun, measured and then cut not only epitomized the lifespan but also the seminal moment of birth. Fittingly, time and fate are sisterly concepts in Greek mythology, woven together in both our collective and personal cosmogonies, our personal origins being the horoscope. Both the Horai and the Moirai were imagined as apportioning time through their participation with nature, the heavens and the gods.

Our contemporary reliance upon clocks to measure time maintains the illusion that time is objective. Hourly appointments, daily rituals, monthly rent, yearly tax returns and 25-year mortgages define the modern-day parameters of our relationship with time. Because it can be defined and divided, time has become a commodity. As a product it can be quantified and sold. We even have a price on what an hour of our time is worth; no wonder we might find it difficult to see time as something other than concrete or fixed. Time has become some-thing, when in essence it does not really exist. What exists is a complex of rules that govern time, but time itself is invisible.

Even though time may be invisible, it is a felt experience. Liberating it from a linear trajectory permits another experience of time. A common occurrence in crisis or when under duress is that the soul experiences a time warp in which seconds feel like hours, the past may be relived or the future confronts the present. The nature of time is a mystery best left to the metaphysicians and quantum physicists to probe. As astrologers, our consideration is how we might reflect on time and the soul in order to apprehend how the astrological symbols reveal themselves through time.

While astronomical timing is quantitative, astrological timing is qualitative. Yet in both practice and theory, astrological timing is commonly thought of and used quantitatively, fixing the timing of a planetary movement to a possible episode in 'actual time', whether that is hours, days, weeks, months or years. When time is fixed literally, astrological practitioners are coerced into anticipating future possibilities.[45] Astrologers find meaning in time, but no moment creates significance until we give meaning to that moment.

From a quantitative point of view, astrological periods are measured by the time it takes for a planet to pass through a particular point in the heavens, whether that is a zodiac sign, a degree of the zodiac or an aspect to another planet. For instance, Pluto moves into Aquarius on 23 March 2023 and will move back and forth across the zodiacal cusp of Capricorn–Aquarius three more times before it enters Aquarius for a stay of nearly two decades on 19 November 2024. On 12 January 2020 Saturn conjoined Pluto at 22° Capricorn 46′. Depending on the 'orb of influence'[46] we can time the period when the two planets will aspect one another. Quantitative time compares these planetary positions with a natal chart to personalize the advance of time. But how we engage with this symbol of time is the key: do we interpret the time or imagine it?

Astrological perception does not operate on the cause–effect spectrum but is a link to the qualities intrinsic in the moment. Qualitative timing is imaginative and symbolic, encouraging participation with the moment. It is not read in the context of a calendar but imagined, involving the individual in reflection upon the astrological image. Through using imagination we make time for soul,[47] not by marking out time but by taking time.

When speaking at an astrology conference James Hillman suggested that by 'setting aside the literalistic attachment to time we might also be free of another dangerously compelling power in astrology: the temptation to predict'.[48] A refreshing thought. But 'setting aside the literalistic attachment to time', given astrology's deeply-entrenched roots in the cause–effect Ptolemaic model, is not a simple task in a world whose dominant mythology is scientism.[49] Ironically, astrology is a model that espouses the meaningfulness of time, yet it is devalued when the qualities of time are literalized. Even 'quality time' in a contemporary sense means an intentioned period of time, defined by the will for a measured outcome, which leaves little room for divine intervention. Similar to the wandering planets, astrological practice needs time and space for the soul to wander along its course until it reveals the significance of the symbol.[50]

Astrology and astrological practice are commonly denigrated by science, sceptics and systems, yet it is not astrology they denigrate, as most have not taken the time to actually become familiar with the tradition. What is denigrated is its mystery and unknowing, its randomness and wanderings which result in revelations. As astrologers we must struggle with our questions on time in a world smitten with explanations and evidence.

The Language of Time

There are many ways of thinking about time; for instance, the ancient Greeks knew *chronos* as the unyielding passage of time. Like the eponymous Titan who devoured his children, time was seen to consume all things.[51] Images of the passing of time, such as the hourglass and crutches, became linked with the god, Cronus, but as an early agricultural god the sickle was also his symbol. While this symbol was associated with power and prosperity, it also symbolized the cutting down of time. Ironically, Cronus also presided over a Golden Age, an era when man lived in peace and prosperity like gods, and 'miserable age rested not on them'.[52]

Once upon a time the age of Cronus was benevolent and undying, but now his time is all-consuming; hence this ambivalence towards Cronus underpins the astrological archetype of Saturn. Cronus time enters our vocabulary through words that represent the passing and recording of time, such as *chronological* or the arrangement of recorded time; *chronicle*, a detailed account of events arranged sequentially; and *chronometer*, an instrument that measures time. But perhaps the word that reminds us most of the troubling relentlessness of time is *chronic*, a mnemonic of the inevitability of temporal corrosion. Cronus remains a powerful symbol of time in our language and his surrogate Saturn remains one of astrology's great chronocrators.

But the Greeks knew another time and that was *kairos*, which had a subjective, even supernatural quality. While *chronos* characterized linear and measurable time, *kairos* referred to a critical moment, an appointed time or the right moment in time. In early usage it was linked with opportunity or the moment when possibility penetrated the present. In ancient Greek terminology it referred to an opening, and *kairos* was the critical moment to enter into and take advantage of the moment. In the Homeric Greek *kairos* was the 'penetrable opening' which may have originated with the archer who seized the right moment to aim at the cracks in the enemy's armour,[53] an early symbolic association between arrows and time.[54] The word was also associated with weaving, which is frequently connected to fate and time, conjuring up the sisterly alliance of the Horai and the Moirai. Metaphorically speaking: 'An opening in the web of fate can mean an opening in time, an eternal moment when the pattern is drawn together tighter or broken through'.[55] *Kairos* is that instant when the veil of time lifts and an opportune moment arises, akin to the idea that the time has come. In contemporary ways of thinking we might align *kairos* with the mysterious process of the ripening of time. *Kairos* might be likened to the birth moment which opens us up to the vital opportunity of life or to other times when a fissure between the worlds appears.

These two concepts embody the quantitative and qualitative nature of time and its literal and fictional qualities. As astrologers we constantly work with both, investing the literal planetary cycles with meaning, using *chronos* timing to become aware of the *kairos* moments of life. It is not the mechanism of time that creates the opportunity, but the willingness to participate freely in its imagined possibilities that astrology aptly outlines.

In astrological thinking each sign of the zodiac contains qualities and essences that characterize the mood of the time. For instance, when the Moon is in Scorpio, time has different features to when it is in Gemini. As Pluto transits through Capricorn, the collective experience of time is different to when it is in Aquarius. Each planetary archetype contributes to the timing of the moment; it is the imaginative skill of the astrologer that tells the time by planetary cycles. Active imagination and participation mystique are fundamental in releasing the symbol from its chronological restraints.

Participation mystique is a subjective practice; a way of experiencing the non-linear and non-rational world through instinct and intuition, not concepts or theories. It is an anthropologic idea inspired by animistic cultures where nature was imbued with soul and unseen forces animated the universe. A characteristic of this form of participation is a fusing of relationship between the observer and the observed; hence a feeling of unity or oneness occurs as boundaries are dissolved. In a way, astrology is animistic. Astrologers perceive the planets as subjective, both as inner and outer dimensions, as well as respecting the unseen forces that give life to the universe. Therefore, the participation mystique with astrology permits other experiences to inspire other intelligence beyond the confinement of rationality. When caught in the grooves of linear time, celestial timing becomes explanations of truthful facts rather than a participation mystique with the eternality of time.

A Question of Time
In our third millennium CE we can measure the passing of time within milliseconds, devise precise calendars for the future and accurately date archaeological findings; yet do we know time? Could our fondness for measuring, ordering and regulating time be a reaction to the lack of control we feel in the face of timeless chaos and uncertainty? A quick remedy for feeling the anarchy of time is to turn our gaze towards the starry heavens. Here we find a 'paragon of order'[56] that reveals the multi-dimensional nature of time. The sky eloquently sketches its cyclical nature and differentiates the passing of time through ever-changing cosmic configurations. Astrology's starry heavens embrace qualities of time through the sanctity of the planets' symmetrical cycles and the eternality of their returns. Each planetary archetype tells its own time, whether that is a lunar cycle of 27 days, a solar cycle of 365 days or a Jupiter cycle of 12

years. Astrology transports us through time, mapping personal and collective moments. Its time is endless and eternal: timeless.

Time does not exist in the same way as physical objects. Nor do we have a sensory perception of time. Time is cerebrally constructed; for human beings time is mainly sensed through change. We are acutely aware of time because of ageing and our ability for episodic recall, to remember past events. Time for animals is not perceived in the same way; it is instinctual.[57] Without the complexity for time perception or episodic memory, animals live more in the moment.

If we were immortal would we feel time? Ageing or the passing of time does not seem to be an immortal concern. Cronus will always be old; Hermes will always be mischievously young; Artemis, lithe and fit; and Aphrodite always sexually active. As humans we live in a temporal world between the instinctual and the divine, bound by the passing of time, unlike our animals or gods who live in a time-free zone. At significant moments we can find ourselves in this time beyond time; hence our experience of time is not always bound by the temporal world.[58] It is this time of which poets and mystics speak.

One of the ways time is deeply felt by humans is through ageing. Ageing confirms our mortality; yet at times we also marvel with a felt sense of immortality. The ancient Greeks wisely differentiated between ageing and immortality through the myth of Tithonus, one of the sons of the Trojan king Laomedon, whom 'cruel immortality consumes'.[59] Eos, the goddess of dawn, fell wildly in love with the youthful beauty of Tithonus. Eos was sister to the Sun-god Helios and Moon-goddess Selene and mother to the stars and winds. Cursed by Aphrodite for seducing her lover, Ares, Eos compulsively fell in love with the attractive energy of youth; the seductive, translucent light which preceded the fullness of day. But, like dawn, youthful beauty is short-lived. When Eos fell in love with the Trojan prince, she carried him away to her home in the Far East; here she and Tithonus dwelt on the horizon separating night from day. Every morning 'Dawn rose from her bed, where she lay with haughty Tithonus, to carry her light to men and immortals.'[60]

Not wanting her love to ever end, Eos petitioned Zeus to make her lover immortal. Zeus granted her appeal, but Eos failed to specify that Tithonus should not age and must remain eternally youthful. The goddess did not differentiate between ageing and immortality.

As the years passed, immortal Tithonus grew older, greyer, stooped and demented. While the original myth ended with Eos locking Tithonus away from sight, a later addition suggested Eos turned him into a cicada so she could hear his voice eternally. The myth so eloquently contrasts human and immortal time, a distinction helpful for discriminating between literal and imagined time.

Does time really slip away, as Eos tried to prevent, or does it just rearrange itself? From an ageing point of view we might find it difficult to do what we once did, but what we can no longer do still exists in another time. While I may no longer be able to do what I did as a seven-year old, an experience of this time exists. Memory is a storehouse of time, not just from our own past experiences, but from those of the ancestors and the ancients. Astrological images of transition and timing stir up these reservoirs of time. Present time is infiltrated by the past.

The Greeks knew of this visceral memory and personified her as one of the twelve Titans. Her name was Mnemosyne, mother to the nine Muses. She personifies memory, not linear or cognitive, but feeling; an instinctual memory stored in the aches and pains of the body, recalled through images, symbols, reactions, impulses, impressions and gut feelings. It is neither lineal nor rational, like learning by rote dates and statistics, but recollected through images and feeling responses.

Mnemosyne's voice is poetic; her memoirs are stored in the fragments of a song, a myth, an epic story or fairy tale.[61] Hermes remembers the details and features of the moment while Mnemosyne recalls its quality and mood. In the *Homeric Hymn to Hermes*, the god's first honour in song is to Mnemosyne,[62] an apt archetypal pairing that reminds us of subjective and objective memory. Both Hermes and Mnemosyne are present at any moment in time. When we reach a turning point on our path in life or are in a dynamic transition, the memory of times past arises. At crossroads we encounter all the other times of life that are resonant with the present. Time 'is not only perceived, imagined and conceived, but remembered as well.'[63] We inhabit a remembered present and astrological time assists in threading these times together.

Time is also entwined with events. While we can time an event and record its circumstances, there are also subjective factors in any particular time: moods, feelings, fantasies, reactions, senses, expectations, hopes, desires and memories. Time is not free from past sorrows or future wishes. The present is punctuated with recollected time and future aspirations, rarely released from its past, nor free of its future. Therefore, we not only inhabit a remembered present, but also an expectant one.

The passing of time is characterized by the ever-changing arrangements in the universe. This is the nature of astrology: it uses the arrangements of the cosmos in the moment to attempt to give meaning to the nature of time that we are passing through. Perhaps not as sophisticated as it might be, nonetheless astrology is a powerful paradigm of time. Each horoscope reflects a different configuration according to the pattern of the cosmos at that precise time. Yet the time recorded by astrological measures not only exists chronologically but soulfully as well.

Walking Through Time
Strolling through an archaeological museum is like walking through time. When the flow of the museum is laid out in linear time the first room you enter is primal time. The natural phases of the Moon, the rising of the stars and the setting of the planets mark time. It is the passing of time without reason: *acosmos*, or without order as we would recognize it today. This is the era before scientific classifications; yet each moment is arranged in a seamless symphony of rising and setting, swelling and shrinking, when the natural world of night and day, dark and full moon and winter and summer solstices chronicle the circle of time.

Ancient Greece had its own Dark Age. Mycenaean palaces crumbled; trade ceased, doors were locked. No sounds were heard from the trinity of generations that occupied this time. In the national archaeological museum in Athens you enter the room that marks the Geometric period when ancient Greece awakens from its dark spell. Ancient vases are painted with algebraic designs; every space available is filled with geometric patterning. The mind is awakened, busily illustrating patterns, shapes, images, ensouling the world that the vase-maker inhabits. Stories from the past illuminate the present.

And next we find ourselves in the Archaic rooms where statuary and architectural chunks overwhelm us. Awed by the ingenuity of our ancestors, we admire the impressive edifices that were built and exquisite votives that were offered to the gods. We are still participating in honouring the mystique of the cosmos, yet now we are becoming mesmerized by what we can achieve. The Geometric period heralds the introduction of the alphabet. Oral traditions wane; poetry and epics are written and spoken. We are building, singing and writing praises to the gods. Philosophy is stirring. We are transitioning between participating with the gods and justifying them. We begin to see an order, identify it and have language to explain it. God-like phenomena are becoming objectified and explained.

And then we step across the threshold to the Classical rooms where the statuary become works of art; movement is introduced, lifelike eyes follow you as you study the statue. Vases are manipulated with colour in an exquisite way. The earth provides the rock for the temples, limestone and marble for the statuary, silver for the jewels and herbs for the dyes. The earth is being commoditized; the human is becoming the cosmic centre. The gods have become the sculptor's model, the architect's inspiration, the philosopher's allegory and the dramatist's conscience; they are separated from us, objectified, distant. Layers of time rest upon one another, but are laid out in linear sequence.

I imagine the process of gestation as being like a virtual voyage through the museum of time where the developing foetus time-travels through aeons of galleries and dreams in collective time, disembarking at birth having internalized these impressions of times past. As the culmination of an epic journey, birth is the destined arrival after a long and demanding migratory journey. Time is not only laid out horizontally behind and in front of us, but spirals back and forth through ancestral and collective time.

The horoscope is the documentation of this causal temporal beginning, based on the first breath of life, the symbolic moment that separates us from the symbiosis with the biological mother and mythological Great Mother. This is the defining moment for the individual horoscope – the archetypal blueprint for the human journey of the soul. It is fixed, unchanging, yet is constantly responsive to and shaped by our participation in time. The four angles of the horoscope give rise to a four-dimensional authenticity that contains a multi-dimensional time. The birth moment marks this crossroads when the human soul becomes temporal, no longer suspended between worlds but locked onto the mortal grid. As we take our first breath, an independent human life begins.

The genesis of birth is a critical time upon which astrologers reflect. Perhaps it is like the exit of the archaeological museum after we have moved through the ages of man and taken in the impressions and feelings of times past. At the exit, as at birth, we forget the enormity of our past and concentrate on moving out into the 'real' world. But the museum of our familial, ancestral, cultural and human past still exists. At birth these experiences and impressions are imprinted upon our genes, branded in our DNA, felt through our emotional memories, impressed upon the unconscious and housed in the soul. The museum of the soul is the sanctuary of the Muses. The museum of Urania, the muse of astrology, is the starry heavens where the artefacts of time are remembered through planetary cycles and celestial phenomena.

The moment of birth marks the entry of the soul into temporal time. There will be other significant and crucial times within the lifespan, but birth is the seminal moment when the first breath symbolizes the spirit incarnating in the mortal body. Astrological doctrine recognizes this as the defining moment of the natal horoscope. Each moment, every event or critical time after birth will have its own horoscope, but these will be secondary to the primary birth chart. These times will exert their unique influences, shape the emerging archetypal responses and even alter the life path. But astrological tradition grounds the authenticity of the soul in the moment of birth. Due to this fixed time, astrologers are extremely susceptible to becoming caught up in the constraints of literal time.[64]

Although astrological techniques allow us to consider the horoscope through time, essentially the horoscope does not change over time. It remains the same. An exercise I do with students is to have them prepare three photocopies of their natal horoscope. The first copy we label the Past; this is the chart that contains what has happened to them, reflects who they were, how they developed, where they have been and also is the chart that is consulted for reflection and meaning as to the why of these occurrences. The second chart is tagged the Present and points towards current circumstances, while the third chart is marked the Future and signifies what lies ahead.

The symbols in all three charts will be the same: the angles, the planetary houses, signs and aspects. An astrologer can apply past, current or future transits and progressions to the chart to put it in a context of time, but ultimately the natal horoscope is timeless: the symbols move in and out of time and through time, but are constant. As our awareness deepens each astrological symbol becomes ensouled and our relationship to that symbol through time becomes more coherent. While all three horoscopes are the same, awareness of the archetype in the present encourages a more collaborative participation with it in the future and a more reflective engagement with it in the past.

Astrological Time and Timing

Astrology is present every time we glimpse the night sky. Carl Jung, when referencing the signs of the zodiac in the Vision Seminars (1930), said: 'astrology may be quite unknown to you consciously, yet to your unconscious it is very intimately known ...'[65] He was referring to astrological rhythms being instinctual: the diurnal cycle of the rising and setting of the Sun, the monthly phases of the Moon, the annual cycles of the seasons, which are all deeply embedded in the human experience. As time is measured by the rotation and revolution of the Earth, it has its footing in the heavens. The starry heavens were the earliest timepiece, whether that was the rising or setting of the constellations, the lunar orbit or the synodic cycles of the planets.[66]

Astrological time is cyclical and spiral, comprising the orbits of all the planets, not just Earth's. In terms of time, each of the planetary cycles maps out its own calendared time. The cycle of planetary pairs from one conjunction to the next also maps out passages of time. These cycles are metaphoric meters for personal, social and collective timing. For instance, lunar time is recorded by the cycle of the Moon and is a metaphor for feeling time and memory, such as the unconscious assimilation of every nuance, reaction, sense, desire, etc. It is a 27.3-day cycle. The Neptune–Pluto cycle lasts 494–5 years and is symbolic of the emerging motives and aspirations of the collective. This cycle is imagistic of the emergence of deep-rooted urges, intentions and ideals that may dominate and influence mankind's direction and ways of being. Since Neptune and Pluto symbolize deep energies beneath the foundation stones of all systems, the cycle represents compelling human attitudes awakened during each cycle's epoch. I have mentioned only two of many planetary time cycles; inherent in each astrological cycle is a symmetry and order that inspires confidence in the intelligence and beauty of the cosmos.

The Eternal Return

Eternal recurrence is a theme which has woven itself through the thinking of the ancient Egyptians and Hindu truth-seekers as well as Pythagorean and later Greek philosophers who wrestled with the idea of return. The forms of return were metaphoric and had many possibilities with many shapes; yet fundamental to the various hypotheses was the notion that a similar situation would recur at some point once again, since time was infinite.

An ancient belief was that history repeats itself 'because the stars return to their former positions'.[67] Images of return and renewal are embedded in astrological cycles, as each planet returns to the same zodiacal degree or to its conjunction with the Sun at some defined point in its cycle. Underlying each astrological cycle is the inevitability of return and the enduring image of the eternal return.

The ouroboros is a cross-cultural symbol which uses the fabled image of the dragon-serpent swallowing its own tail to embody the recurrent nature of the cosmos; on one hand it represents the alpha, the beginning or the head, and the omega, the ending or the tail, yet both are the same point. In astrology we know this point as the conjunction, the beginning of a new cycle marked by the end of the old. This eternal cycle suggests that creation emerges out of destruction, or that life is renewed through death. As the dragon-serpent devours its own tail, its life carries on in a renewed form. Death and rebirth, creation and destruction, beginning and ending, heads and tails mark the eternal return, the never-ending cycle of regeneration.

Early ways of thinking about time imagined it to be cyclical, like the natural phases of the Sun–Moon cycle. At the dark phase of the cycle the Great Mother would take the dead back into her womb to be reborn at the next crescent. With the advent of rational thought, time became more linear with a beginning and end that were no longer the same point. In this way of thinking, rebirth and return are relinquished, detached from the cycle of life. In astrological philosophy the concept of the eternal return preserves this inherent idea that the end is the gateway to the beginning and that each new cycle is reborn from the previous one.

Another perpetual image of the eternal return is the Sun as it returns from its night journey every morning to swallow the darkness, the dawn threshold marking the head, the point where day or the creation of new light devours the dark. The Sun not only demarcates the diurnal return, but also its annual return when it crosses the Celestial Equator, marking the equinoxes, another image of a celestial ouroboros that measures yearly time. Astrologers utilize the image of this annual return to make meaning through the techniques of ingresses and solar returns.

Not only the Sun but the planets, and other celestial bodies and points such as the asteroids and planetary nodes, return to their original position in the horoscope. Returns are natural to human experience. While we may not be familiar with the philosophy or the concept of the eternal return, we know the experience of return instinctually. It is deep-seated and inbred in the soul, having been impressed upon the human psyche for millennia through the experience of daily, monthly and annual cycles.

Astrological Moments in Time

Astrological tradition has cultivated procedures that help its practitioners read the moment of time to bring meaning to it. This act of investing time with meaning can be seen as an act of soul-making. When we collaborate with time we are mindful of creating rituals for the appropriate moment, more conscious of the phases of time and more likely to be participating rather than anticipating.

From past astrological tradition comes a toolbox of techniques such as planetary transits, ingresses, profections, time lords, planetary periods, ascensions and directions which give rise to more contemporary methods such as progressions and returns. As in any profession, the debate among practitioners about the authenticity and dependability of certain techniques persists; however, the success of any system rests with the practitioner. An astrological student learns to be proficient with the techniques, yet it is not the technique that ultimately reveals meaning; hence debates about which method is best limits astrology by tying it to the literality of a measured time.

The moment of time is of specific importance in astrological methods such as horary and electional astrology. The philosophy of horary or 'pertaining to the hour' suggests it is the moment of the question that contains the qualities of its answer.[68] Horary astrology follows a course of strictures in addressing the question, as well as taking into account the nature and authenticity of the query. The time of the question is respected before it can be explored. A series of what is known as *considerations* before judgement is used to ascertain whether the question is worthy. The derivation of the word 'consideration' suggests to 'examine the stars';[69] to consider is to be with the starry heavens in consultation.

At the heart of horary astrology is a great reverence for time. Even if the question is literal, it has a subjective undertone. Horary astrology can inspire an imaginative reflection on the question which engages psyche and inspires consideration. At the very least it brings the nature of concern to consciousness. Horary astrology challenges us to fully participate in the moment of time.

Electional astrology endeavours to synchronize the birth of a project with favourable cosmic arrangements. In considering appropriate times, the astrologer is mindful of the gods of the moment, because underpinning electional astrology is the age-old belief that important passages and events need to be blessed and sanctified by the gods to be successful. While the election for a time of marriage does not guarantee a happy marriage, the astrological process invites each marriage partner to be aware of the gods of relationship; that is, the opportunities and challenges within their union.

Both horary and electional astrology have a reverent attitude to time.[70] In a commercial, outer-directed world where control rather than participation with the cosmos is emphasized, these astrological techniques can become trivialized and directed by desire and will. Yet in a world respectful of soul, these techniques encourage participation in time when we consider our motives and are mindful of the possibilities and resources inherent in the moment.

A technique that also invites us to participate in time is transits, one of the most common contemporary methods used for timing. Simply, transits are the current planetary placements with regard to the zodiacal sphere. As snapshots of situations in time, phases of life and processes of change, each planetary transit characterizes moments in the shifting tides of humanity. The zodiac contains twelve distinct regions, which have linear demarcations or cusps; therefore as the planets pass through the zodiac's signs, the celestial timepiece reflects their images at the moment. Each planetary transit tells a tale of time and is a witness to the synchrony of outer world events.[71] Like a cosmic clock, the transits tell time, they do not make it or judge it.

Progressions are a time-based technique using one clock to measure timelines in another dimension. In speaking on the nature of time, Manoj Thulasidas states that 'time is a secondary sense without any direct sensory percept or reason for its existence' and argues that its measurement is open to interpretation. As part of his thesis he likens the time elapsed from the birth of the universe fifteen billion years ago to forty-five years. In this reckoning the beginning of Christianity two thousand years ago represents three minutes nine seconds.[72] Thulasidas's premise is analogous to the timing of progressions since one period of time can be linked with another in meaningful ways. Using progressions, astrologers observe planetary timing in reference to its secondary expression in time. Progressions challenge us to deconstruct our inclination to understand time chronologically.

Astrology provides ways to open the doors of perception onto the complexity and multi-layered dimensions of time. But to remain true to the astrological symbol through time we must return to the imagination as 'imagination is very much part of our being in time – in fact, intrinsic to it.'[73]

Imagining Symbols Through Time
Astrologers are often criticized for their self-assurance when analysing the past and lack of confidence in deciphering future events. This does not imply that astrologers cannot envision the future, only that they do not see the actual manifestation of the symbol. While symbols in the past have become wedged in the linear grooves of time, the symbols of the future have not yet

materialized. Being so diverse, archetypes can reveal themselves in countless ways. Imagining the possibilities by reflecting on them in the context of their symbolism allows us to be more present in time. Astrologers become stuck in the linearity of time when the symbol is projected forward in the same way that it has displayed itself in the past. To see a symbol through time it must be imagined. Imagination extends us into the fullness of time and encourages meaningfulness beyond the present.

We can imagine what might happen next January. Like the planets, imagination wanders. While astrological timing uses planetary cycles to contextualize time, it also allows the imagination to roam freely focused on symbols. Astrological techniques can be used to frame time, inspiring insight and intuition. In this way astrological timing techniques are like active imagination, which enables us to imagine the future, not predict it. The astrological measurement of time is ritualistic, not explanatory. It prepares us for participation with the uncertainties of time.

3

METAPHOR

'Hope' is the thing with feathers –
That perches in the soul –
And sings the tune without the words –
And never stops – at all –[74]

Emily Dickinson,
'Hope'

'I have run out of steam.' 'I feel as if I am bogged in a swamp.' A command of metaphor helps us to appreciate what cannot be easily articulated, moods not easily expressed or experiences incapable of being defined. Using a likeness of something else, such as another object, action or way of being, animates a particular way of understanding through image. Analogies are constructed to bridge two worlds. Metaphors use images to illustrate the complexities of inner feelings, giving a voice to subjective experiences. For poets, metaphor conveys the complexity of their emotions; for astrologers, the endless breadth of our starry sky is a flawless metaphor for soul.

Leonard Shlain suggested that metaphor is an imaginative contribution to the abstraction of language. Using metaphor, right-brain imagination introduces left-brain reason to feeling and emotion. Through image, metaphor infuses the precision and judgement of factual language with poetry, myth and melody.

When people find it necessary to express in words an inner experience such as a dream, an emotion, or a complex feeling-state, they resort to a special form of speech called metaphor that is the right brain's unique contribution to the left brain's language capability.[75]

While classified as a figure of speech, metaphor has the effect of being able to induce, even enchant, us into new ways of seeing. When used perceptively, metaphors generate insights, activate feelings and reveal meanings by encouraging new avenues of thinking. Using language artistically stirs emotions, stimulates connections and transports us into a way of seeing what could not be understood by words alone or known through a rational process. Indeed, being transported into another realm of knowing is what the word 'metaphor' implied originally. Its origin is ancient Greek, when words were still emblematic and carried us beyond the empirical world to a more soulful way of understanding. Language originally arose out of the imagination; hence etymology transports us back to when words encouraged revelation and aroused the imagination. Images were once embedded in words when image and language were equal; however, with the rise of rationality and logic, words lost their imagination becoming divested of image. Metaphor rouses the imaginative spirit of the alphabetic world, as what is beyond words is given a moving image which animates the feeling life. Metaphor awakens the mood of what is being expressed.

Metaphor combines two ancient Greek words: *meta* – over and above or across – and *pherein* – to carry or to bear; combining these suggests carrying across or beyond. A metaphor helps carry us beyond the observed into an imaginal world that guides us to what could remain unnoticed or unacknowledged. Using metaphors and myths encourages us to see through literal expressions so we can catch sight of a new way of perceiving our feelings, actions or ideas. They are keys that open doors to other ways of witnessing the world and often allow something that is difficult or unthinkable to be communicated.

It is this way of seeing that is essential in working with astrology so that the depth of meaning underlying the symbol can be transferred to others. Without metaphor, astrology is information rather than revelation, words without images. It remains a dead language, an unused prescription. However, with metaphors, myths, movement, images, stories and allegories, the ancientness of astrology can be restored to a living language of life. Being creative astrologically involves the art of transposing meaning in order to bring astrological language to life.

Since astrology's reconfiguration in Hellenistic Greece it has been largely shaped by literacy and rationality, setting aside its images and symbols for delineations and predictions.[76] An astrological chart was now read like the interpretation of a puzzle rather than an involvement with life, even though nature inspired the astrological metaphors. Involvement with the planetary cycles of the natural world gradually gave way to an observation of them. As the planets' rhythms became compartmentalized, the capacity to feel at one with the cosmic environment became impaired. The planets became pointers and signs that were interpreted and read rather than felt through participating with them. Astrology naturally exercises the left and right hemispheres of the brain. But when the left brain *logos* controls the right brain *astre*, information dominates and revelation is compromised.

When philosophical thoughts emerged in the midst of the first millennium BCE, movement towards objective and rational thinking became dominant, revolutionizing the way humans experienced learning, healing and divination. From the pre-Socratic philosophers (ca. 600 BCE) to the post-Socratic period of Aristotle (ca. 300 BCE),[77] the western mind illuminated its left hemisphere. During this period, the creative and cultural flowering was remarkable, but eventually mythology would be replaced by philosophy, and rational thought would become the superior function of the western mind.

Astrologers constantly use metaphors; in fact, we might argue that astrology is itself a metaphoric language. For instance, we use the planets as similes of archetypal human forces; the houses are metaphoric of life's ecosystem; and the zodiacal signs are emblematic of tones of human experience and development. When one is versed in their symbolism, astrological images are metaphors. For instance, an example of an astrological metaphor is Mercury in Pisces. As the messenger god, one of Mercury's many astrological expressions is the style of communication or the thinking function. Pisces is the sign whose images are water, the sea and two fish swimming in different directions. When these two astrological symbols are merged the metaphor of Mercury in Pisces imagines the thinking function as if it were under water. We picture either a very confused, perhaps emotive, communication style, or perhaps being of two minds, perplexed and bewildered. The fusion of two separate symbolic images encourages us to imagine this way of being and communicating, but it also permits reflection upon the self and participation with a greater intelligence.

Variations of the Mercury in Pisces theme have filled astrological texts now for millennia. But these are metaphoric, not literal, explanations. While by the law of correspondences the image may literalize, it is also mythical and metaphoric belonging to an archaic stream continually flowing beneath astrological doctrine. Astrology is an archetypal language, not a literal dialect; therefore it expresses itself through revelatory means including metaphors and symbols.

Rather than astrology remaining metaphoric, it easily becomes prescriptive, literal and a delineation of behaviour rather than an allegory of soul. Astrological doctrines have systematized its symbols to help analyse and evaluate them; for instance, Mercury is deemed to be in its detriment and fall in Pisces, suggesting that the archetypal essence of Mercury is not in its element nor suited to this quality of nature. From a linear and rational perspective it can be easily judged, categorized and explained as being deficient. Astrological tales lose their enchantment when rationalized. Even though astrological delineations and predictions may be uncannily accurate, they are nevertheless still metaphoric. To the initiated, the complexity of astrological symbols can stimulate perception and intuition about an individual and the world they inhabit, but to the uninitiated astrological language sounds like a strange and confusing dialect; therefore, metaphor is indispensable in transporting others into the insightful realms that astrology reveals. To do this we search for images.

To find the image through astrological metaphor I feel we need both hemispheres, the philosophical and the mythological, observation and participation, and rationality and imagination. Astrologers who are capable of translating the factual into the symbolic render the literal world meaningful. When astrologers have this eye for resemblances, they are able to see through the literality of astrological signs and symbols into an archetypal realm that is sympathetic to the individual and the cosmos they inhabit.

The Other Side of Metaphor

Metaphor assists in revealing another reality to that which is factual, tangible or proven. Because this reality is mostly subjective, it is often imaginative, feeling and intuitive, all of which are states that cannot be measured, articulated or evidenced by rational hypotheses. This subjective reality is also real, but not in terms of the objectivist's paradigm. When we fall under the spell of rationalism and the demand to explain ourselves, metaphors become literalized and impotent and no longer carry the ability to transfer us beyond rational boundaries. The myth of objectivism is disturbing as 'it makes both myths and metaphors objects of belittlement and scorn: according to the objectivist myth, myths and metaphors cannot be taken seriously because they are not objectively true'.[78] Since astrology is largely a metaphoric language, it is particularly vulnerable to attack.

Metaphoric language is commonplace and particularly important when trying to express what is intangible or subjective, such as emotions, underlying symptoms, dreams, psychological states, critical periods, complexes or psychodynamic sensations. Using a metaphor helps what is abstract or complex become more differentiated and known. What is subjective or invisible can become more readily accessible through metaphoric images. To an astrological student, Mercury in Pisces is an enchanted way of describing their innate sensitivity to learning or their inspired and/ or vague thinking that is unable to be articulated. It has resonant truth and extends the left brain's boundaries to include image and feeling. A truth is conveyed in a way that words cannot achieve.

However, the intangible that the metaphor uncovers is also at risk of becoming objectified, categorized and conceptualized. Mercury in Pisces can easily become a delineation of character, rather than a soulful image. If this occurs then the astrological metaphor is no longer the felt experience of one's sensitivity, but a label for a way of being. When what is rendered known is diminished to a factual experience the astrological image becomes informational rather than evocative; it tells me something rather than revealing some thing to me.

For instance, the inner child is a metaphor which can transport us into the soulful state of sadness for what we feel we did not receive in childhood, it can stir our sensitivities to not being loved, inspire spontaneous creativity or wake up the simple joys of creation. But so many self-help books have legitimized and legislated the inner child into an object. The inner child has become a category of the Self so the metaphor is no longer soulful or evocative, but just another psychological diagnosis. Even though the inner child is not an object, it has become objectified.

Metaphors collapse under the weight of literality. When overloaded with facts and theories, the metaphor no longer helps us to imagine something else but points us in a specific direction towards certainty, leaving mysteries unexplored and revelations unbidden.

Carl Jung was masterful at using metaphors to reveal images embedded in the psychic landscape. But Jungian metaphors once rich with subjectivity and imagination have also become objectified. The anima, originally the personal voice of a troubled patient talking to Jung and metaphoric of an inner feminine figure, has become literalized, something diagnosable. The shadow too is something we must find or know or at least do something about! When a metaphor becomes fixed it no longer guards the mystery and sacredness of what it intends to keep safe. Lack of metaphors in the day world is akin to lack of dreams in the night world. Without either there is no psychic life.

Anima as metaphor allows us to locate an internal feminine landscape so it may remain sacred and mysterious, not be consigned or reduced to a concept of an inner contra-sexual figure. Shadow as metaphor reveals forgotten, repressed and taboo feelings but it does not judge them. However, when metaphor becomes literalized, shadow becomes pathologized. Ultimately when metaphor becomes rigid it leaves behind its meaning and its ability to carry us beyond. Rather than reflecting on the uncovered projections and repressions, we start doing something about this, abandoning the soulful quality of what the metaphor revealed. When anima and shadow lose their meaning they become diagnostic tools in the hands of clinicians.[79] When astrological metaphors become explanations they become instructions by practitioners who have lost connection to the root metaphor which underlies the vocation of astrology.

Carl Jung stated: 'An archetypal content expresses itself, first and foremost, in metaphors.' Through metaphor, astrologers consider how astrological images express themselves. Metaphor is necessary because while each astrological image may have a common archetypal source, it has countless ways of manifesting in the literal world. Jung uses an astrological archetype to demonstrate his point:

> If such a content should speak of the sun and identify it with
> the lion, the king, the hoard of gold guarded by the dragon,

or with the power that makes for the life and health of man, it is neither the one thing or the other, but the unknown third thing that finds more or less adequate expression in all these similes.[80]

The Sun has many expressions. Even when it is set apart in a sign or house, differentiated by aspect or analysed by astrological techniques, it is archetypal and expresses itself in a chain of sympathies, not pieces of information or keywords. Metaphor allows astrological symbols to become animated beyond the left-brain constraints of literal facts and information. Astrological analogy encourages participation with the 'third thing' that is unable to be known rationally.

Astrological metaphors are vulnerable to the human insecure need to know things, be certain and come up with answers. When symbolic meanings are predetermined they become prescriptive rather than evocative.[81] Therefore what could be metaphoric becomes diagnostic and something to fix, or just another clever way to rationalize temperament. For instance, if we use the horoscopic image of a Saturn–Moon aspect metaphorically, we might imagine a dreary home, an authoritative mother and images of disciplining the habitual life. Or images of creating boundaries or being responsible for others may arise. We may also sense petrified feelings or leaden emotions. Using these images as metaphors invites us to participate with feelings of melancholy or the darker side of our relationship with mother, all images that may be resonant with our inner experiences. Metaphorically the 'authoritative', 'reliable' and/or 'responsible' mother is an image that inhabits the inner landscape of the soul and finds its expression through literal relationships where emotional attachments occur. Astrological symbols are not designed to be wholly prescriptive or factual, but are also ways of revealing and participating with soul.

Astrological Saturn has found its way into the English language through *saturnine*, which describes a gloomy temperament and *saturnism*, lead poisoning.[82] As the Moon, Luna has inspired *lunacy* and *lunatic*. 'Saturnine' and 'lunacy' have their etymological roots in the archetypes symbolized by Saturn and the Moon. When the words and images of Saturn and the Moon emerged out of the collective experience, it was first a felt experience rather than a cerebral one. Astrological metaphors summon the earliest impressions of the planets before they were named, measured or described.

Without metaphor, astrological symbols like a Saturn–Moon aspect describe a literal matter or detail, such as self-esteem issues, depression, perhaps an allergy to milk, an eating disorder or a controlling mother. The metaphor becomes a report of something or a prescription of what is ailing. If a transit of Saturn to the Moon is objectified without metaphor, then the astrological image becomes a literal prediction rather than an allegory of time. It may be described as a period in which we need to take certain action rather than a transitional time when we are engaging with these archetypes. When judging from an objective viewpoint, this astrological image could certainly be categorized as an inferior or unwanted episode, which leads to the fix-it myth of repair and an endless roundabout of trying to improve what is essentially a natural or soulful state of being.

In a fix-it culture with little space for uncertainty or not knowing, subjective interests like astrology are under pressure to conform to the rationalistic paradigm. Astrology is always at risk of attack from rationalists, as its imaginative essence confronts the objectivist myth. Its roots are pre-literate; hence it is images, feelings, senses and inner experiences, not words or reasons that reveal its integrity. While the literality of astrology can be disparaged, its subjective nature cannot. Hence in astrological history we have only a handful of statistics to prove its reliability, yet a mountain of anecdotal evidence from those who have participated in its mysteries. Astrology is a participatory and creative act. But to participate with it soulfully requires the ability to embrace what John Keats called 'Negative Capability'. In writing to his brother, Keats mentions that he was all of a sudden struck with this idea of Negative Capability, and that he felt it was this quality that contributed to rewarding achievement.

> I mean, *Negative Capability*, that is, when a man is capable of being in uncertainties, mysteries, doubts, without any irritable reaching after fact and reason.[83]

Root Metaphors

James Hillman speaks of vocations having root metaphors: 'All of us, no matter what the vocation, work from certain root metaphors. These models of thought stand behind and govern the way we view the problems we meet in our profession.'[84] For instance, a sociologist's root metaphor would be society while a psychiatrist's would be the psyche. In his essay on Oedipus, Hillman suggests that the root metaphor of Depth Psychology is both mythology and pathology.[85] Vocational astrologers also grapple with myth and pathology when confronted with a client and their horoscope.

Root metaphors inform our vocation, not because they are well thought-through philosophies or embrace traditional values, but ironically because they often remain unconscious. What inspires and draws us to our vocations can often be identified when we look back over the course of life. But vocations are not chosen in a rational way; we may actually feel it is the vocation that has chosen us. There is often something fated about how we selected a certain career or course of action. What remains undefined for many individuals about their occupation is the archetypal background that has shaped their profession. In other words, we might imagine the soul of a profession as a living reality which informs the career we have chosen. Being involved with this profession and participating with its soul might also suggest how we make choices in our lives. I imagine a profession's root metaphor as being analogous to its essence.

Would the metaphor that underpins the profession of astrology and shapes its practitioners' worldview be the starry heavens? Astrology grapples with other intangibles that are perplexing and beyond linear and rational constructs. In no particular order I would suggest these intangibles are Fate and Soul which, along with the Starry Heavens, are metaphors at the heart of astrological work. No doubt there are many other seminal constructs that create a base for astrological practice, but this trinity represents the paradigmatic world of the astrologer. The Heavens represent the astrological canvas upon which the patterns are etched; Fate is the pattern herself; Soul is the felt experience of this blueprint. Each of these root metaphors was principal to an ancient way of thinking before rational thought cleaved its distance from the imagination prior to astrology and astronomy being separated. All three ideas focus on the unbroken circle of the day and night forces, a deeply embedded metaphor in astrological practice.

Although Fate and Soul are central to astrological consideration they are not exclusive to this vocation. Religion, medicine and psychology must also contemplate the dynamics of the soul and the patterns of fate in their own way. However, the Starry Heavens are an underlying root metaphor for astrology, which she shares with her sister science astronomy. While astronomy might explain, calculate and catalogue the Starry Heavens with precision, astrology reveals their wisdom through the images, myths and metaphors of the night sky.

Jung reiterated that 'the first knowledge of psychic law and order was found in the stars' but when this 'realm of experience branched off into science, astrology became astronomy'.[86] When the left-brain skills of astronomy divorced the right brain's imagination of the sky, the human ability to experience the wholeness and integration of the cosmos was compromised. Astrology, like other revelations from the night world, became devalued. The circle of the day and night is broken.

When we return to astrology's root metaphor of the Starry Heavens we re-engage with imagination. An archetypal landscape is re-established and the split between left and right, night and day, and astrology and astronomy is addressed. The measured and ordered cosmos reanimates the right brain's capacity for imagination, allowing an integrated and holistic approach to the horoscope. Duality is enveloped and the circle of the day and night is again uninterrupted.

The Starry Heavens

I have fond memories of lying in the high summer grass in northern Alberta looking up at the heavens, watching the clouds shape-shift, seeing their patterns and imagining stories from their silhouettes pressed against the sky. I was nine years old. More recently, on the beach in Tasmania, my granddaughters and I sat on the sand staring at the sky, configuring the cloud formations and musing about them. They saw ghosts and dragons and fairies while I imagined ribcages, houses and planes. But clouds are ephemeral, unlike the stars that reappear each night. Clouds are fleeting; stars are eternal, unwavering in their rising and setting. Clouds are day viewing;

stars are night screening. What seems so momentary in the heavens during the day, at night becomes so reassuring.

Unlike ancient sky-watchers I have viewed the skies from Alberta to Tasmania. The clouds are still transient, but the stars are not. While the visible stars are different in each hemisphere, over time I learn to recognize the regularity of their patterns on the dark canvas. The planets are always there if I know where and when to look. The night sky is heartening; it always reappears, everlasting, timeless and I can trust that its lights will return; a cosmic timepiece that watches over me. Like a blanket carefully placed over a sleeping child, the night sky lays itself over the earth each night. But it is never really dark. The light is always there, the stars and planets are always locatable if I need them to help navigate my way through the dark. These pinpoints of light are admirable and a constant source of imagination and inspiration. Perhaps this is why I have heard so many of my astrological colleagues speak of their childhood fascination with the starry night sky. The heavens have been a muse to countless souls; no wonder the ancient Greeks gave the name Urania to the Muse who watches over them.

Ancient Greeks personified a classical education through their nine Muses who presided over the realms of the imagination, such as poetry, song, dancing, music, comedy, tragedy and the study of the stars. Urania or *heavenly* was the youngest Muse whose vehicle for inspired thought was the heavens; hence she is known as the Muse of astronomy and astrology. In the mythological period distinctions were not yet delineated between science and divination, hence astronomy and astrology were sisters who ruled over the right and left hemispheres of the heavens. Through the starry patterns above, life below could be imagined.

As the daughters of the Titaness Mnemosyne and Zeus, Urania and her sisters reside in the period between instinctual and ordered life. Their mother, Mnemosyne, was the goddess of memory. Being pre-Olympian she inhabits the mythological realm and characterizes memory that could be termed as 'feeling memory'. It is not cognitive, but is memory stored in the body as our aches and pains, in the emotions as our reactions and responses and in our inner life as moods, dreams and perceptions. She is the personification of instinctual memory; not just a record of something that happened in the past, logged in a book, filmed or taped. Mnemosyne is soulful, evocative and affecting. The goddess embodies memory as the act of recollection and recalling, participating with soul-making by internalizing life experiences through the feeling nature. Residing in the right hemisphere, Mnemosyne relies on intuition as a way of knowing.

Zeus orders the world. He personifies the movement from chaos to order and the elevation of the rational principle. He inhabits the philosophical realm and resides in the left hemisphere. As a daughter of Zeus, Urania inherits this natural feeling for the harmony and regulation of life. And as the heavenly Muse, she inspires us to see the orderliness and beauty in the skies above. To Urania and the ancient Greeks, cosmos was order and beauty and it was in the starry heavens that the order and beauty of the cosmos could be seen. Urania, as the Muse of astrology, has inherited the instinctual memory of the heavens from her mother and the appreciation of its timeless order from her father. Her mother is the mistress of metaphor; her father, the master of judgement. Astrology is parented by both.

In statuary, Urania holds a globe in her left hand and a pointer in her right while keeping her attention on the heavens. Balancing the heavenly globe of symbolic wisdom and pointing to the signs in the skies, Urania muses on the imperceptible connection between life in the cosmos and life on earth. As Muse of astrology she personifies the inspiration of the starry heavens, reminding astrologers of the delicate balance between the symbols in the sky and how they are judged and articulated. Unlike her half-siblings Apollo, Hermes and Athena, Urania's destiny was never to become an Olympian. She inhabits an earlier epoch before Zeus's rational world became triumphant and all-encompassing. Astrology too has its roots in an earlier world order where the participation with nature and the cosmos was not yet separated from human experience.

The sanctuaries of the Muses are museums where their inspirational and transformative images are appreciated. Urania's museum is the heavens. As custodian of the heavens, Urania used the patterns of the stars, the movement of heavenly bodies and their interrelationships as the mnemonic device that gives meaning to the cycles and events of life experienced on earth. Through insight and order in the heavens, Urania engenders the felt sense of being an integral part of the cosmos. As astrology's Muse, she personifies the soulful voice inspired through the order in the starry heavens.

Another goddess connected to astrology through divination by the stars was Asteria. Her name loosely means 'starry one' or 'of the stars', derived from the Greek *aster*.[87] Unfortunately, her mythological memoirs remain undeveloped. In later myth she became associated with the 'reading' of the stars, when her name often personified a seer involved in the art of divination.[88] She is named 'the starry one' so we might imagine that she is one of the early personifications in Greek myth of astrology or the reading of the starry sky. And imagine we must, for her myth remains mysterious, like the inexplicable instinct that draws us towards astrological handiwork. Fragments of Asteria's myth from early Greek literature are sparse and contradictory; however, in her family tree there is no doubt that she belongs to the branch of divination.

According to Hesiod, Asteria was the daughter of the Titans, Coeus and Phoebe, both offspring of Gaia and Ouranus; therefore, she inhabits the pre-literate period or the mythological realm. Two ancestral streams influence Asteria: she inherits the starry heavens through her grandfather Ouranus, and divination through her grandmother Gaia. This inheritance is passed on to Asteria's daughter Hecate.

Asteria's mother Phoebe was the third goddess to preside over the Oracle of Delphi. She was given the oracular realm in good will by her sister Themis, who inherited this from their mother Gaia, the first oracular deity. Phoebe gave her grandson, Apollo, named Phoebus after her, the oracle as a birthday gift to the young god.[89] Phoebe's name can be linked to the Greek words *phoibos*, 'bright' or 'radiant', *phoibaô* 'to purify' and *phoibazô* 'to give prophesy', all motifs of early associations with divination and healing. Phoebe's other daughter was Leto, the mother of Apollo by Zeus. Leto is Asteria's sister; Apollo is her nephew. Hecate and Apollo characterize the night and day approach to divination.

After Zeus defeated the Titans, the movement from mythical thinking towards rational order began. As the new god of the heavens, Zeus's domination of the mythological sphere through rational constructs, organizations and commands was precipitated. The mythological sphere was highly influenced by the spirit of the feminine, which now was vulnerable to new values and beliefs. The shift from the mythological to the philosophical is clearly evident in the myth of Metis, the goddess of instinctual wisdom.

Zeus devours Metis when she is pregnant with his child Athena, who then gestates in his stomach and is eventually born through his head to become the Olympian goddess of wisdom. In astrological imagery Zeus/Jupiter is the ruler of Pisces, his mythological realm, and Sagittarius, his philosophical domain. However, in human development and culture, the philosophical sphere has became more valued, creating duality rather than harmony between these two ways of being.

Asteria was no exception to Zeus's domination of the feminine sphere. Desired by Zeus, Asteria shape-shifted into a quail to avoid his advances, diving into the Aegean where she was transformed into a rocky island.[90] By Classical times this was the celebrated birthplace of the god Apollo and his sister Artemis. Asteria's sister Leto sought refuge on the island when she was pregnant, giving birth here to the god Apollo, Hecate's cousin. Leto and her son Apollo, alongside Asteria and her daughter Hecate, are part of an oracular dynasty. However, with the ascension of Zeus and rational order, the divinatory function became separated into day and night. Apollo, the solar god, represents the day force when oracular messages are delivered through a priest or priestess under the auspices of the god. Hecate, as the lunar goddess, represents the night force where divinatory messages are revealed through dreams and rituals such as augury and astrology. When astrology is practised under the patronage of Apollo, oracular messages are interpreted and read; under Hecate's spell they are revealed through participation with the starry symbols of the night sky.

Under Zeus's administration, the illuminating nature of the day function of rationalism dominated the subjective night force. Hence Apollo slays, rather than befriends, the Python that guards Delphi. Apollo aligns himself with institutional religion and all that is reasonable and ordered. Apollo's divination is overlaid with rational constructs while Hecate's is associated with magical arts, mystery and chaos. Yet, before Apollo, it was the goddess Asteria, mother to Hecate and aunt/nursemaid to Apollo, who was associated with oracles and prophecies of night, including dreams and the reading of the stars. Astrology was not yet a science but a divinatory participation with the images of the starry heavens.

Well before Zeus's reign, at creation's dawn, Nyx or night was one of the five primal deities to emerge from Chaos in

Hesiod's *Theogony*. And it was Nyx who produced Aether and Hemera, or brightness and day.[91] In cosmological order, night exists before day.

As astrology became more allied with the day world of science, its imaginative participation with the night world diminished. Ironically, the starry heavens are only visible at night, yet they are still as inspiring and revealing as they were before they were precisely measured and separated; the planets are still as divine and constant as when they were first witnessed. To participate with their revelations and be touched by their spirituality we do not look at them, but through them, to the eternality of the cosmos. And this is the essence of the metaphor that moves astrologers no matter what their beliefs: the starry heavens are the eternal and constantly reassuring experience of a world far greater than our understanding; the starry heavens are beyond our intelligence and perfectly ordered in their own nature. Whenever we refer to the heavens we honour an intelligence far greater than our own and participate with the mystery and sacredness of the spirit that animates the cosmos. Astrology nurtures the pre-rational psyche where the divine is visible every night in the starry sky.

Astrology's starry sky, its root metaphor, underscores all its techniques and methods, no matter what the school of thought might be. No wonder that magic is experienced by those who participate with astrology. But we cannot appease the rationalists nor allay the criticism of sceptics who do not have eyes to see metaphoric resemblances. Carl Jung bottomlined it when he wrote: 'The really important psychic facts can neither be measured, weighed, nor seen in a test tube or under a microscope. They are therefore supposedly indeterminable, in other words they must be left to people who have an inner sense for them, just as colours must be shown to the seeing and not to the blind.'[92]

4

NIGHT

You, darkness, of whom I am born –
I love you more than the flame
that limits the world
to the circle it illuminates
and excludes all the rest.

But the dark embraces everything:
shapes and shadows, creatures and me,
people, nations – just as they are.

It lets me imagine
a great presence stirring beside me.
I believe in the night.[93]

Rainer Maria Rilke,
'The Night'

In describing her son's birth, Rilke's mother confirmed he arrived just before midnight.[94] His horoscope shows the Sun at its lowest point on the Meridian with all seven classical planets below the horizon in the night hemisphere of the horoscope, born, as he says, of 'darkness'.

Like so many other poets and artists, Rainer Maria Rilke valued the shadowy and creative climate of the night, which embraced other presences and other worlds 'just as they are'. In Percy Bysshe Shelley's 'To Night', he invokes his 'beloved night' to come soon; William Blake in 'Night' honours the healing balm of sleep, while Robert Frost's 'Acquaintance with Night' reminds us of our ambivalence about the night. Astrologers have always appreciated the distinct temperament and atmosphere of night.

This division of night and day is at the heart of astrological work, an insightful metaphor which assists in understanding the temperamental nature of planetary symbols. Our astrological ancestors bequeathed us a way of thinking about night and day through the technique of planetary sect. This method differentiated which planets would be more suitably placed if an individual were born during the day or night. Logically, the Sun was the dominant archetype for the day birth and the Moon for the night. The technique values the distinction between day and night and emphasizes a different orientation to the horoscope dependant on a daytime or night-time birth. It contemplates how archetypal responses may be altered when perceived through either a nocturnal or diurnal lens, whether the atmosphere is perhaps Apollonian or influenced by Hecate.

Parmenides, the 5th-century BCE Greek philosopher, referred to the 'gates of the ways of Night and Day'.[95] Metaphorically, these are the gates we pass through each day at dawn and dusk. If you

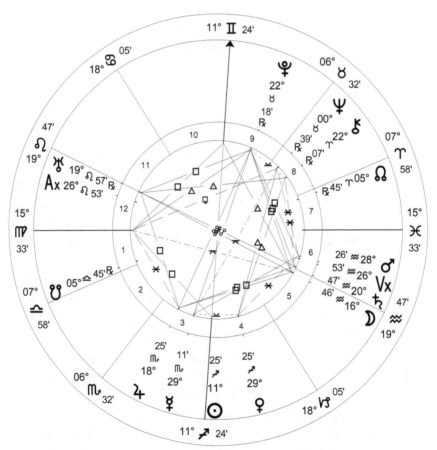

Rainer Maria Rilke, 3 December 1875, 11.50 p.m., Prague

are in your mid fifties, you have passed through each of these gates that divide Night and Day over 20,000 times; 20,000 times you have passed the stream of Oceanus and opened the gate onto Night and 20,000 more you have crossed the River Lethe to find the gate that opens onto Day. These gates are crossroads to another world, each having a different atmosphere and distinct customs. Each world has its own mode of being and knowing: the day world is where Apollo's reason and moderation reign, but the night world is where Hecate's instinct and abandon rule. The day world has the advantage of solidity and continuity but social activities and opportunities are restricted, unlike in the night world where the bondage of time and space is loosened. In the night world of dreams and visions we can meet the gods and our loved ones, dead, alive or as yet unmet.[96]

The metaphor of Night and Day was also central to Carl Jung. He acknowledged two very dissimilar aspects of his nature which were outwardly irreconcilable, naming them as Personality No. 1 and Personality No. 2. Personality No. 1 identified with the mundane world, facts and reason, science, the outer world at the time – his spirit of the times, his day self. Personality No. 2 was the visionary, the magician, the astrologer, the seeker – his spirit of the depths, the night self.[97] Being born with the Sun on the western horizon, his life's work bridged these two worlds of Night and Day. As early as 1911 he wrote to Sigmund Freud about his wanderings into the 'lands of darkness':

At the moment I am looking into astrology, which seems indispensible for a proper understanding of mythology. There are strange and wondrous thing in these lands of darkness. Please don't worry about my wanderings in the infinitudes. I shall return laden with rich booty for our knowledge of the human psyche.[98]

It was Jung's 'wanderings in the infinitudes' of night that opened the portal to the depth of his psychological revelations. *The Red Book* is Carl Jung's 'night book'. In it he details his visions, premonitions, conversations with the dead, active imagination and psychic journeys; calligraphy and mandalas adorn his diary of descent. Whichever way you consider the manuscript, whether as a psychic journal, automatic writing or stream of consciousness, the work pays homage to his personal night visions and conversations. To the day world, it borders on madness. A struggle ensued with his solar self who sought recognition from the establishment for his meaningful explorations of the psychic landscape. Ironically, it was in the lunacy of the night world where he was initiated into the deeply profound, yet paradoxical, nature of the psyche, which dictated volumes of his work. Jung described the years in which he was pursuing his inner images as 'the most important in my life – in them everything essential was decided'. The material that burst forth from Jung's unconscious, the night world, was 'the *prima materia* for a lifetime's work.'[99]

In *The Red Book* Jung writes, 'You open the gates of the soul to let the dark flood of chaos flow into your order and meaning. If you marry the ordered to the chaos you produce the divine child'.[100] This amalgam of the order of the day and the chaos of the night is akin to astrological work where the order of our techniques and methods allows us entry into the unknown territory of the night through the faculty of imagination and the facility of symbols. These gates to the soul are opened when we recognize the symbols. For Jung, symbols made movement to other dimensions of reality possible.[101] Hence this is why he referred to astrology as 'a dark science, a Hecate science',[102] since it defied the strictures of the day world or Apollonian sciences.

Over time the night world has become engulfed by the day world. Darkness, it seems, is a less valuable commodity in a day-ruled world. In a day-ruled world, fascinated with technology and information, it is difficult see the night sky.

Night Emerges Out of Chaos

While differing versions exist of the birth of the gods, it is Hesiod's epic poem *Theogony*, ca. 700 BCE that is the most detailed extant account of how the gods came into being. Hesiod's account is comprehensive, detailing the creation of the copious Greek deities and eventual emergence of the Olympian Gods. But before this emergence of the rational day-orientated gods, there was Nyx, the winged goddess of the original Night. In the beginning was Chaos, a 'yawning' or 'gaping void', potentially the womb of all creation. Through Chaos five beings emerge: the first is Gaia, followed by four other primal deities, Tartarus, Eros, Erebus and Night (Nyx). From the union of Erebus and Night came Aether (Light) and Hemera (Day) as well as Charon, the ferryman of the dead. Day emerges out of Night.

Cosmologically, Night is there right from the beginning. When Night emerges out of Chaos, there is no starry night sky, as neither sky nor stars have yet been born.[103] Night is a primal spirit who parthenogenetically brings forth other personifications of the human night experience: Eris (Strife), Moros (Doom/Foreboding), Cer (a violent or cruel death), Thanatos (Death), Hypnos (Sleep), Kupris (Lust), Momus (Blame/Fault-Finding), Nemesis (Revenge), Oizys (Woe/Misery), Apate (Deceit) and Geras (Old Age). The night world is populated with shades and shadows of waking life.

But Nyx has another face besides this nightly throng of anxieties. She spreads her black wings over the world to bring restful sleep. But, when the day world invades the night, Hypnos or sleep is disturbed and our nightly disquiets are no longer contained by deep sleep and dreams.

Mythologically, Night exists before Day. This is not only metaphoric, but indicative of collective and personal development: the primal gives way to cultural, the right brain to the left, magical thinking to rationality and *gnosis* or intuitive participatory knowing concedes to *episteme* or epistemological knowing.[104] These two ways of being were known to the ancient Greeks as part of our human heritage. Since the Age of Enlightenment the rational, descriptive, factual and purposeful way has largely dominated the imaginative, subjective and participatory way. Day has overrun Night.

Even in the ancient world, Night was a threat to heroic consciousness. Yet to the mystic consciousness of the Orphics, Night was the depth of love and light. Today we favour heroes over mystics – night intelligence is not politically correct. Entering through the night gate into 21st-century life is never easy.[105] Yet this is the gate we enter when we use astrology. When reflecting on contemporary astrological practice, I wonder: have the technical, interpretive and delineative ways of knowing the horoscope overrun the imaginative, intuitive and participatory ways? Have literality and information become the dominant astrological paradigm? Has our astrological night been yoked to the day-world ways of knowing?

To understand the night world's way of knowing I return to dreams. I say 'return', for dreams or 'night letters', many of which are never opened, remind me of the intelligence of the night. What we cannot know during the day can be revealed through dream images. Night images, ghosts, phantoms and Nyx's brood inhabit this world and reveal their messages in the night dialect of story, symbol, image and metaphor. So it is not a surprise that Nyx also gave birth to Oneiros (Dream) or the tribe of Dreams. Dreams are night messages, conversations with the soul. While from the day point of view, in the high-level world of neuroscience, dreams might only be random neural firings, in the night world they are oracular insights from beyond a world bound by facts and reason.

Similarly, astrology is also a night conversation with the cosmos. Astrology is the big dream, the dream of one's life, and each nightly dream re-imagines and re-cognizes the big dream. In listening to the voices of the night through dreams, I have come to listen to the horoscope differently.

Dreams and Astrology: *Daughters of the Night*

Two ancient ways of knowing interconnect through dreams and astrology. Both dreams and astrology are illuminated during the night. As daughters of the Night they belong to a divinatory tradition revealing soul through imagery and metaphor. By engaging with the soulful nature of symbols, memories and felt experiences can be animated and brought to life.

Astrology is also a daughter of Night since the planets and constellations reveal themselves at night, when the Sun is below the horizon. In early Greek literature, Hesiod describes the tribe of Dreams as the daughters of Night. Although astrology is not specified, its birth is implied in Greek myth through Urania and Asteria, as we explored in the previous chapter. Apollo rules the day world of oracular divination; Hecate, the insights from the night world.[106] Both day and night strands are woven into the mantic craft of astrological work.

Although dreams and astrology are divinatory sisters there is a fundamental difference between them. In order to see a dream, the dreamer must be asleep. To see the stars we must be awake. The dream experience is personally felt and experienced and we sense it comes from within, whereas the horoscope, as the reflection of a heavenly moment of time, is less private and outside self. This contributes to astrological images being more susceptible to becoming objectified, literalized, codified and translated objectively without ever touching the soul. But both are divinatory in that they can access knowledge from beyond the bounds of rational control and both involve the gods. In the ancient world dreams were messages from the gods; for astrologers, communication with the ancient gods is evoked through participation with the horoscope.

As children of the Night, the revelations of dreams and astrology cannot be fully developed through the day's sensibilities. Being offspring of the non-rational night world they need metaphors, images, stories and symbols to narrate the soul's journey. While both dreams and astrology can be viewed in the day and analysed rationally and delineated using techniques and manuals, they are naturally reflective by nature and only reveal their depth when we participate with them in a receptive and respectful manner. Their revelations come to life when we suspend our mechanistic thinking and conditioned responses and enter into their dark territory, the state of not-knowing and un-doing.

Dreams are nightly conversations with the soul. As daughters of the Night, dreams adopt the meaningful residue of what has been unnoticed, displaced, forgotten, repressed and/or denied during the day. Therefore the tribe of Dreams are the playwrights for what the soul would like to reveal to the day world. Dream scripts are compiled in images and metaphors, riddles and turns of phrases, unlike the daily composition of language. The dream condenses and ensouls the day's material. The undigested residues of the outer life are the concerns of the soul and become the provisions used to fire up the dream.[107] These narratives of the inner life de-literalize the waking world and return it to soul by revealing the felt experiences and images that have gone unobserved.

Since dreams are the harvest of sleep, perhaps sleep has something to do with this. Sleep is part of the daily cycle where consciousness is reduced, even absent. Or perhaps it is only the solar consciousness that sets, as during sleep much activity, including restoration, memory-processing, brain development and dreaming, occurs. In a way sleep is a daily descent into another reality; however, unlike in death we ascend again into waking. Hence it is not surprising that Sleep and Death were mythic brothers and sons of Night at the time the gods were born. From the mythological beginning Sleep was the land of dreams and closely aligned with Death and the West, where the planets set, metaphorically going to sleep.

How might we, as astrologers, honour the night way of knowing that returns us to the soulful mysteries? Firstly, night is the subjective path, not ruled by being bright nor right. It is a world of participation, inviting involvement with our own way of knowing and our personal experiences, which in turn constellate our uncertainties, ambivalences and paradoxes. This subjective path engages us in our own unconscious process and absorbs us into the chaos of the horoscope that we are reading. It is a world of reflection, rest and sleep, not a world dominated by the need to be recognized or to be correct. It is a world uninfluenced by concepts or words, no matter how dark or feminine or provocative they might be; it is moved by feeling. The language of the night world is image, symbol and metaphor, which facilitate connections to what is not yet known.

Recall that first time when astrology spoke to you, when heaven's gate opened and a connection between two separate parts of yourself was bridged. Something soulful stirred, a deep recognition, a reconnection to knowing there was a cosmic plan, a revelation of something deeply personal yet beyond your biography. But what you heard and felt and experienced was beyond any words.

Yet perhaps in the time since then, the techniques and methods and theories and opinions and house systems and scoring essential dignities have left you with limited access to the mystery and imagination of astrology. If the day world has dried astrology out, try turning it upside down by engaging in or practising not knowing; think laterally, use a metaphor, be paradoxical, take a crack at storytelling, read poetry, listen to music, summon the Muses, reflect on what is behind or below the symbol, perform a ritual or go to sleep with the intent of recalling your dreams. Invoke the night way of knowing. The next time you look at a horoscope in all its precision and array of symbols, pause a moment, hold onto those first thoughts, listen to that niggling feeling, honour the image that floats into consciousness – let confusion and uncertainty be your guides to see through to the starry night that lies beyond the mechanics of the horoscope. Astrology cannot exist without the moistness of the night.

Another subtext of the technique of planetary sect concerned the lunar phases: a waxing Moon was considered diurnal in nature, while a waning Moon was nocturnal. In the ancient world, the night before the New Moon was the time for Hecate's suppers when food was taken to the crossroads to appease the mistress of the Night and her Dead. At the crossroads the restless dead congregated, seeking sustenance from the living. By offering the suppers to the ghosts, the suppliant pacified the dead and honoured Hecate, the goddess of the Night. At night we converse with the spirits of the dead.

Our night world is a metaphoric world, one of symbol and image, which we endeavour to translate into a day dialect. I sometimes wonder if it really matters how literal or commercial astrology becomes, because ultimately She is always a daughter of the night and just the mention of a zodiac sign, a backward travelling Mercury, a Venus pentagram in the sky or that your mother had her Moon on your Neptune returns us to the heavens, something larger than who we are, something bigger than our problems, and something beyond the concreteness of our mundane world.

Logos
Just as Day was born from Night, so Logos is born from Symbol.

When astrology was re-imagined in the Hellenistic period, rationalist thinking had become a prominent gauge to understand the new world that was gradually moving away from the participatory and mythological ways of engaging. It was a philosophical age. The emergence of a more logical worldview had begun to find its dominance over a more instinctual and primal intelligence. A subjective worldview was yielding to a more objective outlook; participation with the gods was becoming replaced by knowledge and scientific inquiry. Day was appropriating Night.

Centuries earlier, when Greece was emerging from its Dark Age, Homer was promoting Zeus and his children, the new Olympian gods, as paragons of order and stability. Zeus gave birth to Athena, the new goddess of wisdom while, in the Hebrew Genesis of a similar epoch, Eve was shaped from Adam. Maleness, light, logic and linearity were emerging as dominant principles. The left brain began to cleave its separation from the prevailing right hemisphere. Hence subject and object became separated, differences became defined, polarities existed and judgements were made. Subjective and objective outlooks were distinguished and data could now be verified independently, not only felt or imagined. The world moved towards empirical knowing, day knowing.

Many centuries later, as Greco-Roman astrology emerges, embracing logical tenets gleaned from the philosophical, methodical and thoughtful Hellenistic period, the dual concepts of masculine and feminine, benefic and malefic, hot and cold, wet and dry were applied to characterize planetary archetypes. The natural division of day and night was suggested, probably in the 1st century BCE. Interestingly this practice, which assigned equal power to the archetypes of the day and night, was misplaced or lost along the way as the cultural equilibrium between day and night became unbalanced.

Two thousand years later, day and night still exist but their experience is not the same. The division between day and night is no longer as distinctive or as well defined as it once was. Artificial light brightens the dark, pills help us sleep and we are encouraged to keep the darkness at bay. The 24/7 news cycle invades our night world with day images; city lights brighten up the night sky, obscuring the starlight; TV, computer, mobile phone and tablet screens brighten our night world with information. The day world invades the night, fuelling the left brain with judgements on the right. Restorative sleep, the boon of the night world, is inhibited. It is acceptable to bring the day world of technology into our bedrooms, but bringing the night world of intuitions, visions and feelings into the boardroom is unwelcomed.

Rilke encourages us to believe in the night and to remember that the dark embraces everything. Astrology is a creative art that welcomes the night and all its images, visions, phantoms and prophecies. Sarah Williams in her poem *The Old Astronomer to His Pupil* beautifully reminds us of the astrology of the night:

Though my soul may set in darkness, it will rise in perfect light;
I have loved the stars too fondly to be fearful of the night.

5

CREATIVITY

To see a World in a Grain of Sand
And a Heaven in a Wild Flower
Hold Infinity in the palm of your hand
And eternity in an hour[108]

William Blake,
'Auguries of Innocence'

We are all familiar with these much-quoted lines from William Blake's *Auguries of Innocence*. These four lines prepare the reader for Blake's poem of paradoxes, which explores the fragility, beauty and imbalance of life. The lines are not just wonderfully aesthetic but speak to a deeply resonant truth not easily explained, nor articulated; truth recognized by the soul, not the intellect.

To understand what Blake is implying, we could make a case that within an hour there are endless nanoseconds and attoseconds; but this would be the ever-restless mind trying to make sense of these images in a reasonable way. However, there is another way: Blake invites us to imagine, to be creative. In these four lines, Blake reminds us of a transcendent sight that sees through nature to other worlds. In a way we need childlike eyes to imagine and play with these images.

As Blake said: 'To Me This World is all One continued Vision of Fancy or Imagination.'[109] For many artists, imagination is the playground that exists alongside the literal world and creativity is the crafting of this imagination into form, like a poem, a play or an astrological reading.

William Blake was a master at crafting his imagination through writing and painting. I was heartened, although not surprised, to see the 5th house, contemporarily known as the house of creativity, well tenanted. The Sun, along with Mercury and Jupiter, images of letters from the imagination, are all housed here. The 5th house is also populated by children and Blake was an advocate for children's rights through his tender and compassionate writing, such as his *Songs of Innocence*. In the 5th house we find a symbolic playground where the imagination of the child has free rein to be creative.

Locating creativity in the 5th house astrologically suggests the creative process is a natural landscape of the soul. Creativity might be considered a biological trait as it is part of our life-lore and experience of living. Innate in each human being, creativity is the natural urge to express the unique and original self in individual and innovative ways. Carl Jung suggested that humans, like nature, have 'the distinctive power of creating something new in the real sense of the word'.[110] Jung conceptualized five main groups of instincts. One of these was creativity, with the others being hunger, sexuality, activity and reflection. In discussing the creative instinct,

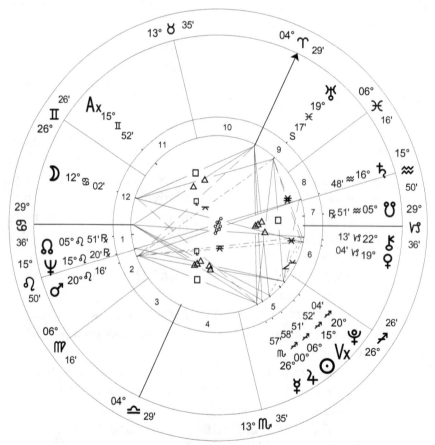

William Blake, 28 November 1757, 7.45 p.m., London

he preferred to categorize it as a psychic factor, like a soulful calling, which arouses a deeper resonant quality.

Psychoanalytically, Freud drew our attention to the similarity between creativity and play, contrasting the artist's fantasies with a child's play. But it was D.W. Winnicott who explored the playground as a creative space where the external world could be imaginatively reshaped without compliance, climax or too much anxiety.[111] In a playful space a creative reaching-out takes place. In the playground, participation with imagination is encouraged and the child's recreation becomes engaged in re-creating their world; for me, this is analogous to an astrological consultation. However, as Freud suggested, the childhood playground is dismantled in adulthood, packed away with the toys of early days. Or as Pablo Picasso quipped: 'Every child is an artist; the problem is staying an artist when you grow up.'[112]

Freud mused that his Germanic language preserved the link between children's play (*spiel*) and poetic creation though words such as comedy (*lustspiel*) and tragedy (*trauerspiel*).[113] Comedy and tragedy were at the creative heart of Greek theatre. In the English language, theatrical productions are called 'plays'; in other words, an engagement with re-creating an imaginative story. Psychoanalysis corroborated astrological intelligence, as creativity and play are linked together in the domain of the 5th, a house known as Good Fortune to Hellenistic astrologers and where the planet of pleasure, Venus, rejoices. Here, in this astrological atmosphere, play is linked with the freedom of self-expression, emotional enrichment and pleasure: it is a sphere of creation, recreation and procreation.

A common perception is that creativity is akin to being artistic. Many clients believe that if they were a writer, poet, painter, dancer or musician, they would experience the passion they feel is missing in their lives. But creativity is not a product, nor is it algorithmic; it is a process. Neither is creativity limited to the arts. Science, engineering, commerce, technology, human resources and astrology can all be creative fields of endeavour when approached imaginatively. Physical, even mundane, work can be creative when the soul is engaged. The work on oneself, development and maturity involve the creative process, an elemental aspect of individuation. Engagement in the process, not the focus on the product or end goal, is vital to creativity.

For many, being creative is imagined as an activity or occupation that will bring a more expressive life. Wanting to know how to access these ambiguous, mysterious and unidentified characteristics of creativity brought many clients to my consulting room. In essence, their longing for creativity was a question of soul. I felt it was my task to use the horoscope to ensoul their experience, not necessarily to offer literal solutions to their complex questions. At the heart of a client's search for creativity is often the question of soul.

Creativity in the Cupboard

Daniel was a client I saw only once. He was at a stage of life where his corporate work was unfulfilling and, as he said, it was time to address his spiritual growth; in his words, 'to identify and work on those issues that are dear to the spirit.' Daniel's appointment was at 5 p.m. on 20 October 2014 in my consulting room in Melbourne.

Daniel was engaged and participatory. What emerged through the process of the consultation was his sorrow at 'shelving' his creativity. He loved music, especially jazz, and as a young man he was strongly connected to becoming a musician. But the reality of earning a living, being a provider and feeling financially secure led him into the corporate world. The stress of the outer world meant his saxophone stayed behind in the closet. Most men would be able to empathize with Daniel's loss of soul because of the demands of the corporate world. I felt that taking the initiative to make the appointment was a step forward in re-engaging with his creative self. Like William Blake, Daniel has a Venus–Chiron conjunction, but his is in Aquarius in the 5th house. This spoke to me of the pain of disconnecting from the pleasures of creativity. At the time of our appointment, transiting Chiron was in a retrograde phase of its cycle, conjunct Daniel's Sun in Pisces in the 6th house. Perhaps it was time to find a way for soul to be reawakened and integrated in his day-to-day life. His Moon in Leo is opposite the Venus–Chiron conjunction, so we amplified the familial and social patterns of creativity and attitudes towards the feminine to try and excavate his authentic feelings around performing and playing.

Two days after our appointment, I received an email. Daniel wrote, 'I would like to share a powerful dream I had Monday night after seeing you.' He then told me his dream:

> I was sitting in the front passenger seat of a car which you were driving and Louis Armstrong was sitting in the back seat directly behind me. I turned my back towards you and looking over my left shoulder started to talk to him. I noticed he was wearing glasses and I asked him a question in the third person, 'Does Louis wear glasses when he is performing?' I noticed I didn't ask him directly and thought how strange that I should do so. I then corrected myself and asked, 'Do you wear glasses when you're on stage?' I can't remember if he responded or not.

He explained that he had dreamt about Louis Armstrong a number of times in his life, suggesting Louis personified his creative and expressive side. He reflected on the dream, saying: 'It seems to me that by addressing him in the third person I wasn't honouring that part of myself.' Ironically or serendipitously, in a real-life cupboard, he had a large framed photo of Louis Armstrong, which he hadn't yet hung up in his apartment. As he said: 'The photographer caught him in a reflective, soulful moment. It's a side of his personality which is not usually captured in images of him. I am now going to hang this photo up within the week.' Like the horoscope, the dream had reminded him to reveal his soulful nature.

Dreams are powerful reminders of psyche's work. Commonly, clients will share their dreams during consultations, as something I have said might trigger a fragment of a dream. Or sometimes clients tell me about the dream they had the night before their consultation. Daniel's dream seemed to be a direct response to the consultation. This dream struck a chord, not only because Daniel's 'creative and expressive side' was about to be brought out of the cupboard to reveal his reflective and soulful nature, but the image of Louis Armstrong was personally meaningful to me. Daniel could not have consciously known, as only a handful do, that my second name is Louis, the name I was christened with and which is on my birth certificate, but which I never use. My parents each chose one name and agreed on calling me Brian, so my name is Robert Louis Brian Clark. My father chose the name Louis after Louis Armstrong, who was his musical inspiration. He always loved Louis's music.

Daniel's Ascendant is 0° Libra 45′; my Sun is 0° Libra 42′ in the 5th house. I contemplated this synastry image as being connected to my driving the car in the dream. At the time of the appointment Mercury was retrograde conjunct the North Node, within a degree of my natal Mercury retrograde, which is conjunct the South Node. When writing this I wondered about Louis Armstrong's horoscope and was delighted to find it had an A rating, and even more delighted to see his Descendant within one minute of arc of my Mercury.[114] Like Daniel, I had turned my back on my father's namesake. Louis also has a 5th house Sun and the dream connection reminded me to make space for play and imagination.

I started our consultation quite apologetically as I had made a mistake in my communication when making the appointment with Daniel. My consulting room in the Abbotsford Convent was Room 1.47, but I had written 2.47. I had never sent anyone to room 2.47 before. Later, when reflecting on this, I recognized that I had sent Daniel to the artist's floor. The second floor of the convent is predominantly artists' studios where there are painters, writers, book designers, photographers, etc. Room 2.47 is an artist's studio, whose resident artist is enormously creative with her installations. Had I sent Daniel to the 'right' floor? He spent 15 minutes waiting on the landing of the artist; therefore we started our consultation late, just as the last degrees of Pisces rose to yield to 0 degrees Aries, Daniel's Descendant.

The Creative Quest
Poets, writers, painters, entrepreneurs, inventors and other original artists frequently describe their creative process like awakening from a dream, seeing a vision or being inspired by a muse or spirit. For instance, Coleridge described his experience of writing 'Kubla Khan' as images that aroused him while asleep, and upon waking he was able to record his impressions.[115] Einstein's solution to the relativity of time coalesced one morning as he arose from sleep. Years of focused contemplation and research had led to this moment. Dreamscapes are unencumbered by rational thoughts and external demands, an ideal setting for the creative process to emerge. In the psychic twilight, when the matrix of time and space is altered, creativity prospers.

Sigmund Freud explored the question of whether creative writers were 'dreamers in broad daylight'.[116] In many ways an astrological consultation is like dreaming in broad daylight. The 5th house of creativity is below the horizon, in the night hemisphere of the horoscope. A creative encounter with each horoscope leads us into the night world where we can initiate, invent, perform and envision. In this transitional setting, connections can be made that may not be able to emerge in any other setting; insights can be gleaned that may be impossible at other times. Creative play, active imagination and honouring transitional space in an astrological consultation are keys that reveal meaning I never would have encountered solely using astrological techniques. I often find myself asking the client to imagine, play a role or change the space.

For instance, Daniel was taking dancing lessons and I asked him to imagine dancing, feeling free, then picking up his saxophone and playing. Gerry felt stuck in a rut at work. I asked him to get up, walk around the room and tell me the story again. Jean revealed she was angry and frustrated with her boss and felt powerless to say anything. I asked her to sit in my consulting chair and tell me, sitting in her chair, how she really felt. Frances was frustrated with her mother who no longer engaged with life in ways that were familiar. I asked Frances to switch roles for a moment, play her mother, pretend to be her. We then talked about what she felt. My intention is engagement with the symbols that have arisen, not therapy, although ironically these playful acts are therapeutic. In a creative space play becomes ritual, which can evoke an encounter with the gods. As an astrologer the horoscope is like a map that invites me to facilitate this encounter for the client.

Astrological Creativity

Clients seek assistance, clarification, confirmation and direction into their career and vocational experiences, often due to a lack of meaning in their job, a conflict in the workplace or feeling undervalued by their industry. One of the most common motifs voiced by clients in vocational consultations is the desire to be creative. But what is creativity? And why do many feel that creativity is the resolution to their vocational dissatisfaction? It is a word often used by counsellors and astrologers in an all-purpose way, but what is implied? I always begin by contextualizing creativity and trying to understand what the client means when they refer to this process.

To me, the instinct to create is at the heart of each vocation, but being creative requires sensitivity and empathy. Its nature involves the capacity to give birth to ideas and activities, to play and imagine, as well as to search for greater meaning. Ironically, creativity is the act of giving birth to the Self in the present situation and circumstances, not being freed by something romantic. Erotic in nature, creativity is life-giving, fuelled by fantasy and filled with possibility. It deeply touches the core of oneself and in this way it also stirs the darkness of melancholy and depression. Creativity awakens the inner life.

Through my work with clients I have found that deeper insights are more accessible when discussing complexities, ambiguities and uncertainties, rather than giving definitive answers or direct advice. Therefore, I became more soul-orientated in my approach to the horoscope, deeply listening and consciously suspending my need to get it right or know the answer. In participating with the client's contradictions, confusion and despair, deeper feelings behind the astrological images and symbols are revealed. I came to develop the ability to not give advice and the art of not knowing, which to me are essential in developing a creative way of thinking.

Dane Rudhyar wrote that 'to cast an astrological chart in the way it is done today is just as symbolic a process as painting an oil painting.'[117] For, like an artist, when an astrologer is immersed in the psychic waters of the horoscope, something precious and productive can be created. In this way astrology is a fine art, because like any authentic art it speaks to the ultimate depths of the individual, revealing and inspiring images and revelations. While art may be decorative and mesmerizing, its function is exploration and investigation. Similarly, astrology can be appealing and compelling, but like all art it teaches us how to perceive the world we inhabit and see through it to deeper realms. Like an artist, an astrologer constellates insight, using his craft to find meaning in the heavenly images symbolized in the horoscope.

The language of art, like astrology, is logical but not in a rational way, as it opens up a conversation exploring what is unknown rather than focusing on a fact or definitive answer. Creativity can often be conceived through a conflict of ideas. However, it is born from the ability to perceive something beyond the literal, conventional and traditional implications. Astrological creativity is born from the ability to connect images, sense the many nuances of a symbol and synthesize these impressions into a meaningful image for the client. Like art, astrology inspires us to explore the mysteries, confront our realities and question our authenticity. While an artist might use textures, natural materials, illustrations or sounds, the astrologer uses the symbols of the horoscope to communicate.

The art of astrology is the skilful use of symbols in the context of the moment. Intellectual agility and confidence are needed to be creative, but empathy, intuition, perception, sensation and feeling are also essential. In the chapter Metaphor, we introduced John Keats's 'negative capability', which highlighted the creative values of uncertainty, mystery and doubt over the respected sciences of facts and reason. Although he did not use this turn of phrase again, it was always implied through his exploration into his own creativity. In a later letter he amusingly summarized the feelings of his marginality as a poet: 'What shocks the virtuous philosopher delights the camelion Poet'.[118]

While astrology is a remarkable merger of poetry and philosophy, it can also be used factually and conservatively. When astrology is reduced to cause–effect explanations, bound by techniques and systematized, its character becomes practical and productive, which may still be of value but is no longer divinatory. In other words, the symbol becomes a sign leading us in a certain direction towards a conclusion, highly useful when seeking certainty or an exact answer. However, this approach can become formulaic, removing the mystery, soulfulness and art of astrology. When the mystery of divination and the creative power of the symbol are no longer part of the astrological equation, astrology becomes a system rather than a creative act.

Locating the creative process in the horoscope is fluid, as there are many ways to shape one's imagination. As a guideline I explore the 1st, 5th and 9th houses as the embodiment of the creative process, as these habitats align with our baptism into Self. These houses address an aspect of creativity, whether that is birth, self-expression, play, inspiration or the search for meaning. And each house in the trinity leads to a house of 'substance' where the creative process can be grounded and expressed in the world. The dictionary defines 'to create' as to bring something into existence or being. Creativity is more than imagination and inspiration; it implies incarnation, an embedded truth in the astrological wheel, for the houses of incarnation, matter and substance follow the houses of birth, creativity and play, and inspiration respectively.[119] In essence, all environs in the horoscope can be creative; however, the 1st, 5th and 9th houses encapsulate creation.

Genius is often associated with creativity, describing an individual who expresses special and outstanding abilities. This concept of genius became more widely used in the 18th century in reference to an individual with an exceptional inborn talent or a natural creative disposition. In Latin, the verb *genui* or *genitus* is akin to birth, to create or produce. However, in ancient Rome, the earlier usage of the word *genius* referred to a guiding spirit or personal or familial deity. Since gifted and creative people were influenced by their *genius*, the word began to be associated with talent and inspiration. In the 18th century the English translations of *One Thousand and One Nights* anglicized the Latin *genius* into the word 'genie', the guardian spirit at the command of the person who had released it from its captivity. Like genius, creativity too has a divine nature, for to be creative the individual needs to release the genie and follow their guiding spirit.

Astrological tradition also used the idea of *genius* or guardian spirit through the enduring and mutable concept of the *daimon*, also contextualized over time as a power, a demon or spirit, even personality and destiny.[120] It appears literally in the names given to houses 11 and 12 as the Good and Bad Daemon as well as named in the Lots. Its image has been used to describe planetary deities or noteworthy planets in the horoscope. Astrologically, each planet could be seen as having its own special creative qualities. However, while each planetary archetype may be inherently creative, it is the approach to and use of the energy that constellates the creative act. What is Mercury without a puzzle; Mars without a battle or Saturn without a commitment? Creativity can be encountered through each planetary archetype when engaged authentically in the moment rather than rationalizing or fixing it.

As with alchemical work, there are stages in the creative process. The initial struggle with the creative urges is followed by an interval of incubation where the pain of creativity surfaces through self-doubt, anxiety and despair. It is during this phase of anguish that seeds are planted, and if they take root the consequence is inspiration. The final phase grounds the creative process in the world of form, where it is given shape and substance.[121] The process requires both ego strength and surrender; receptivity and activity. Therefore, it is evident that creativity is not a commodity to be obtained, but a deeper psychic process that requires the ability to be open to its complexities and ambiguities. Imagination and symbolic thinking are valuable, as is the capacity to be fluid and accepting. While many clients feel that doing something other than what they are doing would be meaningful, ironically it is the involvement with their current life process, and working through its stages and troubles, that is creative.

Creativity is fostered by agreeableness, openness to new experiences, an interest in ideas and aesthetics, the cognitive ability to manipulate abstractions, to think laterally and a willingness to be marginal. Behind each creative life are introspection, questioning and the urge for self-actualization.[122] Creative beings are often 'astonishingly productive'.[123] But rather than typifying creativity or imaginative individuals, perhaps these observations suggest that the creative impulse is located on the edge of chaos, outside organized systems and independent of hierarchical dominance. In other words, creativity is akin to originality and uniqueness, on the frontiers of the unconscious, animated by the imagination and sustained by productivity. Astrology lives and thrives in this domain; hence engaging with astrological images is potentially always a creative act.

6

SYMPTOM

I am not a mechanism, an assembly of various sections.
And it is not because the mechanism is working wrongly,
that I am ill. I am ill because of wounds to the soul, to the deep
emotional self and the wounds to the soul take a long, long time,
only time can help and patience, and a certain difficult repentance[124]

D. H. Lawrence,
Healing

Illness raises more questions than can be answered, despite the remarkable advances in medicine: 'What is wrong with me? Why did it happen to me? What is going to happen because of this thing that has gone wrong?'[125] 'Why me?' remains a common question. Modern-day medicine's answer has become narrower. Illness has become objectified, reduced to something that we get, no longer something that is part of us. Disease is referred to as an enemy, something to battle, separate from the soul. The instruments and means of modern medicine are a marvel and very persuasive, yet biomedicine is not always able to heal. The subjective, intimate and personal questions about disease have been relinquished to the Church, the New Age and alternative counsellors.

As a counselling astrologer, I often witness the personal question, 'Why me?' which has been asked of me in so many ways: 'Why can't I fall pregnant?', 'What is this pain the doctors can't diagnose?', 'Why did the cancer come back?' I am alert to the images and reflections that arise from the discussion of the symptoms, not in an effort to fix or prescribe, but to honour the soul's capacity for healing and acceptance. Although the horoscope can be effective at diagnosis, if I become too literal I will collude in abandoning the personal and turn the illness into a thing, renouncing the soulful voice under the symptom. If I am too conceptual about the imagery of the illness, then I might inflame remorse about wrong choices. By listening to the client's symptoms, considering the horoscope's patterns and then engaging in dialogue with the client, something that makes all the difference is often revealed.

When Illness was Divine

In Greek mythology the divine healer has always been acknowledged and petitioned. This tradition is traceable all the way back to Paean in the Mycenaean period through to Apollo in Homeric epic and his son Asclepius, the god of healing, in the late Archaic and early Classical periods.[126] In the later 5th century BCE, Hygieia becomes the personification of health and the embryonic concept of well-being. Before the emergence of Hippocrates and rational medicine, the transmission of healing passed from Paean to Apollo to Asclepius and Hygieia.[127]

Chiron emerges in Greek literature as the 'righteous' centaur, first mentioned in Homer's *The Iliad*. By the 5th century BCE, Euripides had forged his image as the kindly mentor of healing and warfare.[128] As Greek medicine developed, it reiterated the cosmological motif of order triumphing over chaos. While medical progress characterized the Greek doctrine of rational order, the developing cult of medicine created a coherent medical mythology by aligning the healer Asclepius, first mentioned in Homer's *The Iliad*, with Apollo and therefore the gods. When rational medicine emerged, Hippocrates was legitimized as the founder of medicine by linking him to mythic Asclepius. Ironically, this created a cohesive pattern in the transmission of medical knowledge and acknowledged both doctor and divinity as attendants at the nativity of medicine. Hippocrates' ancestral chain reached back nineteen generations to claim descent from Asclepius, the mythic healer of Epidaurus who was schooled in the arts by the wise centaur Chiron from Thessaly.[129] Western medicine rests on this divine ancestry.

An artefact of ancient medicine is an awareness of the amalgam of wounding and healing. In antiquity, both were the authority of the gods; wounding and healing could not be separated. What wounded was also an agent of healing and the god who wounded was the god petitioned for healing. Both disease and cure were divine, as is clearly illustrated in early Greek literature and myth.

In the archaic mind a lack of virtue was the precursor of disease. Within *The Iliad* and *The Odyssey* the notion that misfortune is the inevitable consequence of recklessness or immoral action is apparent and this moral emphasis is confirmed at the very beginning of both epics. Early Greek thought suggested that evils are born from our own irresponsibility. Two millennia later, in a monotheistic ethos, Paracelsus reiterated the authenticity of the divine disease:

> You should divide the disease of men … into those which arise in a natural way, and those which come upon us as God's scourges. For take good note of it: God has sent us some diseases as a punishment, as a warning, as a sign.[130]

It is still common to believe that transgression against the sacred justifies illness. Even in our technologically sophisticated medical atmosphere, the transitory thought after a complicated diagnosis or onset of a critical illness has moral undertones. The mind regresses to connect sin and impiety with the commencement of sickness. In spite of everything, even the marvels of modern medicine, disease remains mysterious and bewildering, as intimated by the universal question the patient poses: 'Why me?' Yet illness also reconnects us to a more authentic and imaginative life, reawakening an inherent religious instinct and, at the very least, engendering meaningful reflection. With the diagnosis of a serious disease the patient is confronted by their mortality and this critical realization often shifts the course of their lives in a more soulful direction.

Chiron's Legacy

The mysterious fusion of disease and healing, curing and wounding, is visible in the mythic figure of Chiron. The discovery in 1977 of Chiron coincided with the burgeoning awareness of complementary medicine and alternative ways to practise healing. One of Chiron's archetypal images is the wounded healer. James Hillman reminds us that the 'wounded healer' is a personification of a kind of consciousness.[131] Chironic healing arises from the consciousness in the wound; therefore, our injuries and our illnesses reveal the soul's intent.

When health and sickness are split, we are confined in a binary state which exacerbates the pain. Chiron is positioned in the split, inhabiting the space between the medicine man and the medical doctor, acknowledging both body and soul. The Chironic archetype acknowledges wounding as part of the welfare of the whole constitution. When included in the astrological pantheon, Chiron initiates us into this ancient way of healing. Honouring this archetype suggests an awareness of the divine in both the wound and its cure. In the horoscope it reiterates the ancient intelligence that healing consciousness is brought to light by participating with the wound rather than triumphing over it. Chiron challenges our fix-it mentality – its very essence suggests that the wound is an aspect of the soul yearning to be heard.

Broadly speaking, we could categorize two strands of healing. Both are woven through the fabric of medicine, symbolic of the two snakes that entwine the caduceus, the icon of medicine. In a modern context we could define these two ways as the biomedical model and complementary (or alternative) medicine. Both can be effective rituals of healing, yet over time they have become polarized.

This was not always so. As Greek medicine developed in the later 5th century BCE, the Hippocratic tradition was devoted to rational medicine while the Asclepian tradition practised psychological healing through dream incubation and attending to the divine. These healing fibres are threaded together throughout the history of medicine, categorized as the strands of rational and religious medicine.

In the rational approach to medicine, disease is seen as a physical ailment requiring objective intervention. Symptoms are indicative of imbalances in the body, a genetic proclivity or weakness, a virus or bacteria undermining the immune system. Inherently, the source lies within the body and the treatment relieves the symptoms, often by battling the disease. Treatment is prescriptive or pharmacological and comprises a course of action.

The alternative approach also acknowledges disease as an imbalance, but psychological, ancestral and spiritual factors are recognized as being part of the syndrome. Symptoms indicate psychic or soul disturbances, such as trans-generational losses or complexes of feelings that have not been acknowledged or freed, the impact of *in utero* or precognitive trauma, stressful change, childhood loss, abuse, tension or disturbance, etc. Therapy helps to make contact with the source of the wounding in order to loosen the complex and liberate the trauma. Healing is ultimately an amalgam of both the rational and the religious, because an effective union between the two affords a greater possibility of healing.

Soul and Symptom: Psyche + Soma = Psychosomatic
Since the first treatises of medicine, pain has been considered to develop from imbalances in the constituents of the body. Pain is *in-between*, a space between the body and soul, an ancient idea referred to as *metaxy*. This in-between healing space is Chiron's province.

In a psychological sense, pain is the expression of unacknowledged tension between two different ways of being, a split or unattended opposition. While Hippocratic doctors were comfortable treating diseases that had physical roots, patients with symptoms connected to 'invisible ills' were referred to the Temple of Asclepius. The Hippocratic doctor was aware that if *Tyche* or Chance was a component of the illness, then *Techne* or technical knowledge was not effective. What needed to be healed was the soul and that required another therapeutic methodology. At the dawn of rational medicine there was a great respect for the divine disease or what has come to be coined 'psychosomatic' illness.

Our contemporary definition suggests that psychosomatic illness is a physical disorder that is caused or notably influenced by emotional factors. Common themes in a psychosomatic disorder are trauma and unacknowledged loss, such as the loss of an attachment figure early in life, abandonment by a parent or caretaker, early childhood abuse or trauma, parental neglect or lack of support. The loss seeks recognition through a physical symptom or a mental state. Losses from previous generations also impact the psyche. Like phantoms, shades of the disturbance continue to haunt successive generations; hence the invisible pain and underlying aliment are difficult to diagnose. The unspoken loss of a child or a parent, unacknowledged trauma or violations held in secret seep out into the pool of familial feelings to be absorbed and expressed by others in the familial environment. A grandfather's depression from an untended emigration wound, a lost inheritance or an unsuccessful parental career pulls future children into its abyss to be acknowledged and healed.

Although early medicine fully acknowledged the divine in the disease as being a vital aspect of wellness, the psychic component of disease remains neglected in consulting rooms, hospitals and healing centres today. As medicine became dissociated from the divine, the gods were no longer in the diseases; hence the soul became ignored in medical treatment. And as James Hillman quipped: 'Dead Gods can hardly heal.'[132]

Astrology remains one of the few tools that still acknowledge the divine in the disease. Its medical associations identify the influence of the gods. In contemporary terms, these resident gods of the unconscious are personalized through the arrangement of astrological symbols. From a contemporary view, divine diseases are akin to psychosomatic ills. Bodily complaints and symptoms are imagined as the pronunciation of the soul's discontent, and astrology can imaginatively link the symptoms of the body to the signs of the soul. In the hands of a complementary practitioner, the horoscope is an exceptional tool to assist in imagining the root disorder of the symptom.

To know its core, the symptom must be read, not in a literal sense, but using metaphor and image to reach the heart of the ailment. *Semeia*, the ancient art of reading divinatory signs and symptoms, is compatible with astrology because astrology attempts to read the symptom through planetary images and symbolism. Reading symptoms requires fundamental listening skills such as active silence and the ability to hear what is not being said, as well as the use of metaphor and imagination. Creating a safe and sacred space is also vital. A brief family history is important as it often reveals the reoccurrence and timing of the psychic disorder.

To find ways to imagine the underlying disease one needs to find words to express the symptom, and these are metaphorical, not literal. These images belong to the soul, not the body, although it is the body that becomes the screen for these projected psychic images. Conversations with the soul use the poetic language of symbols, signs, symptoms, omens, slips of the tongue, reveries, imagination, fantasy, feelings and, of course, metaphors. Jung suggested the gods have become diseases, no longer honoured on Mount Olympus, but now manifesting as 'neurotic symptoms':

> We are still as much possessed by autonomous psychic contents as if they were Olympians. Today they are called

phobias, obsessions, and so forth: in a word neurotic symptoms. The gods have become diseases.[133]

Jung's way of thinking is consistent with astrological imagery in that we can align planetary gods with symptoms. Dishonoured gods of the horoscope become likely dis-eases. Astrological images encourage us to consider what underpins them. Often the link between the astrological image and the disease is apparent; however, the reflective task is to let the soul reveal itself through the images of the chart rather than theoretically delineating the astrological images. Astrological theory is profound, but when contained and held in the reverence of the psyche something beyond the Self emerges. We cannot get a soul history from a case history and neither can the soul reveal itself through the astrological image if technique and logic are directing the delineation.

There are numerous ways to think about psychosomatic ills. When authentic aspects of the individual are unlived or denied they may find their way into conscious expression through poor health. Pre-verbal, *in utero* trauma, early childhood abuse or emotional distress are often the source; however, this too is likely compounded by trans-generational suffering. At the core of the psychosomatic pain is a soulful urge that wants to be acknowledged. Since the astrological horoscope is a metaphoric map of the psyche, the imaginatively rich poetry of astrology can help guide us. But I would like to emphasize that it is a guide, not a forecast, for the prognosis is revealed in the voice of the symptom. Before the mechanistic model of disease began to prevail, symptoms were honoured as voices of the divine. Today the soul's voice may be unheard, often numbed by medication or ignored in treatment. Astrological intelligence encourages the soul's voice to be heard through the symptom.

Planetary Symbolism: Gods and Diseases
Acquainting ourselves with the planetary archetypes from the perspective of health assists in understanding what lies behind the symptom, the soulful source of the discontent. Not being medically trained I have developed my own way of thinking about symptoms and the soul by listening to the symbols and images of clients' pain and ills. Symptoms may be physical or mental; in other words, the

core of the distress is either projected into the body or absorbed by the mind. In astrological wisdom this embraces the 6th–12th house polarity where the soul voices its disorder somatically or psychologically. The tradition of the 6th house is akin to *physical* illness while the 12th suggests *mental* health.

While astrological patterns can help reveal the core of the psychosomatic disorder, this is only possible when listening to an individual's story. Astrology can offer the archetypal picture but the individual will supply their personal experience of how this pattern penetrates their well-being. Psychosomatic disorders are often entrenched in trans-generational chaos, as ancestral disagreements, rejections and the disowning of authentic values and morals pollute the soul's legacy. For successive generations at critical stages this might resurface as illness, disease, depression or dissatisfaction.[134]

Complex aspects between the outer planets and the inner planets, in particular the Moon, hold strong personal urges often compromised by patterns greater than the individual. Difficult aspects to the Moon are highly vulnerable to absorbing grievances only to have them surface later through symptoms. The feeling life has difficulty in finding words or expressing itself logically or directly. More akin to image and emotion, the Moon reflects its distress more easily through the somatization of pain; therefore the Moon is often the master key to unlocking the defence manifesting as the disorder. My experience is that complex aspect patterns involving the Moon often correspond with the diagnosis of syndromes.

When dramatic aspects between the outer and inner planets occur, the formation of identity and attachment may have been severely compromised and later this difficulty may surface somatically. A way of thinking that I use is that the inner planets present as the personal urges. When strongly aspected by either social planet Jupiter or Saturn, personal urges may be compromised by social strictures such as family beliefs, ethics and morals, religious ideologies, cross-cultural taboos, migration or rules, authority, expectations and responsibilities, anxiety and inappropriate boundaries. When a personal planet has a difficult aspect from an outer planet, I imagine the great force of ancestral and communal fate impinging upon the personal. The outer planets suggest the influence of energies beyond the comprehension and understanding of the system; therefore, they are often the most likely symbols for psychosomatic and trans-generational disorders, especially when they are in complex aspect patterns with inner planets, when the archetypal realm has punctured the personal.[135]

When considering psychosomatic illnesses it is important to *read the symptom*, remembering that every symptom is an attempt to cure.[136] A symptom is a sign, which images the essence of the wound; therefore, a symptom describes itself best though its own composition. Knowledge of the planetary archetypes helps to creatively explore the soul's malcontent that underlies the symptom. For instance, when an illness does not respond to physical interventions such as diet, treatment, herbs or pharmaceuticals, I engage the client with their associations with the symptom. When disorders are misdiagnosed, mysterious unresponsive to medical tests and treatment, I am alert for aspects between the inner planets and Neptune or Pluto, as both planets are masterful at disguise.

Exploring ways of thinking about the soul's discontent and how it finds expression through the body or the mind was an aspect of early forms of healing. To begin to read symptoms, reflect on the archetypal nature of the planets involved and imagine how these might express themselves either mentally or physically. Bear in mind that personal planets are probably voicing the personal concerns, while the social planets are stressing a set of laws and conventions that might not support the personal. The outer planets compound the soul's stress when they represent collective urges that are contrary to the personal or signify the rejection of authentic values trans-generationally.

Medical astrology has bequeathed us a fine system of rulerships to awaken our imaginative process. Medieval astrology handed down the melothesic man (the zodiac man), and today the first-year student knows the parts of the body that are ruled by the signs of the zodiac from head (Aries) to toe (Pisces). Traditional astrology has delineated the houses of health, and medical astrology has set guidelines for planetary correspondences to health. If we can read the astrological symbols that correspond with the physical or mental wound, then these symptomatic symbols will help to illustrate its origins and the place where healing is located. Like Achilles, who was trained by Chiron, we know that the agent of wounding will also be the means of healing.

By nature, the Moon's inclination is to absorb and retain or instinctually respond. Its disposition is to hold; therefore, it symbolizes the containers of the body such as the breasts, the womb and the stomach. When stressed, feelings are either held in, unable to be expressed, or flung out in reaction, leaving the feeling nature unacknowledged. Over time, including the generations of time, these unexpressed feelings could coalesce into symptoms to bring the complex to consciousness.

I have developed a faith and confidence in astrological signatures; not that they suggest illness, but if the theme arises, then symptoms are reflected in the astrological images. But each case is unique and the task of connecting with the client and developing a dialogue is always a priority. For instance, I have had many cases where the lunar focus is on fertility and pregnancy, and while the aspect patterns may be similar, each individual's experience of this is personal and individual.

Jennifer had a Chiron–Saturn–Moon T-square and was never able to bring a pregnancy to full term. She endured three miscarriages and was downhearted at the prospect of never being a mother. I asked about her mother's experience when she was born. There was an instant reaction. 'I'm adopted,' she said and her tone of voice suggested this was a touchy issue. I proceeded cautiously and when I said 'I wonder how your mother felt carrying you', her response was tinged with anger. 'I don't know and I don't care and I have no intention of finding out by finding her,' she barked back. I indicated I was not implying that, but for a moment could we just imagine how difficult it must have been to know that you were carrying a child who you knew you would have to relinquish.

Jennifer went quiet. I remained silent as well. The image in the chart felt tricky to hold onto without negative feelings. Then I said 'I just wondered if there might be something deeply felt that makes it difficult to hold this jumble of feelings.' She looked away and started to sob. I felt she was crying for herself, her mother and her unborn child in a way that she had never cried before. Then she said 'Do you think that there is a connection?' I felt she was asking my opinion about the connection between her miscarriages and her own miscarriage of feelings around her own birth, her mother and her relinquishment. I replied 'I don't know, but it seems a worthwhile question to consider.' We continued to explore many previously unspoken feelings about being abandoned and adopted, rejected, yet loved. Jennifer fell pregnant shortly after our consultation and gave birth to a healthy daughter.

Martha was just past her Chiron return at the time she came for a consultation. She also had a Moon–Chiron square; however, this was in a Grand Cross with Jupiter and a Venus–Pluto conjunction. She sobbed when we spoke of the children she always wanted, yet could never conceive. Physically there were no known reasons why she could not conceive, yet it had never happened. She said her tears weren't sad tears and I wondered if she meant they were soulful tears in recognition of her fate. She was a medical researcher and worked in IVF, helping women to conceive. And so her painful wounding of never being able to conceive called her to be engaged in the process of helping others to do what she could not. The labour she would never experience became a labour of love for other women. I wondered if this was Martha's way of participating with her loss. For Martha, the image of Moon–Chiron opened up a soulful encounter with the nature of her work.

This way of working with planetary images and symptoms can be applied to all the planets. These are only ways of thinking about the archetypal imagery in the horoscope, not prescriptions or delineations. For instance, Mercury rules the lungs; therefore it is associated with lung disorders and diseases, breath and breathing, asthma, respiration and respiratory problems. Ruling movement and the linking mechanisms in the body, Mercury is connected to mobility and the nervous system and therefore associated with the nerves, restriction of movement, lack of flexibility and the lack of coordination. Lack of flexibility in the limbs triggers the question about feeling out on a limb or being stranded on a limb. Mercury is mental and cerebral by nature; therefore the lack of ability to speak up or express an opinion, having a speech disorder or learning difficulties could be part of the Mercurial constellation in the horoscope. Therefore, nervous disorders, anxiety and mental imbalances resonate with this archetype. Learning abnormalities such as dyslexia can be traced to Mercury, as can speech and hearing difficulties. The soul's disturbance might be connected to deeper feelings of not being heard in the family, lacking a voice to speak out; perhaps one voice or one opinion may have controlled the family's flow of ideas and communication. The inability to speak up or articulate feelings may be a deeper aspect of the family shadow caught up in trans-generational learning patterns or restricted movement. Trauma may be interlinked with learning or moving. For instance, in the familial past there may be unexplained severances from educational patterns, strong biases against or in favour of education and familial stories and experiences around teaching and learning that have disturbed the soul of the family.

This was especially true for Lillian whose parents were both hearing-impaired. Pluto ruled her 3rd house and squared Mercury; she described growing up in a vacuum without sound or stimulation, a dead space. Jupiter was in the 12th house opposite her Aquarian Sun–Mars conjunction in the 6th, all squaring Chiron in the 8th. Her father's lack of education and violent familial experiences had left him an embittered, angry man who in turn was brutal to his own children. Since childhood, Lillian had suffered anxiety and numerous related symptoms. When she first saw me, her progressed Moon was in the 6th house exactly opposite Jupiter; progressed Mercury had reached her South Node, synchronizing with memories of how unintelligent she felt. When we explored the motif of her father's aggression and lack of education that might underpin these symptoms, new learning possibilities presented themselves. We discussed her anxiety as a calling to embrace her own knowledge and brightness, as well as the reservoir of her abundant source of energy that wanted focus and direction.

The subjectivity of astrological symbols allows them to become personal, intimately connected to the client's experience and background; therefore, the astrological images are powerful healing agents when we support them in revealing the core of the wound from a soulful perspective. If our symptoms are an attempt to cure, then we must truly ask 'Why me?' Astrology is a remarkable tool to aid in this reflective process. A soul symptom seeks meaning for its cure. And sometimes that is enough: an acknowledgment of a truth always known, yet never allowed; a shameful feeling shared and heard without judgement; a way of being acknowledged without feeling condemned. While I hear and witness the story, I am also the custodian of the client's horoscope during our session. Reflecting back the archetypal images of the horoscope allows the client to connect with this part of themselves. For me, healing takes place in the recognition that the symptom is an invitation to soulfully reflect on the underlying condition.

7

FATE

> There is no puny planet, sun or moon,
> Or zodiacal sign which can control
> The God in us! If we bring that to bear
> Upon events, we mold them to our wish,
> Tis when the infinite 'neath the finite gropes
> That men are governed by their horoscopes.[137]

Ella Wheeler Wilcox,
'To an Astrologer'

As the 20th century dawned, new branches of spiritual study sprouted. Theosophy, Spiritualism and the Rosicrucian Order reworked and reinvented long-established philosophical concerns. Ella Wheeler Wilcox was involved with these 'new thoughts'. Being an advocate for the New Thought Movement, her poetry was positive and uplifting, echoing the group's beliefs in karma, reincarnation, free will, the omnipresent divine and the eternality of the soul. Astrology was also re-establishing itself in this period and recent ideas and developments influenced new ways of thinking astrologically. Yet, whether in Hellenistic Egypt, medieval Europe, turn-of-the-century Great Britain or contemporary America, the age-old questions concerning fate and the divine are intimately intertwined with astrology. Each astrological practitioner is confronted with the need to develop their own ways of thinking about fate and the divine.

If astrology helps us to perceive patterns of our own and others' fate, then what is it that is fated and how do we witness it and respond to it? By its very nature astrology is fatalistic, as fixed patterns are woven into each horoscope at birth. Whether these are predetermined by the soul remains an open question, yet these patterns are distinct, set into the horoscope by the time and place of birth. An astrological consideration encourages self-awareness, as each horoscope invites its owner to become conscious of these fixed designs and reflect on how to participate with these greater patterns of one's life. As astrologers, we need to consider astrology's overarching connection to fate in order to place our beliefs, our theories and our experiences in the context of the fixed patterns of the horoscope.

Reading Liz Greene's *The Astrology of Fate* in 1985 liberated my ways of thinking about fate. This thoughtful text amplified fate through different lenses. Like 'soul', 'fate' is a potent and challenging word, and over time it has inspired a host of deliberations, differentiations and considerations.[138] As a motif of unconscious patterning brought to light by the horoscope, the model of astrological fate is reflective and revealing. I began to appreciate the word 'fate' as being the framework for the patterning of the horoscope. That could not be changed. But what could be changed were the attitudes and viewpoints brought to bear on the astrological patterns. I began to consider fate so I could find my own beliefs and ways to place these in the context of my work. This took me back to the mythic beginning when Fate first emerged from the womb of Night.

The Question of Fate

As discussed in Chapter 3, one of the most compelling root metaphors that underpins astrology is the question of fate. Fate confronts the individual – indeed, humanity – with a core philosophical question of whether life is predetermined or flexible. Is it God's will or free will? Since 'God's will' suggests a desire not always in step with our conscious choices, Carl Jung suggested that 'the man who submits to his fate calls it the will of God; the man who puts up a hopeless and exhausting fight is more apt to see the devil in it'.[139] This echoes two approaches that are often coupled with fate; one identifies it as something we can do nothing about; the other surrenders to its will. These two views are evidenced from the times the gods were born. There is also a third perspective which acknowledges the power of participation and presence: how we might consciously cooperate with the threads of fate already spun so that the tapestry of our lives can be woven in the most satisfying way. Ralph Waldo Emerson captured this essence when he wrote: 'Deep in the man sits fast his fate, to mould his fortunes, mean or great.'[140] The perspective that fate is our inherent temperament and the horoscope reveals the temporal beginning of embodying that nature was a way for me to comfortably begin working with fate. It was person-centred, not ego-centric, as it honoured the calling to be aware of and part of the larger, pre-determined patterns woven into the horoscope.

Like fate and free will, fate and destiny have become inseparable. 'Fate' comes from the Latin *fatum*, 'to speak'. A fatum was something that had been spoken, such as a declaration or a prophetic utterance of the gods. 'Fate' suggested what was decreed by the gods for humans, something set or laid down, over which there was not much control. 'Destiny' also has Latin roots suggesting to determine, appoint, choose, make firm or fast.[141] Interestingly, both the Destinies and the Fates are daughters of Night in Hesiod's *Theogony*, the first epic to detail the birth of the gods.[142] From the beginning, fate has a dualistic nature.

It is the Greek word for fate, *moira*, that has come to characterize weaving the threads of fate. The word refers to a portion, a division or allotment, from which we derive the image of our lot in life. Fate is the heart of Greek tragedy. Fate is enmeshed with tragedy, but the Greeks also demonstrated how ignorance or refusal to be involved with the gods inflames misfortune. Sophocles's Oedipus demonstrated how being unaware of the pattern ignited his personal hardships. Fate and destiny are the same in death. This is both our fate and our destination, and to not accept this fate raises the possibility of tragedy. When used in the plural, 'Moirai' generally refers to the trinity of Fates, the three sisters named by Hesiod in the *Theogony*. Two genealogies for the Fates are revealed in this epic, as if Fate can be parented in two ways. Hesiod's first reference lists the Fates as the daughters of Nyx or Night. Parthenogenetically, Nyx gave birth to a fearsome strain of offspring. These creatures of the night personify dreaded human experiences such as Doom, black Ker, Death, Blame, Distress, Nemesis and Strife.[143] The Destinies and the ruthless Fates are their siblings. Later the Fates show up again, now as daughters of the ordered gods Zeus and Themis, both custodians of justice. They are identified and named Clotho, Atropos and Lachesis.[144]

These two genealogies reflect the ways that Fate has been conceived in the human experience. As daughters of Night, the

Fates are fearsome, unordered and worrisome. Undifferentiated and impersonal, they personify the fate that is laid down, pronounced, without choice. It is fixed, unalterable and inflexible. It is this fate that inhabits the mythological period when goddess cults were predominant and even gods were subject to *moira*. Herodotus tells us that Apollo could not deflect the Fates and, in *Prometheus Bound*, Aeschylus says Zeus 'cannot fly from Fate'.[145]

In this pre-Classical age gods and goddesses had power over human affairs; Fate was instinctual and natural. Fate was not just biological instincts or inborn patterns of behaviour, but was the authority of the gods. Fate was one's lot; literally the lot that was bestowed by the gods. Should someone try to take more than their share, Fate would punish the transgression. Fate's role seems to be what one is allotted in terms of the quality, station and length of life. In this epoch, the concept of personal will was not in the conscious mindset; therefore, neither was the notion of 'free will'.[146]

Another word closely related to *moira* in ancient thinking was *heimarmene*, which is derived from an ancient verb referring to the action of allocating or allotting; that is, the act of allocating the lot.[147] Jung likened *heimarmene* to what psychologists would call the 'compulsion of the libido' or perhaps what the mysteries might refer to as the 'compulsion of the stars'.[148] The purpose of the mystery religions was to be freed from the grip of *heimarmene*. Jung aligned the psychic energies and patterns of compulsions with fate through *heimarmene*. He suggested that this 'low level' and 'primitive form' of self-awareness 'was the psychological situation of late antiquity, and the saviour and the physician of that time was he who sought to free humanity from bondage to Heimarmene'.[149] In a contemporary context, Fate's first bloodline links it with libido, whether that is physical or emotional drives, instincts and compulsions, or the fatality of incarnation.

Hesiod's second pedigree records the Fates as daughters of Themis and Zeus. As daughters of order and justice, they are more differentiated, being named and identified with specific roles. Clotho, the Spinner, with a roll or a spindle, twisted the threads of life. Inherent is the image that our threads of life are spun before birth, yet the fabric that can be woven from these has not yet been crafted. Lachesis, the Apportioner, measured out the threads.

She characterized the time and amount of thread we are given to work with. Like Urania, the muse of Astrology, Lachesis was pictured with a pointer and a globe. The third Fate was Atropos, the Inevitable, who cut the thread at the apportioned length. Her main symbol was a severing instrument but she also carried measuring scales, a scroll and wax tablets. The Fates have also been linked to weaving the bodily tissues connecting fate to genetics, the gestation process and the body itself.[150] The concept of the genetic load of family fate was clearly identified in Greek mythology, as the Fates wove their threads into family patterns passed down through the generations. Some philosophers would later locate fate in the body and the freedom from fate in the mind.

As daughters of Themis and Zeus, the three Fates inherit their parents' penchant for judging, measuring and weighing. From a developmental perspective, Fate is beginning to be considered, evaluated and moralized, as Fate becomes positioned under Zeus's domain. One epithet of Zeus was the one 'who knows everything that happens to humanity, what the Fates grant and what they determine shall not be.'[151] This was Zeus Moriagetes, the leader of the Moirai, who now are under his jurisdiction. Under Zeus, fate is an ordering principle; it is just and the lot becomes the law. Fate is being aware of which gods to honour, being measured, moral and rational.

Homer, through the voice of Zeus, suggested that we conspire in writing our own fate: 'Oh, for shame, how the mortals put the blame upon us gods, for they say evils come from us, but it is they, rather, who by their own recklessness win sorrow beyond what is given.'[152] Zeus overthrew the chaotic age and with the new gods a more 'reasonable' era emerged. Freud echoed the same sentiment 2,750 years later: 'When a man is pursued by a malignant fate it usually turns out that he has arranged the events himself'.[153] Fate's second bloodline aligns it with rational order and the capacity to judge. We are in a position now to consciously cooperate with Fate.

Perhaps the two parentages of Fate – Nyx and Zeus – are nodal points on the Wheel of Fortune. When conceived of literally, they are assigned to two poles; one is the darkened Fate born of Nyx, a random predetermined force, which is preordained. This is the fate of the night driven by our compulsions and complexes. On the other pole, Fate is born out of ordering and contextualizing instinctual chaos. As chaos and compulsion subside, we are more capable of ordering our fate. Both truths are experienced in different ways at distinct times. In this complex pedigree of Fate the two bloodlines are intertwined: one as daughter of Nyx or Night, shadowy, unclear and mysterious; the other as the daughter of Zeus and Themis, just, ordered and lawful. But each one is Fate. In primordial times, when we are in the dark, lost in despair, caught in dread, overwhelmed by grief, haunted by compulsions or driven by obsessions, fate is unfair and punishing. In Classical times, when we can reflect and conceptualize the larger schema of our life, then fate can be appreciated and accepted.

Right from the beginning Fate is innate. When the natural laws of Nature were violated, then the Moirai would avenge the sin.[154] Freud also referred to the laws of Nature as forms of fate.[155] However, we have lost this sympathy for natural law and cycles, alarmingly visible in the way we disrespect the normal life-cycles of the animals we raise for produce, and in the way we desecrate the earth for its resources. Death is our destiny but even this nodal point is no longer our fate. Who dies any more of natural causes? We die by some-thing, rational causes such as cancer, heart attacks, respiratory problems or strokes.

By the Classical period when Sophocles was setting out his Oedipal tragedy, philosophers were inquiring about the nature of the human soul. One of the constant companions of soul in western thought has always been fate. Given other names and clothed in different garments, this question of fate accompanies the soul. Of interest to me is how our concept of fate shifts as it emerges out of the mythological period into the minds of philosophers. Fate herself remains the same, but our experience of her is altered as we move from a primordial and predictive world-view to a more psychological outlook on life. As philosophical ideas develop, fate becomes more aligned with the body, while free will sides with the soul, as it is free from corporeal reality. On the cusp of the Classical period, Aeschylus, through his character Prometheus in *Prometheus Bound*, gives us a prelude to the emerging philosophy of freedom from one's fate. He says:

Fate fulfils all in time; but it is not ordained
That these events shall yet reach such an end. My lot

Is to win freedom only after countless pains.
Cunning is feebleness beside Necessity.

Yet when the chorus asks who controls Necessity, Prometheus is quick to respond: 'The three Fates and the Furies, who forget nothing'.[156] Both Fates are always there.

By the 5th century BCE, Plato portrays Necessity as the mother of the Moirai in the Myth of Er, his visionary tale of the spiritual world. Necessity, the great mother of Fate, spins the cosmic spindle around which all the revolving spheres of the planetary orbs and fixed stars are turning. Necessity is affixed to time through her three daughters: Lachesis sings of the past, Clotho of the present and Atropos of the future. Fate is timeless. Each soul is asked to choose a new cycle of life which will be theirs by necessity. The life that is chosen will be their destiny. It is clear that each man has his own virtue and choice, so blame rests on the individual, not the Fates.[157] Plato paves the way for the soul to be liberated from Fate through right choices.

Marsilio Ficino was a voice of the Renaissance who endorsed the Platonic hypothesis that an individual regulates his fate by virtue and righteousness. In 1472, when writing to a friend, Ficino ended his letter: 'My dearest Giovanni, if we follow this golden rule of our Plato, with the wind of heaven behind us we shall circumnavigate successfully this vast whirlpool of fortune, and, quite untroubled, sail safely into harbour'.[158] Plato's golden rule that Ficino is referring to is to respect the divine virtues of prudence, piety and justice. It is through this attempt to be as god-like as possible that freedom from the oppression of fate could be achieved. Ficino valued Plato's counsel to move away from bodily attachments and worldly affairs towards the cultivation of the soul. 'Otherwise, we cannot avoid evil'.[159] Evil, born from corporeal attachments, becomes our misfortune and fate. 'Evil' is 'live' spelt backwards!

Ficino placed free will outside the body, as the embodied world was subject to fate. He says 'Every soul should withdraw from the encumbrance of the body and become centred in the mind, for then fate will discharge its force upon the body without touching the soul. The wise man will not struggle pointlessly with fate.'[160] The concept that free will is outside the body in the non-corporeal sphere of Plato's 'intelligible' world of spirit seems psychologically similar to bringing consciousness to bear upon these compulsive patterns of our lives without moral judgement. Hence, like the field of astrology, psychoanalysis needed to consider its position on fate.

Psychoanalysis struggles with fate and destiny through its in-depth contemplation of human nature. James Hillman said: 'Character reintroduces Fate into psychology. Substitutions for character eliminated this ancient connection. "Ego", "personality", "self", "agent", "individual" reduce psychology to the study of human behaviours – to processes, functions, motivations – and omit the fateful consequences implied by the idea of character. Psychology shorn of fate is too shallow to address its subject, the soul'.[161] And, like psychoanalysis, astrology loses its ancient connection with fate and destiny through rigid techniques, interpretations and moral judgements.

Fate, Archetypes and the Unconscious

Jung's language of the unconscious and his work with primordial imagery and archetypes is a great boon to astrology. Today, the term 'archetypal' seems more fitting than 'psychological' to encapsulate this symbolic approach to astrology. Jung's amplification of archetypes gifted astrology with a wider vocabulary and insight into its own archetypes, reminding astrologers of the discipline's inherent symbolic attitude.

Here the synergy between Jungian concepts and astrology is most apparent, as both systems recognize the 'inherited *tendency* of the human mind to form representation of mythological motifs'.[162] In mapping the landscape of the psyche, Jung recognized some major archetypal images which astrologers could recognize from their own planetary pantheon. Each planet is archetypal in that it represents the similar faculty of soul for every human, what the Greeks suggested as *ousia*, a soul essence. Both astrological and Jungian images are representatives of archetypal forces and patterns that shape and govern the human experience; it is a match made in heaven or the unconscious, depending on which team you are on.

Jung emphasized that archetypes are inborn. He also drew an analogy between instinct and archetype. Instinct is embedded biologically, but archetype 'clothed in its archetypal image is the psyche's experience of that instinct, the living force expressing through every movement of every fantasy and feeling and flight of the soul'.[163] Jung suggested that archetypes, like instincts, are collective phenomena. The following quote is the first time Jung uses the word 'archetype'.

> ... we also find in the unconscious qualities that are not individually acquired but are inherited, e.g., instincts as impulses to carry out actions from necessity, without conscious motivation. In this 'deeper' stratum we also find the *a priori*, inborn forms of 'intuition' namely the *archetypes* of perception and apprehension, which are the necessary *a priori* determinants of all psychic processes.[164]

Previously Jung had used the term 'primordial image'.[165] As with Hesiod, we have two metaphors: one is primordial, an unconscious impulse, while the other, archetype, gives us a way to reflect through myth, symbol, image, associations and considerations. Jung recognized the connection between fate and archetypes, suggesting that perhaps 'these eternal images are what men mean by fate'.[166] Astrological doctrine implies that each individual's archetypal disposition is embedded in the birth chart and knowing the planetary archetypes helps to map a diagram of individual fate. Of importance for astrologers is the differentiation between the inherited tendency, which is collective, and the personal manifestation of the archetype. For instance, Mars in a personal horoscope suggests the impulse to act or react, but does not indicate how this will be personalized. Astrology's symbolic framework can contextualize the archetype in an individual's life through its zodiacal sign (quality), its house (environment) and planetary aspects (influences), informing the individual of its astrological pattern, timing and how the archetype might personalize, but this is a tendency, not an explanation.

Jung's concept of archetypes reminds astrologers to differentiate between the inherited complex of the planetary archetype and the myriad of personal associations and experiences that envelop it. The horoscope symbolizes the archetype, not the personal matters that gather around the core of the complex. Planets bear the names of the gods that embody their characteristics and patterns; therefore, astrology is well suited to an archetypal perspective, as it helps us imagine both the individual's personal temperament and the deeper archetypal patterns of psychic life that underpin character. An archetypal perspective is intimately entwined with the question of fate.

C.G. Jung provided many definitions and descriptions of archetypes throughout his collected works. For astrologers, the importance lies in the link between an archetype and the gods and goddesses of antiquity, which were named for planets and other bodies in the heavens. Human beings inherit a physical and psychic history which the horoscope symbolizes. The 'collective unconscious' is the landscape of our species' inherited psychic history, containing instinctual patterns that have been laid down through human history. These archetypal patterns reveal themselves as images, hence the term 'archetypal images'.

Archetypes are inborn propensities to react in certain ways to a wide range of situations faced by us all, such as birth, death, marriage, loss, love, attachment and relationships. Being inborn, instinctual patterns of knowing, they can be triggered in response to recurring events in the outer life; therefore, the outer event often symbolized by a transit or astrological image of transition brings to life the underlying archetype. The astrologer can then stay with the image of that planetary archetype to try and amplify meaning in the context of the individual's life. Every society and culture has images and mythic stories to do with such phenomena as creation, birth, death and rebirth, magic and demons. While specifics vary from culture to culture, the underlying themes are similar. It is these universal archetypal patterns that play a significant, mostly unconscious, role in how we both perceive and react in our everyday lives. Astrology reflects these patterns and the horoscope assists us in working with them. Archetypes are ways of seeing and modes of apprehension which can shape our behaviour and, as Jung always implied, our character and fate as well.

Aside from myths and astrology, the other obvious place where archetypes manifest themselves is in our dreams and our astrological horoscope. Astrological archetypes carry a transcendent, mythic quality; yet they also have very specific psychological expressions, such as the desire for love, the experience of beauty, what we value and appreciate (Venus) and the impulse towards forceful activity, aggression or courage (Mars).

Horoscopic imagery helps to honour the depth and image of the archetype in a personal and soulful manner.

The Daimon

The concept of the *daimon* has been used in many ways. It has been equated with a demon, spirit, genius, personality, destiny, power and a guardian angel. In philosophical thinking, from Plato onwards, the personal *daimon* was like an overseer or leader of the soul – the conductor of the archetypal orchestra, so to speak.

In more modern psychological language, Hillman talked of his acorn theory, 'which holds that each person bears a uniqueness that asks to be lived and that is already present before it can be lived'.[167] The soul of each of us is given a unique *daimon* before we are born, and it has selected an image or pattern that we live on earth. This soul-companion, the *daimon*, guides us here; in the process of arrival, however, we forget all that took place and believe we come empty into this world. The *daimon* remembers what is in our image and belongs to our pattern, and therefore our *daimon* is the carrier of our destiny.[168]

This concept is very astrological and interesting to ponder. Does a powerful planet in our chart characterize our *daimon*? Astrologers have identified the *daimon* in terms of houses, such as the 11th house being the house of the good *daimon* and the 12th as the place of the bad *daimon*. Sometimes Hellenistic astrologers saw the ruler of the Ascendant as the *daimon*. There may be other ways to imagine the *daimon*, such as the final dispositor, which is the planetary archetype connected to each planet through a chain of rulerships. These astrological ideas are ways of imagining and understanding how the *daimon* might manifest through our experience.

Freedom is intimately woven into the fabric of fate. Freedom is not 'free will' because our struggles for freedom are finite. We cannot freely choose our destinies when we are conditioned by genetics, predisposed to afflictions, traumatized, abused, addicted, uneducated. As Jung said: 'Not only is "freedom of the will" an incalculable problem philosophically, it is also a misnomer in the practical sense for we seldom find anybody who is not influenced and indeed dominated by desires, habits, impulses, prejudices, resentments and by every conceivable kind of complex'.[169] Destiny is freeing the compulsion through reflection on the image. The daughters of the dark, night terrors and nightmares, do not change. But perhaps character does, through self-reflection, questioning and a willingness to transform its relationship to the forces of fate.

How has our concept of fate changed and how might we change our encounters with fate? Our experience of fate shifts as we move away from a purely literal and predictive model to a more participatory and psychological approach to life. When we are able to meet, reflect and take meaning from the experiences that happen to us, we are more likely to feel more accepting and less restricted. This is often the role of religion as it offers a moral context for Fate. Through conscious intention and reflection, we awaken to find a religion of our own.[170]

While fate may not alter in its fundamental nature or timing, perhaps it might change its expression with the application of consciousness. Inner work may not change the patterns and designs of our fate, but the level of conscious awareness brought to bear on these patterns allows it to be experienced in a more authentic way. When the horoscope is used in service to the Self and the soul, it has a revelatory, may I say divine, quality that encourages our awareness of fate and reintroduces us to our personal *daimon/s*.

My continuing reflection on fate has helped enormously to free me from self-righteous morality, judgements and criticisms of ways of being. Although fate is continuously linked with the cycles of heaven and 'the stars', to me, working with fate became a way to develop and elaborate compulsions, tragedies, traumas and uncertainties using planetary archetypes, not through explanation or classification, but with reverence and respect for the gods of life larger than we are. Being a witness and a listener, open to each life mystery, assisted me to be present when Fate's tragic plot unravelled. I try to be sensible and rational about the depth of what the soul can reveal, but sometimes I am carried away by an image, a voice, a sense, a feeling, and I take this as my involvement with the mystery of astral fate. Sometimes I become emotional, holding onto my tears in the face of a heroic client who braves her fate. And sometimes I sense a healing breeze penetrating through the cracks that the encounter with Fate has opened. I have always recognized astrology to be a profound tool of healing, and am grateful to have witnessed many of its mysteries.

8

DEATH

There is no armour against Fate;
Death lays his icy hand on kings:
Sceptre and Crown
Must tumble down,
And in the dust be equal made
With the poor crookèd scythe and spade.[171]

James Shirley,
'Death The Leveller'

While researching and reflecting on death, I read two memorable and poignant books by adult children writing about their mother's death. The first, *A Very Easy Death*, by Simone de Beauvoir, is a beautifully written and moving account of her emotional journey with her mother through the final passages to death. In contrast, David Rieff, the son of Susan Sontag, describes his mother's desperate struggle to cling to life in *Swimming in a Sea of Death*.[172] Simone's and David's mothers confronted death very differently. What is similar in each version during the dying phase is their kaleidoscopic experience of loss, grief, despair, guilt, remorse, anger, sadness and relief, intermixed with their own encounter with mortality and uncertainty.

From an astrological perspective, death is part of a greater cycle which continually yields to rebirth and renewal. Embedded in the human soul is the template of the dying and renewing Sun. Planetary cycles end, only to begin again. Astrologically, the house of death precedes the house of long journeys. Astrology offers hope and insight into the archetype of death, as it differentiates the human encounter with death from the soul's perspective.

Death reawakens the abyss between body and soul; it re-engages us in its mysteries. Renaissance is possible with the soul but not necessarily the human body. Over the years of consulting,

I have spoken with clients facing their own death, the death of a parent or partner, families in conflict over an estate, a will and/ or funeral arrangements, a grieving parent who has tragically lost their child or the death of a pet which has unleashed a legacy of loss. As a witness to their grief, I often found it necessary to acknowledge the reality of their encounter with death by retracing the dying passage and process that they mourned. For the most part I was practical and purposeful when discussing their return to life in the face of the losses that death had dealt them.

My underlying questions to myself were always, 'How can I help ensoul the experience of death and bring meaning to this process without platitudes or concepts? How do I find my way through the emotions and beliefs to the special relationship that death has with the soul?'[173]

Helen's Gift

Helen was a long-term client; ironically, I have her recorded time of death, yet not one for her birth.[174] My last consultation with Helen was on her seventy-first birthday. A few weeks before, Helen had phoned to tell me she had been diagnosed with ovarian cancer and was not seeking treatment. The prognosis was 'months, not years'. She asked if I would come to her house for an appointment, as she could not make it to the office. Serendipitously, the date we chose happened to be her birthday.

I first met Helen on Monday 10 November 1986. It was 12.30 p.m. I know this, as this was my first appointment with her. I noted that it was my Venus return and, since Venus was retrograde, it would return again. Mars was rising at this time and transiting my MC.

For the next twenty-seven years I would see Helen at least four times a year. At the beginning of our professional relationship I often saw her once a month, but in the last years perhaps four times a year. We always consulted her horoscope, which she found to be useful and engaging. Astrology became a boon for Helen, as it supported her feeling that the complexities, turbulence and the difficulties that she so often described were part of her life journey. She recognized that she had the choice to participate with this or not. Even though it was difficult to understand why anyone would have such a lonesome and difficult road to travel, astrology helped map out her life and gave her an opportunity to consider and reflect upon it.

Helen was recommended to me by her psychotherapist. He wondered if the chart might be able to provide some alternative images for their therapeutic encounters. We made the appointment. She was so sure of her birth time that I did not question it, which I usually do. In my notes of the session I noted her reaction to my description of her 12th house Uranus–Moon–Saturn constellation squaring the North Node–Sun in the 3rd. In my notes I had recorded: 'Helen cries when I approach the question of whether she had felt abandoned or disapproved of from an early age.' I now wonder how I had actually phrased these thoughts in that moment during our session. How did I express these to Helen? Often they come in the moment, arising from the felt experience of the interaction, the nuances of conversation. Sometimes the symbols speak, not

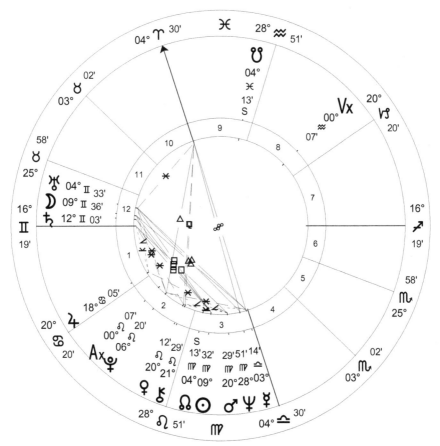

Helen, 3 September 1942, 1.52 a.m., Melbourne, Australia

dictated to me but appearing in the space between myself and the client, through an unknown process I think of as my imagination.

As we have been exploring, imagination is often thought of as being the polar opposite of truth; something fanciful, constructed and unscientific. Yet it is imagination that allows us to form mental images of something that is not tangible or present to the senses. Generally I find when imagination is present in the consulting room there is a participatory and meaningful relationship between myself and the client, each of us struggling to make sense of the horoscope, not just me as the specialist and them as the passive client. At the beginning of the consultation I try to make contact and build a relationship, so that I feel comfortable in struggling to articulate the images of the horoscope.

Just before she died, Helen told me that whatever it was I said that very first day twenty-seven years ago was so very important to her, as it had helped her feel understood and valued, not judged. It was as if something in that symbol made sense to Helen, an authentic confirmation of her felt experience from a non-judgemental, yet personal, perspective.

Maybe there were grounds to what she felt. Perhaps her feelings of dread and rejection were authentic for her soul. And perhaps if I could see that in her horoscope, then maybe she could know them in herself in a different way. I do not remember what I saw or said. But whatever it was, it was important to her and helped her to feel known and seen.

I could not tell you how or why we forged our relationship for all those years. Helen was difficult to contact; perhaps this is why the psychotherapist had suggested she have her chart read. She was in constant pain. Her fibromyalgia included the physical ailments of chronic fatigue, joint pain, bowel and bladder abnormalities, along with severe depressive episodes. Conventional medical and psychological treatments did not seem to uncover any cause or provide any means of relief. Helen was also bulimic. In the early days of seeing her, she would binge on creamy cakes and then purge. Afterwards she would find herself driving across Melbourne's West Gate Bridge, fighting with her inner demonic self-judgements and suicidal fantasies about whether to jump off the bridge. It seemed that her call to death was stronger than her desire for life.

I would mostly listen to the full account before commenting. Helen had a way of detailing a story. She was a great storyteller, down to the last minute detail. But when she'd go off on another tangent or tributary, I would take an opportunistic break in the narrative and give her a little nudge to come back to the thread of her story. And she did. Helen needed to tell her story, again and again, and she needed someone to listen. I became a witness to Helen's life. But in the last stages of her life, I realized she had also been a witness to mine. Working in astrology to earn a living and provide for my family does not come with a guaranteed income. Astrology can be trivialized and marginalized as a profession, but Helen was one who valued and respected what I did. So just by being who she was, she witnessed me in my true vocation. And for that I am ever grateful.

Helen had a privileged childhood, attending private schools and specialized courses. She gained her architectural qualifications, worked in London and travelled through Europe in her mid twenties before she felt compelled by guilt to return to Australia because her mother was ill. Letters from home pleaded with her to come back. But her mother recuperated quickly upon her arrival home; Helen felt duped. She never got to visit Europe again.

She took an opportunity to redesign the new architectural premises where she was working, creating huge swathes of colourful cloths with bold designs to hang on the walls and from the warehouse ceilings. So catchy and vibrant were these designs that she and her partner decided to start a business manufacturing bedlinen, drapes and wallpaper featuring Helen's designs. It was the Seventies, long before IKEA arrived in Australia. Helen's designs were very successful. In New York there was a Macy's display; her fabrics were a bestseller in Japan and showcased in the *International Design Yearbook*. But I met Helen after this part of her life, after she had disengaged from the expression of her creative self. I only knew her talent for design by the colours and patterns she wove through her stories.

A convergence of events had taken place leading up to our first consultation. The business manager made a series of poor investments that bankrupted the design company; her partner left her; and when getting out of her car on busy Chapel Street, Helen was knocked down by a truck. From that day on she seemed to collapse under the weight of both her physical pain and the legal ramifications that the accident brought about. Helen's father, her Rock of Gibraltar, had also died. By the time she walked into my consulting room, Helen's struggle had metastasized into serious depression.

Her relationship with her mother had never been close, no attachment had ever developed and it was four years after I starting seeing her that I found out why. When Helen arrived for the appointment that day, she said she had so much she needed to talk to me about. I listened and listened for the punchline, as Helen wove the story of her dying mother's confession and what had been revealed to her. But first Helen retold stories of the many times her mother had been consciously cruel and hurtful throughout the course of her life. Perhaps it was to understand that the revelation she was about to tell me had context and continuity. Of course it came as a surprise, but when she told me, it also seemed to fit perfectly, like Cinderella's slipper.

Helen had discovered she was adopted.

For the next year she traced her origins and the story of her adoption. Her father's sister knew the situation but was reluctant to tell her the full story, but with persistence Helen managed to piece the account together. Her adoptive mother had two miscarriages and a stillborn child, Robert, born in 1938. Whether her adoptive mother could no longer have children or whether it was the fear of losing another child, the parents decided to adopt. But before they did, they wanted to make sure they were adopting a healthy child. Helen discovered that she had been in foster homes until she was adopted at seven months old. A local doctor had been an advocate in this process; so Helen came to join her family when she was already half a year old. Forty-eight years later her mother told her of the adoption.

Helen had never questioned her mother about her birth. The birth certificate had listed her birth but there was nothing to question regarding its authenticity. Like many born in this period, there was no time recorded and it was difficult to access original hospital records as most had been destroyed. The birth time she gave me was from a kinesiologist who had dowsed her time, as her mother had said it was early morning. We continued to use this time.

When she found the name of her birth mother Helen did not want to pursue her or any connection to her birth family. In a way it was confusing, yet in another way it made perfect sense. She reminded me how often I had said to her, 'Are you sure you're born in Australia?' I was always aware that Helen was more European than Australian.

When her mother died a few years later Helen rallied somewhat, but her depression had set in. She had withdrawn and was mostly reclusive, which for me was difficult to understand, as she was animated and funny, socially aware, bright, well-read and knew the political and financial landscapes. She made me laugh. Three weeks before her death she regaled me with the story of the pastoral counsellor who wanted to sit and pray with her. She told me that she told him: 'The last thirty years of my life I have been ill and a recluse and I used that time to find my own spirituality and my own religion, so I do not want your institution in care of my soul.' I chuckled. I could just imagine Helen being blunt; she never could be hypocritical.

During our sessions we relocated charts to the places she loved and hated, talked about the horoscopes of her adoptive family, why her creative life was never as successful as she imagined it would be. We went back through her life to turbulent times to discuss the transits and progressions, and each year we looked at the solar return. She asked about friends, famous people, and when she had an inheritance from her aunt, she asked about financial astrology. Whatever interested Helen or whatever she needed to explore, I tried my best to join her world.

My last appointment 'professionally' with Helen was on her seventy-first birthday. I went to her house as she was frail. 'There's only one thing we need to speak about today,' she said. 'When is the best time to die?' We spoke about the timing. The fact that Helen would die in the next few months gave the horoscope a context. It had the feeling of an ancient manuscript, one that we had tried to translate and decipher over the years, but now we were closer than ever to its meaning. In the face of death, the astrological signatures seemed to have this deeper reverent sense.

I was aware of an enormous grief during this consultation, as I knew it to be the last, but was able to contain the feeling. Our times together triggered existential and collective anguish. I was mourning losses, perhaps not just of Helen's life. How had this happened: this bright, creative, stylish, funny, intelligent and interesting woman being confined in a painful body and solitary life? I was in grief for all the injustices in the world beyond our understanding. Our professional life had ended and I had a choice. Were my feelings for Helen only contained by our professional relationship or did they extend beyond that framework into something more? After twenty-seven years of intimately witnessing Helen's life, I felt it was something more.

'Whatever you need or want me to do,' I said to her on the phone the next week. 'Are you sure?' Helen hesitated. 'Of course', I said. And that's when she asked me to take her to the hospital and wait while her abdomen was drained of the retained fluid that builds with ovarian cancer.

When she was admitted to the hospice I visited many times. We knew when it was time to say goodbye and we did. Again she affirmed how important our relationship had been, and its value and meaning in helping her prepare for this final transition. I had witnessed her story; now I was not just a witness, but a participant.

I saw Helen thirty-six hours before she died; she laid still, no responses. They say hearing is the last sense to go, so when I was ready to leave, I waved goodbye from the threshold of the doorway and said 'I will miss you. But I'll see you again.' She died on 10 December 2013 at 5.45 a.m. The Sun was rising. Its rising degree was conjunct Helen's Descendant; therefore it was setting in her chart for the last time, yet just about to rise in the world she was leaving behind.

Jupiter was retrograde at the same degree as hers. She was in the midst of her sixth Jupiter return. New horizons appear at these times and new journeys are made. Neptune too was in the midst of its transit over the South Node, a haunting image of release. The progressed Sun and Venus were joined with transiting Saturn while the transiting North Node conjoined progressed Mars. The progressed Ascendant had reached her North Node; many images of the progressed chart in accord with the transits and natal chart gave me a sense that something had finally come together for Helen.

Helen bequeathed me some valuable gifts, not just material ones, but the gift of being part of her life and her acknowledgement of my work and value. But her precious gift was in our relationship; maybe it was only twelve hours a year but in each of those moments we engaged in the task of interaction with the horoscope and each other. She left me with an awareness of the honesty of creating a relationship. The horoscope was illuminating but the relationship we created was healing. And not only for Helen: I was also touched and changed by our encounters. She will always remind me that in each engagement with a client and a horoscope, an intimate relationship is possible. The ancient parchment of the horoscope opens doorways to deep and private relationships beyond our physical and problematic existence.[175]

Judith's Question

My consultations with Helen had involved many discussions about suicide. She was a member of Exit International and was aware of all the ways and means to take her own life, which she often graphically shared with me. In a way she had prepared me for my consultations with Judith.

Judith – or Jude, as she wanted to be called – was recommended by another client. I never met Jude in person as she was confined to a wheelchair and lived in another state; therefore our only option was to make a phone appointment, which we did for 14 February 2002 at 2 p.m. Melbourne time. Today my consultations are mainly conducted by Skype or phone, but at the time of my consultation with Jude, it was an exception.

I took note that it was Valentine's Day.

Having no idea why Jude was contacting me, I began by asking her why she had made the consultation. Briskly, she said that she had regularly consulted with an astrologer for many years who had told her that when she was fifty-six it would be the best year of her life. She was angry; her mood was hostile and I felt attacked. I thought to myself, 'I would never say that', but I also realized that I was only hearing her side of the story, so I replied: 'But how can *I* help you?' She responded that astrology had always been a helpful guide and she would like to ask me a question. I gathered that fifty-six was not the best year of her life and, given the transits, I pondered what her question might be, not expecting what was to come. 'Yes', I said.

Jude answered: 'When is the best time for me to commit suicide?' She must have felt my response on the other end of the phone, as she asked if I was still there. 'Yes, I am, but I need a few more details to understand what you are asking me,' I said. Her anger was turning to frustration as she said she had told the story a million times. I said perhaps she had, but I had not heard it.

From the age of thirty-four, Jude had suffered from scoliosis. By the age of fifty-four her spinal curvature had worsened to such an extent that the pain prevented her from standing and even lying down, except on hot water bottles. Her pain was aggravated by other conditions including Sjogren's syndrome, which affected the moisture-producing glands, and agonizing tenosynovitis in her hands. She was exasperated with the medical profession who could not help and also felt abused by the health system which offered little consideration.

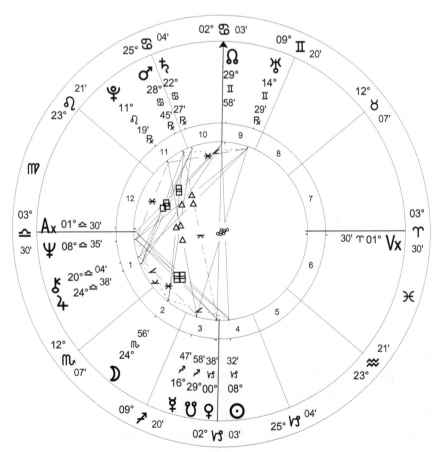

Jude, 30 December 1945, 11.50 p.m., Adelaide, Australia

Jude had made one suicide attempt in February 2000. Having taken a dose of sedatives she positioned a suicide bag over her head, but after she passed out she instinctively tore off the bag. This resulted in Jude being detained in hospital for a fortnight and, as she said, traumatized by psychiatrists and hospital staff who doubted the level of pain she reported. In the previous two years her suffering had become unbearable and she wanted to die. We discussed some options. One she said was to wheel herself off the jetty in her wheelchair. We laughed, and in that moment I felt she had begun to connect with me.

Throughout the year the Chiron–Sun motif was highlighted. Chiron was approaching the conjunction to her Sun in the 4th house. After being exact in March, it would retrograde back over the Sun in May and complete its third exact pass over her Sun in December. In April, Jupiter would aspect the Sun for the last time in its oppositional passage through the 10th house. Saturn, too, would make its final quincunx to the Sun from the 8th. This meant that these planets would also be aspecting Jude's Neptune on the Ascendant, which was square the Sun. On that day of her first consultation, the transiting Sun was conjunct Uranus on her 6th house cusp. In the light of the question and her impending death, each image seemed steeped with meaning.

The image of Chiron crossing her Sun came to life through her story, aligning her essential self with her suffering. It encouraged me to try to find a way to speak to her soul, the deeply private part of herself still contactable beneath the anguish and the trauma she was experiencing. The end of every cycle is often the most meaningful point; the last time is the most poignant and the conclusion is full of soul. I felt in the moment that her question beneath the pain and the anger was how to make the ending successful, not physically, but soulfully. I was reminded of T.S. Eliot's lines from 'Little Gidding': 'And to make an end is to make a beginning', echoing the astrological intelligence of cycles. I asked 'If you could begin again what is it that you would do differently?'

Her voice softened and she said, 'My relationship with my daughter.' A traditional image of the 4th house is 'the end of the matter', and with the Sun there in Capricorn so strongly highlighted at that moment in time, I wondered what lay unfinished. And what she might be able to do to set her soul free from the guilt and regret.

We spent the rest of our session focusing on her relationship with her daughter, her fear of her daughter finding her body and her humiliation at being in this predicament. I appealed to her integrity and authority, taking back control of the situation and being as vulnerable and honest as she could be with her daughter. Together we imagined many ways to start the exchange.

We had three more sessions; the last phone consultation was on 8 June 2002 at 2.00 p.m. In these four months she had spoken to and found peace with her daughter. Another topic had arisen through the horoscopic images. Transiting Pluto had begun its passage across her Mercury in Sagittarius in the 3rd house and Saturn would soon oppose this. On the date of our last consultation the Sun was opposite Mercury, while Saturn had just opposed it and the North Node would do so in a few weeks. Therefore the South Node would soon pass across Mercury. The Sun's proximity to the Node signalled the solar eclipse that would happen in two days opposite Mercury. The progressed Moon at this time was also within a degree of conjoining Mercury; for me these all felt like potent images of expressing the power of her feelings through letters.

Jude had been a journalist. Through these present symbols converging in time with the horoscope I felt sanctioned to encourage Jude to keep her diary and compose letters about the right to die. We talked about her ability to write about a meaningful and dignified death. This consultation seemed very different, as Jude felt less troubled about her daughter and empowered by what she could put in writing, not just for herself, but for others in the future. As always I left it open if she needed to call. But that was the last time we would speak. Her Mercury was conjunct my Descendant; therefore Pluto was in its approach to my Descendant, while the South Node was exactly on my Descendant. Saturn, the North Node and the following eclipse were conjunct my Ascendant, as was the Sun that day. Upon reflection I could not help but marvel at the alignments across my own horizon, an axis that spoke of the dying and resurrected Sun, birth and death.

The friend who had recommended Jude wrote to me in August to say Jude had died. She had successfully committed suicide. In the envelope was an article from the front page of *The Australian*, a major national newspaper. It was an open letter from Jude about her plight and plea for the right to die. The friend also told me

Jude had left her diary to the euthanasia society so others were able to access her story. I felt a deep sense of gratitude that Jude was finally free from her agony and that she had left a legacy that made a difference.[176]

9

MYTH

There was a time when meadow, grove, and stream,
The earth, and every common sight
To me did seem
Apparelled in celestial light,
The glory and the freshness of a dream.
It is not now as it hath been of yore; –
Turn wheresoe'er I may,
By night or day,
The things which I have seen I now can see no more.[177]

William Wordsworth
'Ode on Intimations of Immortality from
Recollections of Early Childhood'

Mythology values soul by honouring the stories of our shared childhood. Myths are located in a time when rituals and traditions were sustained through participation with and service to the gods. As a template for early human development, mythology is a guide to our personal and collective history. Mythology transports us back to primordial times where we re-encounter original and authentic states of being.[178] Cosmogony and creation, humanity's infancy, along with the distant memories of our ancestors, are preserved through mythic tales. When we engage with myth, primal layers of psyche are reactivated.

Beginning with conception, through gestation, perinatal experiences and during the dawn of our childhood, we encounter the heroes, hydras, caretakers and chimeras of mythic storylines. These experiences are often discounted as belonging to the imagination of childhood, but that does not make them any less genuine. We tremble with fear at what we imagine or squeal with delight at what we feel, whether 'real' or not. Mythology nurtures the imaginative world before the advent of rational thought explains it away.

Alongside myth, astrology addresses the soul's purpose and its journey. Both exist before the construct of theoretical paradigms. Myth narrates our miracle of birth, conceived by a god yet reared by mortals. Birth is the culmination of an epic journey, incarnating after a long and demanding migration, and it is this moment that astrology mythologizes through the horoscope.

But childhood, like the mythological period, ends. No longer participating with the otherworldly storylines of our childhood we enter a world where divine forces are explained away and our encounters with them wane. The philosophical period dawns, *logos* arrives and our awakened ability to reason seals the portal to the mythic world.[179] The right-brained world of mythic participation gives way to the left-brained discipline of certainty, as Wordsworth poignantly describes above.

The innate development of cognition and objectification creates new perspectives on the natural world, and the imaginative and mythological realms recede. Childhood's end is characterized by the transition from magical perception to rational thinking. Myths have imaginative ways of perceiving the mysteries of creation and life, honouring the divine and the sacred; but mythological epochs end with ages of reason. Myth expires with 'good sense', even though it offers a way to re-imagine a world with soul.

An individual in search of soul soon discovers that 'the soul is entangled in myths' and that 'to know ourselves we must know the Gods and Goddesses of myth. We must face the Gods'.[180] Astrology, like mythology, invites us to face the Gods so we can re-envisage a world with soul.

The Myth of Astrology

Astrology is mythic by nature as it imagines our human story. Underpinning astrological practice are ancient ways of thinking about who we are and the world we inhabit. Like myth, astrology leads us back to primordial times to help make sense of psychic chaos. Contemporarily considering images in the sky as archetypes and patterns of unconscious human concerns continues the tradition of the ancient mythmakers who observed their divinities in the planets and stars. Astrological discourse reveals which gods or archetypes we must be mindful of, and at which god's altar a sacrifice is needed. Astrological imagination reveals the incarnation of archetypal images and events.

Yet, while astrology's own natal chart was birthed out of the mythic and creative unconscious, ages of reason with their theories and hypotheses have covered its imaginative nativity. Astrology encourages us to deeply consider our relationship with the soul; however, that suggests finding our way back through the layers of doctrines and theories that have left it languishing in the dimly-lit backrooms of our culture. Astrology invites us to return to the primordial images that first animated the heavens.

Embedded in the constellated images of the starry heavens are myths, which infuse astrological symbols with images that inspire an imaginal way of knowing. Carl Jung suggested that the 'psyche contains all the images that have ever given rise to myths';[181] however, it was the starry heavens that inspired many of our ancestors' mythic narratives. Our skyful of stories consists of myths of psychic life. The very nature of myth defies explanation because it shape-shifts in the company of the storyteller and the listener. We may be listening to the same narrative, but each one hears the story from their personal experience and understanding. With each narration of the myth something new is created and revealed. When we are relieved from having to believe it or accept it as truth, myth calls us to another way of knowing. As it meanders, we wander away from our ordinary world that is bound by time and place. We are coaxed into leaving the literality of our usual frame of mind for a timeless and placeless world. Through its imaginative and universal language, myth unfastens a psychic portal and invites us to step through. Classicist Mircea Eliade suggested:

A myth tears man away from his own time, from his individual, chronological, 'historical' time – and projects him, symbolically at least, into the Great Time, into a paradoxical moment that cannot be measured because it has no duration.[182]

Astrology also 'tears man away from his own time' as the power of its symbolic language divines the mechanistic constructs of the heavens. This is the astrological *mythos*.[183] Congregating underneath each zodiacal animal are images, symbols and myths which tell stories of the qualities, tasks and seasons of life. Each planet is an eponym; underpinning each one is a god or goddess whose mythic history reaches back to an animistic aeon when planets were not just physical masses revolving around the Sun, but embodiments of deities that governed the cosmos.

Each horoscope is animistic and polytheistic. Every time an astrologer reads a chart, the ancient gods are reanimated. Astrology is a way of seeing mythic narratives through patterns in the heavens and it was one of the earliest attempts to link the world outside of us with the world within. Yet its mythic roots have become truncated, and over time attempts to revive the mythic underpinnings of astrology have been susceptible to explanation and interpretation, disconnecting the potency of myth from the corpus of the craft. The horoscope is a document based on the first breath of life, the symbolic moment separating the newborn from the symbiosis with the biological mother and mythological Great Mother. It is fixed, unchanging, yet is symbolically responsive to and shaped by the punctures of time.

Carl Jung's life's work involved the use of mythological explanations to psychologically understand the larger patterns of human experience. As he succinctly said: 'Herein lay the vital importance of myths: they explained to the bewildered human being what was going on in his unconscious.'[184] The unconscious is another world, shadowed in the brilliance of the rational one. We could imagine the unconscious as a mythic realm where gods and goddesses are forces in control, the monsters bring the fears and insecurities, and the heroes personify the human spirit that strives to perfect itself. Jung suggested that the 'whole of mythology could be taken as a sort of projection of the collective unconscious' and suggested that this was most evident 'if we look at the heavenly constellations, whose originally chaotic forms were organized through the projection of images.'[185] The mythic images projected onto the constellations arose out of the depths of the collective psyche before science had measured and categorized them. These images, projected onto the planets and the heavens, are archaic psychic illustrations, not on the walls of a cave, an Attic vase or a holy shrine, but on the canvas of the sky. The planets were personified as gods and goddesses, while stars and sky images became shaped into constellations of animals, heroes and sacred objects. The night sky was animated by myth long before it was subjected to dissection.

Engaging Myth

Analysis and clarification cannot be applied to myth in the same way that it can to history. It is not a diachronic portrayal of times past, nor a record of human actions. Myth is more akin to a soul history, a commentary on the universal and archetypal experience of being human; it is the sound of primordial knowing.

One way to orientate oneself to myth is to consider it as a dialect of the soul. Mythic storylines awaken primitive images. They are strung together with fabulous images of monstrous intent and heroic deeds, antagonistic gods and fierce goddesses, set in fertile valleys or on mountain peaks in battle and in love. Soul is nurtured through myth as it is imagistic and ageless, reminding us of an 'other' world beyond literal space and time. Beyond the limits imposed by rational thought, myth offers an original view of our natural world. When we engage with its stories or speak in mythic tongues we suspend our beliefs and certainties about who we and where we come from and cross over to a dimension where these realities are less personal. They are everyone's realities, not just mine, but I perceive and participate with them from my private perspective. Myths are a 'collective dream'[186] that engage the imaginative self and encourage participation in its creative process.

Myth assists us to 'see through' physical form and matter into a subjective world where imagination is the primary way of knowing. It de-literalizes the world we live in, rendering other worlds more accessible. Mythological narratives inspire us to participate with this other way of being and knowing that lies beyond the shores of waking reality. It is an extraordinary place not bound by linear time or hinged to facts. When we engage with myth, paradoxes are not contradictory, physical boundaries are not limiting, death is not the end and everyone shares the same concerns, trials and initiations. Myth narrates the stories of our humanity without judgement and with compassion. During consultations I often use mythic fragments to normalize or put into perspective difficult feelings or situations.

Myth is alive in every culture and in everybody. Yet in a postmodern culture whose residents mostly respond to facts and proof, the idea that myth has its own authenticity alarms most people. Theories have replaced fairy tales. Dictionaries define myth as falsehood; therefore in a contemporary world where truth represents what is measurable and observable, myth along with its deities has been dismissed.[187] Yet the prevailing paradigm of scientism is itself a myth, one whose dominance marginalizes any other forms of myth-making. Modern myths of technology and economics are spellbinding since they are 'real' and 'true'. Under this regime all other myths become unreal and untruthful, and the word 'myth' becomes a fictitious narrative, generally regarding the supernatural, which has been its main definition since the Age of Enlightenment. 'Myth' has come to mean an irrational, illusory, non-scientific tale, something which is fabricated, perhaps an elaborate story; certainly one that is not to be trusted as any form of intelligence or truth. Astrology is a myth in that it is imaginative intelligence: imaginative, not imaginary.

Truth is multi-dimensional. Myth legitimizes the unseen world of subjective feelings and responses: 'Myth is truth which is subjective, intuitive, cultural and grounded in faith.'[188] Hence myths do not conform to rational analysis, measurements or theories, as myths are not literal accounts of outer events. There are no standard versions, sequels, nor happy endings. Myth is not concerned with facts or literal causes but invites us to deepen our thinking and free ourselves from a binary reality of certitude and structure. Carl Jung suggested that myths are a way to consider the 'inner, unconscious drama of the psyche'. As astrological myths are 'mirrored in the events of nature', they also lead us to primary psychic processes, but the path does not follow an interpretive and calculated course.[189]

Mythological stories embrace the spectrum of human experience, reminding us of the anxiety, fragility and vulnerability of being mortal. Yet myth also reminds us that we are not alone, nor are we the first to have this experience. Mythic motifs contextualize our human experiences and allow us to understand them as part of the human condition, no matter how painful or shameful.

John was a regular client for many years, many years ago, but I fondly remember having the opportunity to tell him about a lesser known segment of Heracles's myth. Mercury, Venus and Uranus in Gemini were within a degree of each other in his 11th house.

The Moon in Gemini was also close by. In our second consultation, when exploring the images of this pattern, he tentatively told me that he was a cross-dresser. This urge would come upon him when he caught a reflection of his feminine self in a mirror. To me the astrological image resonated with this urge to cross over to his feminine side where beauty could be expressed.

I was aware of how difficult it must be for John to share such an intimate aspect of himself. But I felt it was also a soulful, perhaps shamanistic, part, as many myths tell of the initiations and mysteries of crossing over. Heracles, who served Omphale, the Queen of Lydia, after his twelve labours, dressed in women's clothes, exchanging his rough persona for a soft and receptive one. In a way his heroic cross-dressing is symbolic of an ability to cross over into another world, embracing what had been lost to consciousness. On the island of Kos, in honour of Heracles, bridegrooms would dress as women on the eve of their wedding. John appreciated that the depth of compulsion he felt was part of a heroic tale and not an aberration.

When Grace expressed her anxiety about meeting her relinquished son for the first time, I drew on the myth of Callisto and Arcas to acknowledge the ancient pattern she was feeling. Callisto was devoted to Artemis, but Zeus desired the maiden. In the guise of Artemis herself, he approached the innocent girl and ravaged her. When Callisto fell pregnant, she tried to conceal this from Artemis, knowing she could no longer be under the goddess's protection. Eventually Artemis discovered her secret and exiled her into the wild where she gave birth to her son Arcas, who was raised by Maia in the land that bore his name, Arcadia. Hera, enraged at Callisto for carrying her husband's child, transformed her into a bear and banished her into the wild. During Arcas's adolescence, fate drew him and his mother together again. While hunting wild beasts, Arcas came face to face with his mother. Unable to recognize her in the shape of a bear he raised his spear to kill what he believed to be a ferocious and menacing force. But as they stared into each other's eyes they recognized their eternal bond and were placed together in the heavens as the northern bears Ursa Minor and Ursa Major. Grace recognized the fate of the pattern and, although still anxious about the meeting, she could also appreciate the blessing inherent in the return. She was eighteen when she relinquished her son, who was now also eighteen; the nodes were returning for them both, and Jupiter was about to transit her Moon.

Mythic Enmeshment

To the ancients, myth-making was a creative act of soul-making. Since mythic templates are intrinsic to appreciating the soul, they became advantageous to psychoanalysts in the early exploration of the unconscious. Mythic characters, symbols and storylines were exposed in the excavation, but so were their affect. Myth blurs boundaries, so when we objectify or justify myth, we 'lose the plot'. Alternatively, myth invites us to subjectively participate in its plot.

Sigmund Freud suggested that biographers have a special affinity for their central character. Their chosen subject evokes their own personal emotional life, as if the character voices the writer's destiny. Freud's personal entanglement with Oedipus confirms his perception.

In his *Interpretation of Dreams* he suggests:

> The *Oedipus Rex* is a tragedy of fate ... His fate moves us only because it might have been our own ... It may be that we were all destined to direct our first sexual impulses toward our mothers, and our first impulses of hatred and violence toward our fathers ....[190]

Through his sympathy for Oedipus, Freud presented a new premise to psychology, and his cornerstone theory of the Oedipal Triangle resonated throughout 20th-century psychoanalysis. But the myth closely aligned with Freud's own childhood fantasies. Was it because of his personal identification with the storyline that he assumed it was everyone's childhood pattern? Or was it through his enmeshment with the myth that he could become its narrator? No doubt, like Sophocles, Freud's Oedipal complex was a great work of the imagination, but it became simplified to a formula through literality and explanation.

Freud's Oedipus is a prime example of how mythic patterns underline the fate of the human soul.[191] Oedipus was as animated in Freud's creativity as he had been in Sophocles's tragedy two and a half millennia beforehand.[192] While details in the Oedipal tale were similar to Freud's biography, universal patterns were there too, especially the heroic labour to become conscious of our blindness and, when unsighted, how we mistake interrogation for reflection. But perhaps, above all, Freud's Oedipus illustrates how we can become engulfed and entangled in mythic storylines when we objectify the patterns, rather than take part in them. Perhaps if the course of living involves being possessed by a myth, consciousness implies being a willing or 'in-sighted' participant with the mythic material. Freud's biography was Oedipal; hence it resonates with mythic patterns in so many ways. No wonder a dramatist knows his characters so intimately; the therapist, his patients.

When subjective truth becomes legitimized as fact, observed through case studies and bound up as a theory like Freud's Oedipal complex, its imaginative and soulful essence withers. The myth becomes diagnostic rather than agnostic, becoming foreseeable and symptomatic rather than uncertain and mysterious. When we generalize a personal connection to a myth as a collective reality, rather than a personal or cultural motif, we become seized by it, blind, like Oedipus, to its power over us. Rather than a conscious participation with the storyline, we become enmeshed in its plot.

Although Freud's Oedipal enmeshment identified a psychic plot already entrenched in the collective, his choice of myth to delineate his theory actually demonstrated the intensity of mythic identification. Christine Downing, whose mythological writings have also revealed her emotional life, says: 'Myth study is never disinterested, objective; perhaps Freud's main contribution is this insight. The analysis of myths, of primitive thought, is always in part self-analysis, and self-analysis is always self-creation, therapy.'[193]

Working with horoscopic signatures is similar to working with myths, a form of self-analysis, at times 'self-creation' and 'therapy'. But when the astrological symbol is explained and interpreted as the pattern, we run the risk of being blindsided like Oedipus. Or when we generalize an astrological signature without knowing the symbol subjectively, we run the risk of becoming enmeshed in its pattern. While there are many distinctions between astrological symbols and myth,[194] they both invite us to stand inside the process, not outside.

Myth and Astrology

Like many other cultures the Greeks personified their myths in the constellations. By the Classical period[195] the constellations that the planets passed through were being mapped out as a celestial highway known as the zodiac. Characterizing the early zodiacal signs were instinctual images embodied as animals; hence the constellated figures of the zodiac are not just smatterings of haphazard images but representations of collective psychic energy animating the skyscape.[196] While myths underpinning the zodiacal constellations seem unrelated, almost random in their selection, a cohesive schema of life energies emerges as we imaginatively unravel their storylines.[197]

The word 'zodiac' is borrowed from the Old French *zodiaque*, derived from Latin; however, the original source is Greek.[198] The Greek root of the word refers to a circle of sculptured animal figures: *zoion*, suggesting a living being, an animal or life. This circle of animals or wheel of life symbolizes an instinctual, yet deeply divine, layer of the human soul. Embedded in the zodiac is this archaic wisdom; hence why it came to be known as the 'seat of the soul' or the 'temple of the spirit'.[199] In effect, the zodiac is one of humanity's first picture books, characterizing the instinctual human journey, an imaginative way to view the schema of life and an early depiction of the individuation process. The animal motifs symbolizing its primitive and instinctual nature are much older than the zodiac itself. Therefore, as we participate with the primitive and instinctual nature of the zodiacal myths we are no longer in chronological time but primordial timelessness.

The ancients distinguished the 'wandering stars' from the fixed ones and these came to be known as the planets, derived from the Greek verb *planasthai* meaning 'to wander'. The ancients imagined the planets as deities wandering amongst the constellations along the zodiacal route. Therefore, planets were named after the gods. Today, the names are Latinized but the Babylonians and the Greeks knew them by the names of their deities: for the Babylonians, Venus was Ishtar, and to the Greeks this was the star of Aphrodite; Babylonian Mars was Nergal while the Greeks knew it as the star of Ares. Consequently, set into each horoscope are the names of ancient gods, who are animated every time a horoscope is consulted.

While astrological language was filled with mythic allusions, astrological practice was never largely impregnated by myth, although at times along the way the gods would reappear in an astrological context. During the Renaissance the gods were reclaimed and in the 15th century CE Marsilio Ficino was a spokesman for them in *Three Books of Life*. The third book, *How Life Should be Arranged According to the Heavens*, reimagined astrology.[200] In the 20th century Carl Jung repositioned the gods in the midst of psychological work. As 'personifications of unconscious contents',[201] the gods revealed themselves through the psyche. Jung's investigation of the unconscious and its archetypal inhabitants was akin to early Mesopotamian thought, yet now the gods were no longer enthroned in the sky but positioned on the psychic landscape.

It is ironic that even though the tradition of astrology disregarded its mythic origins, astrology remained a custodian for classical myths throughout the Christian era. The textbook for my Classical Mythology course at the University of Melbourne credited astrology for helping mythological names survive into the modern age:

> ... astrology was too much a part of late classical and early medieval culture to be extirpated. It therefore survived the coming of Christianity and with it the classical gods prolonged their existence ...[202]

I take pride in the fact that our craft has such a time-honoured tradition and that in the midst of monotheism our practice honours the pantheon of classical gods. Since each chart is polytheistic, every time we look at a horoscope the multiplicity of our ancient gods is reanimated. As contemporary astrologers our challenge is how we converse with them.

Astrology is liberated when it returns to its primordial roots and faces the gods. These roots are sunk into the mythological soil. Mythical literacy kindles the imagination. Astrology is a way of seeing the mythic narratives that occur through patterns in the heavens, one of the earliest attempts to link the world outside us with the world within: as above, so below. James Hillman suggested that mythology was the 'psychology of antiquity';[203] however, we could also suggest that astrology was an earlier psychology of antiquity as its intention was to study the soul, the rightful nature of psychology, through movements in the heavens. The myth of astrology was and still is another way of comprehending the world around us; a very potent myth, as it references the ancient gods, goddesses and the heroic stories through its symbols in the starry heavens. Their images, patterns and stories narrate the soul's archetypal journey. Without a mythic base to astrological language, the practice of astrology can become obtuse and oversimplified, a lost language understood only by its advocates.

During the 20th century Dane Rudhyar proposed a 'transpersonal astrology'[204] that illuminated astrological symbols in the light of the inner and divine life. He suggested that astrology 'can, and I believe should, be considered a symbolic language – indeed a great *mythos* that could inspire and lead to much needed psychospiritual realizations.'[205] While Rudhyar used the Greek word for myth, he was not referring to mythology per se, but to astrology's capacity for intuitive commentary and meaningful revelation through its archetypal patterning. The *mythos* of astrology encourages an involvement with not only the literal world, but the subjective and personal cosmos.

Inspired by the work of Carl Jung, Liz Greene was at the forefront of a generation of astrologers who used myths to infuse astrological symbols with deeper meaning.[206] In the last quarter of the 20th century the mythic underpinnings of the zodiac and the planets became more established. Using a psycho-mythological framework, some astrologers began using myth to amplify astrological configurations, thereby potentially broadening the tradition's foundations.[207]

However, when myths become explanations, rather than images of astrological signatures, they no longer inspire or disclose meaning. When Persephone's abduction is a Pluto transit or the *psychopomp* is Mercury retrograde, the fertile landscape of myth is rendered barren. When archetypes like the anima are no longer evocative symbols of the psyche, but a man's Venus, or when the shadow becomes a troublesome aspect ruled by Saturn, then the mystery of the symbol and its ability to bring meaning to light is compromised. If astrology's gaze remains focused outside self with formulas and facts, then the mystery of the soul's story remains unobserved.

On the other hand, the mythological and archetypal ways of thinking that are now available for astrological practitioners provide a great opportunity for them to ensoul their practice; however, another way of knowing is required. It is not an objective knowing about things but a participatory exchange 'which changes you or which you have to change to know'.[208]

James Hillman's 'archetypal psychology' reconnected psychic patterns with gods and goddesses, a proposal already consistent with the astrological blueprint.[209] Astrology has always embraced this idea, although at times it has been unspoken and unwritten. Through the planetary deities and their interactions in the horoscope, astrology offers a plan that can amplify personal and archetypal patterns. It supports this primal view through its synergy with myth. Even with a lack of awareness, myth lives in each horoscope, offering its multi-layered narratives.

Underpinning each horoscope is a mythic landscape where the roots of each planet and zodiacal sign are deeply buried in primordial soil. Depending on their astrological placements, the personal journey of the soul can be imagined in the context of a contemporary time and place. But, like myth, astrology is not an objective or factual discipline, but one that belongs to the spirit of the gods. Astrology has been and still is a curator of myth. Its mythic foundation infuses the horoscope with timelessness and respect for the divine agents whose patterning underpins our life.

10

VOCATION

Two roads diverged in a wood, and I –
I took the one less traveled by,
And that has made all the difference.[210]

Robert Frost,
'The Road Not Taken'

In Robert Frost's poem 'The Road Not Taken', 'knowing how way leads on to way', he took the road less travelled, aware that he might never return to this fork in the road again. To me this captures the way of vocation: how one path opens onto another and then another throughout the course of our lives. Whether through personal intention or by divine decree, we follow this vocational path, guided by an inner purpose.

This question of vocation is one of the main themes that clients bring to my consulting room, often when work has lost meaning and fulfilment or when there are two paths to choose from. An astrological consultation can be beneficial in contemplating what path to potentially follow, as the horoscope contains an abundance of images evocative of vocation. A horoscope does not detail literal careers, as vocation unfolds over the course of life, but it does offer suggestions as to what occupational skills, qualities and essences can assist in shaping the way of one's life to be more in tune with one's calling. Vocation is not just a career or profession, but includes hobbies, volunteer work, activities, creative projects and courses of study. Our vocation does not always present in the form of a line of work. It is how we 'make a living' in a way that is authentic and resonant with soul. An individual's career questions are often symptomatic of a larger question about individuation and self-development; therefore, it is helpful to listen carefully to hear if the underlying question of vocation is about who we are, not necessarily about what we do.

As a map of raw material developed in the laboratory of life, the horoscope offers so many ways to reflect on the vocational components such as talents, resources, money, creativity, work satisfaction, career direction, professional development and timing.[211] A fulfilling vocation is neither granted nor denied, but is the product of focus, discipline, hard work, effort, passion, patience and consciousness. The vocational path is never linear or certain, but like the heavens is constantly in flux. In many ways Chance plays her role in our future through opportunities, encounters, appointments and assistance experienced on our vocational quest. Reflecting on astrological timing through cycles and transitions enhances our sensitivity to vocational patterns, assisting Chance to be an integral part of the process, not something separate from it.

Vocation is a calling, an inner voice, not one originating in the outer world. The English word originates from the Latin *vocare*, to call, and in early English this was understood to be a spiritual calling, an intimate invitation to follow the course of one's passion. The root *voca* means 'voice' and the original implication of having a vocation was that one followed one's inner calling. Vocation is an internal tone; a poignant moving feeling that there is a place for us to be in the world. Vocational impressions are inborn and often accessible through early memories, and certainly through images in the horoscope, but one of the main obstacles in understanding vocation is literality. Mistaking an internal image or a symbol for a specific indication of a profession puts an end to further exploration or amplification. It also perpetuates the myth that vocation is something that exists outside of us, already established in the world for us to find; not something that emerges over the course of our lives.

Since the language of the inner world is articulated through images and feelings, this inner voice is not logical but experienced intuitively and imaginatively. It arises through images, symbols, felt senses, fantasies and dreams; therefore, it is often ambiguous and unclear. Nonetheless, it is deeply felt and lives through our imagination. And because vocation is deeply felt, it prompts us to give it meaning, form and life. It demands something of us, but that something eludes being identified or articulated. It is a yearning, a sense, a hope, a drive that even our creativity, work or profession cannot appease. It often remains a spiritual calling until we participate in its mystery and work towards shaping its presence in our everyday lives.

Following the *Daimon*

The question of vocation is not static, nor fixed, but lifelong. Vocation is more than our work, our activities, our creativity or our career. While it encompasses our livelihood, vocation is how we find meaning in making our living. It is about purpose and what we feel we are meant to do. It is a process, not an end goal, as vocation is a deeply intimate part of who we are. The astrological horoscope helps us to consider our vocational *daimon*.

The *daimon* is akin to the passionate force that leads us in certain directions. It is there from the beginning and drives us in certain ways, often along untraveled roads. In the earlier chapters of our vocational story it is more difficult to know what it wants of us, but when the *daimon* stirs in us, we are invited, even compelled, to follow. As we age, perhaps more evident in our sixties, the *daimonic* pattern is clearer, where the ways and the steps along the path become more apparent when we look back. The *daimon* is a force, an urge, and has its own intelligence which is not always easy to follow, but follow we must. Creative and vocationally fulfilled individuals who have successfully followed their *daimon* are often surprised at the feedback from others about what they have accomplished. They know they cannot take all the credit – what they have accomplished was not something they planned and did, but more something they were driven to do and so they followed the prompts.

Carl Jung suggested it was *vocation* which induced an individual to follow his own soul and become conscious. He proposed that vocation was 'an irrational factor that destines a man to emancipate himself from the herd and from its well-worn paths. True personality is always a vocation.' More than most, Jung knew the courage and strength needed to follow the *daimon* and break away from the 'herd'. The herd is the well-trodden path of what is acceptable to the consensus reality of our society, our parents and our ancestors. To follow the voice which summons one on their authentic less-travelled path demands the individual be 'set apart from the others'. As Jung reminds us, 'Creative life always stands outside convention'.[212] Vocation demands that we risk being marginal, in touch with our own need for individuation. Vocations do not come with job descriptions, opportunities for promotion or a guaranteed income. No doubt work and career are aspects of vocation, but we cannot appease this deeper longing for individuation and self-fulfilment solely with a literal job. Individuation *is* a job, it *is* a task; it *is* the 'opus' of one's life. Therefore our vocational task continuously unfolds throughout our lifetime and its success depends on our ability to follow our *daimon*.

As Tom Moore reminds us, following our creative and vocational *daimon* is complicated; 'expect a struggle', he says.[213] He acknowledges that Jung's *daimon* led him into the deeper mysteries of life. Along this road less travelled, in the dark depth of the unconscious, Jung's archaeological discoveries of the soul informed his life's work. Moore quotes Jung: 'There was a daimon in me. It overpowered me ... I had to obey an inner law which was imposed on me and left me no freedom of choice. A creative person has little power over his own life. He is not free. He is captive and driven by his daimon.'[214]

While struggles and setbacks are part of the *daimonic* terrain, so are mystery and magic. For me, following my *daimon* has been an act of grace. Building my practice as a full-time counselling astrologer was not easy in a world where the external values were not in sync with mine. Crafting a living that allowed me to support myself and my family was a struggle, but each year, as I visited my accountant, I was reminded of how much I owned, not in a financial or material way, but from a psychological perspective, since I was following a creative course that felt right for me. So I cannot explain how the path opened up and allowed me to travel and teach and write in ways I never could have arranged by myself. I can only say it feels as if another force guided me along the path and I had the courage (or naiveté) to follow its call. I still can see my accountant shaking his head as he could not quite reconcile the year's income with how we lived a life that was abundant in many ways. When looking at horoscopes from a vocational perspective, I drew on the confidence that I gleaned from following my *daimon*. It helped me build the trust to confidently support others in following their own call to vocation.

Being called can sometimes be quite literal for some people: a voice, a vision, a deeply felt knowing. But it is a subjective force, an inner force. Being so deeply personal, it is important not to 'read' it factually, but to allow the symbol to reveal its meaning through a more reflective and contemplative approach. In my book *Vocation* I have used this example of a client who heard a call which changed his direction in a way he could never have imagined.

For a period of three years Jeff, a young man on the cusp of his third Jupiter return and entry into the mid-life passage, consulted me about career and life direction. He was a solicitor in a high-ranking legal firm and while his work was financially and professionally lucrative, it was emotionally and creatively unprofitable. But for a young man with family responsibilities, it was not easy to risk following his passion.

Jeff was passionate about writing and had considered journalism, but law was a more secure option. With his angular Mercury squaring Neptune on the MC, the image of an imaginative thinker

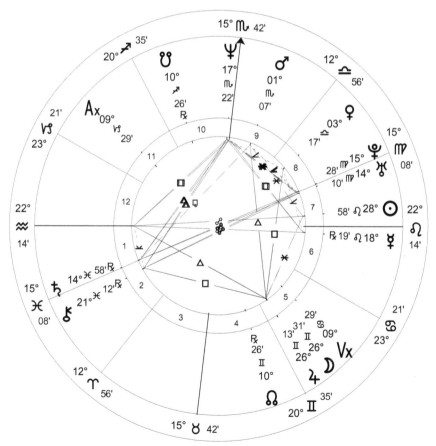

Jeff, 22 August 1965, 5.14 p.m., Geelong, Victoria, Australia

and storyteller was very apparent to me. Having his North Node in Gemini, with Jupiter conjunct the Moon in the Mercurial sign in the 5th house, his enthusiasm to express himself through words, images and ideas felt right.

Throughout our time together, Uranus transited his Ascendant. When it was in its retrograde phase across the Ascendant, Jeff's severe back pain led to an unexpected operation for a prolapsed disc. Five days after the operation, on his last night in hospital, he awoke in the middle of the night. The room was filled with light and he heard a man's voice say, 'You are supposed to be a psychologist'. His third Jupiter return would be exact that month and later in the year Uranus would turn direct and pass over the Ascendant for the last time; the chart was indicating a new life phase.

Jeff phoned to tell me what happened and that he felt motivated by his vision to research how he could become a psychologist. When we were able to resume our work together his clarity about becoming a psychologist had faded. We spoke about the voice and its message. Our word 'psychologist' comes from the Greek *psyche* and *logos* which together suggest 'a student of the soul'. And perhaps this man's voice was a reflection of Jeff's, his *daimon*, an inner calling symbolized by his angular Neptune square Mercury that Uranus was also triggering as it crossed the angle. Perhaps the voice was the clarity of knowing that he needed meaning in his work or he would continue to feel the burdensome weight of purposelessness on his back.

Jeff had been awoken and had been called. By the next year, when Jupiter crossed into the 6th house and Saturn transited his Jupiter–Moon conjunction in the 5th, work changed. Earlier in the year an unexpected opportunity to teach law at an innovative university had arisen. He followed the lead and moved into a new career, a new state and a new phase of life. Jeff's passion was being a student of the soul and he followed his way that would lead into new avenues of vocation.

Work and Soul

Our need to tend to soul in what we do in the world is always present. Without nurturing this need, an individual feels empty, incomplete, unfulfilled. An essential aspect of the Self feels lacking. Out of this empty place an individual seeks answers.

Feeling dissatisfied with work, disliking one's job or knowing there is 'something more' are often the motivating factors as to why individuals book an astrological appointment to explore the realm of vocation. There is often the belief that the 'right' career will be the solution to what is missing. However, the answer is never simply a particular profession or a definitive course of action or even pursuing an exciting job, even though this can be enormously helpful.

So often in my consulting room individuals have described the strong sense of something they feel they were meant to do. Yet the same individual does not know what that is, or what to do about the feeling. They only know they are meant to be doing something more than what they are doing. The fantasy is generally that if the right path or the right career were to be found, these feelings would subside. The urge to find soul in the world is often projected onto the image of a profession, which seems to address some of the missing components of the individual's current life. The longing to find a soulful connection to the world is prone to becoming inflated and fuelled with fantasy. James Hillman warns that 'vocation is a very inflating spiritual idea'[215] if it is attached to believing we are chosen or meant to do something special or definite. Believing that literal 'creativity' or the perfect job will nourish the longing and appease that hunger is fraught with disappointment since an external position cannot fulfil such a deep aspect of the Self. So often our vocation is what we already know or simply what we already do. It is inherently a part of our character, which unfolds over time. A literal career or profession, no matter how enlightened, is not necessarily the answer to the soul's longing. As vocation is an aspect of the individuation process, its path is not predetermined but forged over time through the interrelationship of the inner self with the outer world. Vocation demands its own set of rules and insists on its own laws.

Because work is how we make a living we often identify work as something we do rather than something intrinsic to who we are. Some professions can bestow such prestige and status that we may be drawn to a profession because of what it can offer the ego, not the soul. Some careers offer the financial rewards that provide a wealthy lifestyle, which outwardly appeases the need for self-worth. However, midway through the second Saturn cycle, in mid-life, it becomes evident that these career bonuses are never enough if vocational urges are still unmet; therefore, the midlife crisis often centres on coming to terms with life's vocation. Even when all the objective criteria seem to suggest a successful career, the soul is often despondent and unfulfilled. It is at this point that I often meet my clients, who are drawn to astrology rather than career counselling, as the model lends itself to reflecting on the course of one's life.

An astrology that respects soul can be highly constructive in addressing the loss of the sacred in work and in re-visioning and redeeming aspects of the Self that seek expression in the everyday world of work. I was heartened to recognize that many of the words connected with vocation have a sacred origin resonant with soul. Words are also symbols and images. Apparent underneath our vocational language is the soul's urge to be occupied and employed through craft, skills, talents and, most importantly, though ourselves. The deeper essence of these vocational words echoes through many of our astrological houses, signs and images. The connection between our profession, our life's work and our religious needs is an ancient part of us all. However, after the Industrial Revolution, which reshaped the sphere of work, our usage of these words changed. Work became something outside of us, devoid of soul and disengaged from the spiritual. When we become disconnected from the soul's intention and are no longer occupied with a meaningful path in life we are disconnected from the wellsprings that renew and revitalize the Self.

We have already mentioned vocation as being the call from deep inside the Self, an internal voice, the calling to attend to soul in the world, not a literal mission. 'Profession' is from the Latin, meaning to declare aloud or in public, to profess one's vows. Inherent in the word is the act of making a vow to the world. While its earliest form referred to the vow made by individuals entering religious orders, it later came to mean an occupation that required a professed skill or qualified training, which is its contemporary meaning.

A profession is our declaration to the world, our vow of intention. Today we mistake qualifications, degrees, networking and supervised experience for professionalism; therefore we can become disheartened when the pursuit of degrees or membership of prestigious and elite organizations does not satisfy a deeper yearning. Over time, an internal connection with our own authority is forged by following our authentic professionalism, but when it is projected onto external authoritative standards we are at risk of losing integrity and an inner connection to the wisdom of our own authority.

'Career' is from the French, and means 'racecourse' or 'a road for vehicles'. In Latin it refers to a carriageway. It implies a runway or racecourse, and later referred to a run, usually at full speed, or to rush wildly, hence to career off course. Our career is the course of our life. It is the way through life's transitions and stages, and like any course it is neverending; hence a career is often the focal point for the journey through life. Astrologically, 'career' implies that the gestalt of the whole chart is important to consider since it suggests a fuller process of self-actualization.

'Employment' is from the French, meaning 'to devote' or 'to apply', with its suggestion of being applied to a purpose, being involved, engaged and connected. This reminds me of the need for intensity, application, passion and Eros in work that engages mind and body. When we are employed we are focused and centred. Without connection or engagement to soul in what we do, the mind wanders and is anchorless; therefore, any vocational analysis needs to ascertain areas that can employ the individual's interest and focus, as well as engage their creativity and life force. In a medieval context, occupation was the act of holding or possessing land or goods, taking possession in order to occupy. In terms of vocation, this is akin to occupying a place in the world or taking possession of a business. Our occupation is the place where we are engaged, either by choice or by fate. The word also refers to being taken or seized, which we can feel when we are carried away with our job, being fulfilled and focused in what we do.

Sometimes we may feel we have drifted into our work, and it now occupies our time and space, rather than us being occupied with it. When this occurs, the central focus for our occupation is outside us, rather than internal. Tom Moore expresses it this way: 'Most people tell fate-filled stories of how they happen to be in their current "occupation". These stories tell how the work came to occupy them, to take residence. Work is a vocation: we are called to it. But we may also be loved by our work. It can excite us, comfort us, and make us feel fulfilled, just as a lover can. Soul and the erotic are always together. If our work doesn't have an erotic tone to it, then probably it lacks soul as well.'[216] To be occupied is a passion we seek through our work. To be occupied with our work is to be fulfilled by it. It is an aspect of our fate and, as such, exerts a powerful urge to be known. Being 'unoccupied' suggests we are not being guided by the *daimon* of our vocation. Astrologically we are alerted to the necessity to take account of the intense, creative and erotic aspects of the chart when analysing the vocation.

'Trade' refers to a path, track or course of action, such as footsteps along a track. A trade was one's path through life. Later, trade became associated with the traffic of commerce, trading as in buying and selling items of value, such as shares and commodities. In a contemporary sense, work has become a trade for monetary reward, yet without a soulful connection to one's life course one's trade cannot be satisfied without a meaningful exchange of resources. Whether we have a trade, or trade is our career, the earlier root of the word reminds us of our path in life. Many vocations are a trade, as in trading services or expertise; therefore, it is important to acknowledge what we are capable of sharing and trading.

The earliest root of the word 'livelihood' is also linked to a course of life through making a living. This suggests the soul's quest to enliven our world through our contributions. Today, making a living often refers to a wage rather than finding the connection to life through who we are. In a contemporary sense this is one's 'lifestyle', the urge to integrate work with all aspects of one's life.

Etymology reminds us of the deeper urges to fulfil our Self through vocation, yearnings often implied beneath the client's questions about his or her career. Vocation and the urge to ensoul the world through our work is an archaic, yet potent, force that informs the choices we make on our career path. As astrological counsellors in an age when instability in the career sector is escalating, it is helpful to remember that the astrological blueprint helps us to consider not only the finite images of a vocation but the infinite ones as well. The horoscope reveals more than a job description. It offers us a reflective model to address the soul's longing to be fulfilled in the world.

A Considered Vocation

Fulfilment in the world is more a product of who we are, not what we do. The vocational nature implies a path of individuation, a road 'less travelled', perhaps a road still under construction. A client's anxiety about their direction is often persuasive enough for us to delineate careers and jobs rather than explore the larger question of vocation which underlies their uncertainty. From a wider perspective a vocational analysis of the horoscope needs to address the spiritual longings to help bridge the connection between their calling and the outer world.

Astrological consideration of a vocation needs to be placed in the context of the individual's life cycle. For adult clients, especially those on the verge of midlife, the urge to find meaning and purpose through vocation is often the priority. Here we need to draw on the many resources in the horoscope to help articulate which paths into the world will nurture the soul best. Adolescents will greatly benefit from a traditional examination of the vocational patterns in the horoscope to help confirm and inspire their career plans. Many of my clients have brought their adolescent children for an appointment, specifically to address the vocational strengths of the horoscope in order to help them choose subjects for their final years of high school or plan for further tertiary study.

Selene's mother recommended that her daughter make an appointment with me to discuss her choices for university courses. Selene was pressured by the system to choose eight potential courses of study in the next month and she was afraid of making the wrong decisions. She was also concerned about not knowing what she liked or even what she wanted to do. Her best friend was applying for journalism, another friend for architecture, but Selene said she did not feel passionate about any field of study. Therefore our consultation centred on her inability to choose, the pressure she felt, and her needs, interests and strengths. By the end of the session, with her horoscope as a guide, we developed some strategies for helping her to meet the deadline. We also discussed alternatives to university in the year following her high school graduation and why her path in the world was different from that of her friends. We talked about courses she felt drawn to and how she could feel comfortable with her choices.

Towards the end of our session she told me that she had taken many tests with her school's career counsellor and that our consultation had confirmed what he had said. When I asked Selene in what subjects she received the best marks, she answered, 'Psychology', so I asked her whether she also liked this subject best. When she said, 'Yes', I asked her 'Why?' 'Well, nothing is as it appears to be', she said. I asked her if she could think of an example of this. 'Take the Moon on the horizon' she replied, 'it appears bigger than it really is!'

I smiled and said, 'Do you know that you were born when the Moon was on the horizon? Not only that, but your name belongs to the Greek goddess of the Moon.' This synchronicity relaxed her, and she seemed to become more willing to be engaged with me. Her Moon in Libra was on the Ascendant, ruling her Cancerian MC. In myself I felt that Selene's unconscious was confirming that the symbol she chose illustrated that her paralysis in making a decision appeared a bigger problem than it really was. I felt more confident to respond that I felt her choices and solutions would lead her in the appropriate direction. Besides, a lifetime lay ahead of her.

11

PLACE

They cannot scare me with their empty spaces
Between stars – on stars where no human race is.
I have it in me so much nearer home
To scare myself with my own desert places.[217]

Robert Frost,
'Desert Places'

Who can explain why we are attracted to certain places from a young age; perhaps we have a penchant for moors or deserts, while others are distressed by them. Why are some fascinated by caves, others by open spaces; some prefer cities, while others villages. Innately we yearn for place. We feel homesick or sometimes speak of being in the right place, whether that is our physical home or not.

As humans we generally associate place with safety, consigning it to either end of a spectrum that stretches from the security of home and sanctuary to the anxiety of remoteness and isolation. Place can inspire a sense of well-being, belonging and a feeling of coming home; yet on the other hand certain locations ignite dread, overwhelm us with loneliness or leave us feeling secluded or imprisoned. Place has that ability to engage or repel us; in essence, it arouses the soul.

Astrology offers us a way to reflect on place through images in the natal horoscope as well as through applying relocation techniques. From a soulful perspective the natal and relocated charts help us to understand our reactions and patterns to places in our lives. The natal chart implies how we might orientate ourselves to home place or whether we might travel to find this. At times, relocation techniques even help us to address our sense of fate about certain places.

Soul and Place

Soul responds to place. Some landscapes are vivid and vibrant as if the spirit of the place energizes and awakens it; other landscapes remain soulless. Places hold memories and inspire imagination; hence soul is set into the landscape, not just by what happened there, but also by what we imagine happened. An ensouled place is historied; it reveres nature and has an archetypal presence. The divine is at home in the countryside; hence physical topography is often ensouled by locating spirits or deities within the landscape. Phantoms, nymphs, fairies, dryads, elves, even ghosts, dwell in the natural features of our environment.

I live at the base of an ancient volcanic plug known as the Nut that rises 145 metres out of the sea and dominates the town, which is surrounded on three sides by water. The town is at the end of an isthmus that stretches 7 kilometres out into the strait. The territory is affectionately known as 'the edge of the world' and the Roaring Forties blow uninterrupted from South Africa, identified as such because of the winds along this latitude. When these westerly winds subside, the Antarctic winds blow cold. They say it's the freshest air on the planet.

Despite being such a tiny town, it was the birthplace of an Australian prime minster and graces an Australian postage stamp which shows the Greek goddess of the sea, Amphitrite, linking the Nut to the Australian mainland. In 2014 DreamWorks transformed the town back to the 1920s for the set of a major motion picture,

The Light Between Oceans. The main street was gravelled, shops were transformed, extras were dressed in period costume and old cars drove up and down alongside horses and buggies. As I stood watching the filming it was as if a thin membrane separated me from stepping over the makeshift boundary into 1926. The place itself had turned back time.

For me this place has always been enchanted and timeless. It invites the imagination. Ironically, for someone who moved every three–four years, loves to travel and likes the pace of the city, this isolated place at the edge of the world feels like coming home. My house is on the main street of this remote seaside village set on the north-western tip of Tasmania. Seemingly so far removed from the rest of the world, I hear French, German, Chinese and Japanese accents as people pass by my window.

Legend relates the Nut as being a sacred site for Aboriginal women. When I see this rock formation, I imagine it as an acropolis. From the top of the Nut the view is spectacular as the ever-changing weather conditions reveal a different landscape each day. Some days the wind forcefully stirs the ocean while other days it is so calm, not a ripple is to be seen. Some days, when the tide recedes it leaves abundant seaweed strewn across the sand. Other days it draws back to leave a virgin beach. The ocean is multicoloured; Mediterranean blue when the sun is high, but as it sets it is like the colour of Homer's wine-dark sea. It is mesmerizing. After the sun sets, a canopy of stars crowns the land, uninterrupted by city lights or pollution.

But the place does not appeal to everyone. Recently, an acquaintance stayed in a cottage nearby and her experience was that it was cold, dreary, it rained nonstop and there was nothing to do. And another acquaintance who told of her visit said the town was haunted. Place is personal space, forged and differentiated by the soul. Natally, Saturn is in my 4th house, but it relocates to the 9th in this part of the world. Jupiter, the only planet above the horizon in my natal chart, is in the 8th house; in my relocated chart in Stanley, Tasmania, Jupiter conjoins the Ascendant. Both images relocate Jupiter and Saturn from houses associated with endings and family to ones connected to life and creation. Jupiter sees a different view of the horizon located here than it does in my birthplace.

Archetypes and Place

Archetypes are located everywhere. Place gives ground to the archetype; therefore we imagine certain archetypes embedded in particular settings. Myth locates the gods in particular landscapes and alludes to what takes place in these settings due to their archetypal affinity with the area. Athena was named for and located in Athens; her temple was built in the heart of the city. Hermes was on the road, unsettled, nomadic; Hestia was in the sanctuary of the home, dwelling in the hearth, while Artemis's realm was the glades and forests. When we feel the soul of a city we are in Athena's province, but when we are at home in front of the fireplace, Hestia is there.

We know Hades as the god of the Underworld; he is its personification. Entrances to the Underworld are usually located in remote and wild areas, accessed through caves, chasms with underground pools or springs, fissures, cracks in the surface of the earth or hidden underneath a lake or body of water. When we are in a cave, a graveyard, a basement or when the psychic landscape is inaccessible and despairing, we are in the realm of Hades. Through image and symbol, archetypes remind us that the outer landscape reflects the inner one.

In a way the gods all have their natural residences: Zeus's is Mount Olympus; Poseidon, the seas; Demeter, the fertile valleys; Asclepius, the healing place; Chiron, the cave of learning; and Ares, the battlefield. When we are in one of these environs we are in that particular deity's sphere of influence. In the ancient world the site was marked out as a sacred sanctuary in respect of the native deity. This image is transmitted into astrology, where the astrological gods have their own residences. Mars's domains are in the first and eighth signs, while Jupiter's are the ninth and the twelfth. When we are in these astrological sanctuaries, the archetypal ruler of this domain is animated. In divinatory practice the god is petitioned.

The spirit of a place is imagined through the fairies and dryads, who caretake the gardens and arboretums of the natural world. These spirits are embedded in the architecture, alive in the marketplace, on the roads and sensed in the overall ambience of the location. Personal history and attachments deepen our connection to place, while the site's social and cultural life stimulates its spirit. Place sustains its well-being through traditions, festivals and rituals, while its myths, folk tales, narratives, music and art illustrate the psychic life of its community. The concept of genius was particular to the Romans who used the expression *genius loci* to refer to the spirit of place. The Romans also honoured the household gods, the Lares. Like many other cultures they recognized the spirit of place as well as the spirits of the house.

When a dwelling is historied it has soul. When personal memories are placed in an area they connect us to that district, even if it is a temporary connection. A special picture, a photograph, a sacred object, an heirloom, a piece of art or a child's drawing brings feeling to the setting and supports the continuity of life. Objects with feeling-value become agents of the soul when placed within their particular context. We can also ensoul our collective space and the world we live in by honouring and respecting the spirits of the place. Places become spirited through folk tales, myths, history, culture, celebrations, landscape, nature, parks, rivers, landmarks, architecture and monuments; therefore we honour the spirit of the place when we participate in its culture, respect its environment and care for its well-being. When soul is in place there is depth and sanctity. We consciously cooperate with ensouling both our personal and our collective places by attending to and participating with where we are.

Ancient philosophers reflected on the importance of place. Archytas, a Pythagorean friend of Plato's, was one of the first to write about place. He argued that 'it is the first of all beings, since everything that exists is in a place and cannot exist without a place';[218] hence place had to be earlier than what first occupied it. Our being needs to be located. Place is before, always there, waiting for the soul to find it. It is ancient. Place exerts its influence and at times it influences our choices, develops our character and changes the direction of our lives. Place both holds memory and gives us meaning. Archytas's attitude seemed to suggest that we needed to be located to exist.

The Greek root for place is *topo*, hence 'topophilia' expresses the love of place or the affective bond between people and place. Its opposite, topophobia, suggests the fear of place. But these are 20th-century words that reflect the long-standing idea that we have an emotional relationship with place. For instance, *atopos* or 'no place' was the ancient Greek word for out of the ordinary or bizarre. Being placeless or out of place does evoke strange and unusual reactions.

When I think about the soul geographically, I am reminded of both place and space. The concept of space seems more universal and collective. Outer space is the wide force field that surrounds the Earth through which our planet and all life travels. But place feels more personal, more subjective and something to which we are emotionally bound. Place is differentiated space, something we can attach to; therefore, place comes into existence when we endow it with meaning. When we name a place we separate it from the undefined space that surrounds it. Once place exists it is an emotionally bound area where there is attachment or aversion, sometimes both. Once place has feeling and an emotional charge it becomes ensouled personally, socially and/or collectively. Since places are soulful, they have a fantasy factor, fill our hearts and become our muses.

Hence our place of birth is a soulful setting as this is the place where the soul incarnated. Here is where our soul awoke from its collective dream into a personal one and where it placed itself in space. But unlike the time of birth which is fixed and unalterable, we can relocate ourselves from our birthplace. Astrologically, our time of birth fixes the planetary degrees, signs and aspects of our horoscope, but place constructs the houses of the horoscope. Therefore, as we travel away from our birthplace, we experience different perspectives on the placement of our natal planets.

Place is a vessel for the soul. Changing place does not alter the imprints of the soul, but like a turn of a kaleidoscope it gives us a different view. But first we must know the archetypal arrangements from the birthplace before we can contemplate how the gods react in different locations. The natal chart is always the primary source. It is the vessel for this lifetime, so a relocated chart is secondary.

Without place there is no ground. While archetypes may be found everywhere, our natal horoscope houses them in specific habitats. The space of the horoscope is bound by twelve houses which represent place literally, emotionally and soulfully. For instance, the 12th house represents places that are secluded, isolated and not

open to the public, like a prison or an asylum. But it is also the place
of sorrow as it is the resting place for family secrets and denials.
Yet soulfully the 12th house is also an access route to the inner
world through dreams, reveries, fantasies and active imagination.
If the relocated 12th house now holds planets that are from other
domiciles of the natal horoscope, these archetypes are placed in a
new position to view the inner life from a different perspective. As
a young boy, Jiddu Krishnamurti was taken to London, which was
a lonely and isolating place for him, yet here he began writing and
became the official head of a new organization, the Order of the
Star in the East. By relocation, natal Saturn in his 9th now occupied
the 12th house. London was a place of solitude and seclusion, yet
in this place a depth of soul was being forged.

Soul gets into place through our memories and our imagination.
When we endow places such as our birthplace, special or dream
places with meaning, then they become internalized, a part of us.
Other places that become significant are places of pilgrimage, even
though we may not consciously be aware of why we are drawn
there. This is where the relocated chart may be of value in helping
us reflect on how soul interconnects with place. In a way, the
archetypes of our life are re-placed for a moment so we can see
them from a different angle.

Houses as Habitats of the Soul
House is an archetypal symbol of shelter, a place where we feel at
home. A house can provide 'the most immediate opportunity for
awakening soul to the outer world'.[219] When we feel at home, we
are grounded, more centred. Houses have many layers, literally
and metaphorically. On the surface we see the literal house, but its
lower storeys contain emotional, psychological and soulful levels.
A house is ensouled by the feeling life of its inhabitants and stories
of its past. In a technological age we have come to know the stories
of a house, not as memoirs or life histories, but as height.[220] In a hi-
tech society the soul of a house is often sacrificed for functionality
and space. I wonder if in soulless times we sacrifice the depth of
storey/story for height.

The house is the space we inhabit, the place we come home to,
where we dream and wake up each morning. When we inhabit that
space we are essentially home,[221] accommodating the soul. In every

house there is soul activity; therefore, houses are symbolic of the soul's dwelling place, often appearing in our dreams to remind us of our deeper needs. The houses of the horoscope are evocative images of places of the soul.

Astrological Houses as Habitats of the Gods

The astrological houses are metaphors for our habitations. Astrologically, the twelve houses are the symbolic places we inhabit: our in-habits or inner patterns, so to speak. They represent both the outer surface of our lives as well as its inner planes. We can live on the surface of our astrological horoscope, experiencing the chart as it seems to appear, or we can become more conscious of its inner design.[222] At the deepest level, the houses reveal the place where the archetypal longings of our lives find solace and meaningfulness. When we begin to explore the terrain underneath the astrological houses, we encounter a deeper understanding of the patterns in the outer world. At the deepest level of the houses we locate meaning that can be applied to the experiences of our lives.

Although the houses were moulded from the twelve signs, they differ in that they represent place, locale, environment and atmosphere. They are the 'where' of the life experience. The horoscope provides a manual of how we might learn to live in accord with our environment by understanding the deeper layers of the houses. These are the places of our lives and these twelve places symbolize the environment that surrounds our being. We could imagine the houses as places where traces of the soul are interred and contained. As we excavate the houses we discover a deeper resonance with the provinces of our lives, such as our personality, our talents, our language, our home, our creativity, our employment, the other, intimacy, meaning, vocation, community and spirituality. These are the places of our lives and each place symbolizes the environment and surrounds of our being.

Astrologically, houses represent place, whether that be an outer location or an inner landscape. The angles of the horoscope direct us through life. They are the principal tracks laid down over the cosmic landscape, boundary markers that traverse the horoscope's topography. The Greeks understood that a boundary was not to keep something out, but to contain the presence of what was sacred. The *temenos* was the boundary line which contained the sacred. The Ascendant–Descendant is the horizontal *temenos* of the horoscope. At the Ascendant the soul is present to life. The MC–IC is the vertical border line that encloses the sacred history of the soul.

Astrology offers a way to reflect on place geographically and symbolically through images in the natal horoscope. Planetary archetypes are located in specific houses, allowing a reflection on how this archetypal force is best accommodated. We might imagine planets in houses as the spirits of place.

But First, Home is Where We Start From

Essential to place is being, then being in something that covers, contains, shelters and holds. At the innermost level, the 4th house symbolizes the home place, the foundation stone for life. From this foundation stone, psychic functions connect us to feeling placed. This space governs feelings of belonging, being at home and being connected. This innermost depth of feeling, whether light or dark, is also a doorway to the soul; hence it is through reflection and contemplation of our familial patterns and legacy that a deeper narrative of our soul's journey with place can be appreciated. 'Places, like home, are where we start from, and they are also where we come back to in homecoming.'[223]

At a much more unseen and speculative level, the 4th house may relate to the infant's felt experiences of the family environment, even impressions from the atmosphere, perhaps prenatal senses and feelings from the family of origin. These unconscious feeling reactions are part of the internal make-up of this house and an aspect of creating a secure base. These experiences shape our trust, our habits and our level of safety. The 4th house is where we develop a base that is secure enough to strengthen our capacity to feel we belong. It is where we start from. The 9th house is known as the house of journeys and it is here or in its derivatives that the call to find a more worldly place is strong; hence combinations between these two places in the horoscope often suggest the burning urge to find where we belong.

Each planetary archetype has its unique orientation to place and attitude to transition. For instance, the Moon is an archetype of belonging; hence its placement in the chart reveals our instinct for place and a felt sense of belonging. It suggests how we make transitions between places, as well as what we need in order to feel safe in these transitions. Jupiter heightens the call to move away from our safety net to explore beyond home place, to stretch out in our life. Saturn supports the urge to identify and commit to place. But it is the planets beyond Saturn that challenge us most with place. These are the planets beyond the traditional world, not bound by conventional systems or familial places. Being collective, they are often more comfortable with space, rather than place, attracting such aphorisms as 'displaced', 'spaced out', 'space cadet' or 'dead space'.

Re-placing Ourselves

Moving or travelling to certain places, whether they are places of our dreams, pilgrimages or work, can be powerful transitions in our lives. For many, moves have been involuntary or out of personal control. Displacement from the birthplace, country of origin or a beloved home can be highly distressing. In the family history there may be unresolved family trauma around moving, migrating or emigrating. Trans-generational migrations may have left the wound of feeling homeless, disconnected or marginalized lingering in the family atmosphere.[224] In these cases, reflecting on place and the fate of place can be revealing.

Are we destined to move? This would depend on our belief system; however, my experience has been that there are repetitive themes around those who relocate, live abroad or travel considerably. Settling and resettling is the dominion of the Moon and therefore aspect patterns involving the Moon are significant. For instance, the Moon in the 9th house is a symbol of home on foreign soil. The archetypes of Jupiter and Uranus are concerned with travel and disconnection; therefore, Jupiter or Uranus in aspect to the Moon, on an angle or in another prominent position may be significant. Other signals would be 4th house considerations, 3rd or 9th house planets, or planets in Gemini or Sagittarius, or perhaps the cardinal points 0°Aries, 0° Cancer, 0° Libra and/or 0° Capricorn being occupied.

In considering astrological times when travel or moves are highlighted, I am alert for major transits to the Moon, the IC and the other angles, as well as through the 9th house. Transits of Jupiter or Uranus to the inner planets are significant, as is the progressed Moon moving through the 4th or 9th house. These are ways of thinking about general indicators but, as always, each individual and each horoscope is unique.

By relocating our horoscope to different places we can contemplate how certain archetypal arrangements may become re-placed, perhaps dis-placed. From a soulful point of view, the natal and relocated charts shed light on our feelings about certain places through their archetypal connections to geographical places.

Jim Lewis was an American astrologer who developed Astro*Carto*Graphy, a brilliant technique which projects the planets of the horoscope onto a map of the world, showing where planets were angular – that is, where they rose, set, culminated and were on the lower meridian – at your time of birth.[225] At a glance we can follow the angularity of each planet geographically by following its 'line' on the map, whether that is the Ascendant–Descendant or the MC–IC lines. I fondly remember Jim regaling

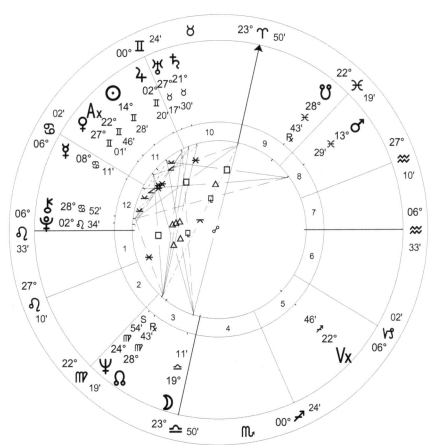

Jim Lewis, 5 June 1941, 9.30 a.m., New York, NY

us with wonderful stories of places and angular planets, but I was witness to the following story.

Jim was looking forward to his trip 'Down Under' where he would visit Sydney and Melbourne for astrological seminars. Off the coast of eastern Australia, near Sydney, his 8th house Mars was on the Ascendant. In other words, at the moment he was born in Yonkers, Mars was rising in Sydney. Jim's chart allows us to view a map, as if our psyche was projected onto the world, revealing places where each planetary archetype is intensified. At the time of Jim's visit, Jupiter was transiting natal Mars and therefore the relocated Ascendant as well. Part of Jim's thesis was that we are drawn to certain planetary lines or places when transits or progressions activate the resident planet there. And so Jim was bound for his Mars rising line under a Jupiter transit.

I was meeting Jim at Melbourne airport. Uncharacteristically, Jim was not in the first batch to deplane, nor the second. Finally I saw his tall figure hobbling towards me on a pair of crutches. My first words of greeting were, 'What's happened?' Laconically, Jim answered 'I was hit by a red car crossing Military Road in Sydney.' I was concerned about his mobility and well-being, but after he assured me he was fine, we shared a good laugh. We dined out on the story for the next few days, as the textbook Mars symbols of the red car on Military Road were too real to be true! But being a reflective and considered person, Jim knew the symbolism was deeper than the literal event.

Like any technique, for it to be of value it must be considered. Since place evokes the soul, I have found great benefits in reflecting on place astrologically, using the houses and angles of the relocation chart. But some of my most difficult clients have been those who arrived with Astro*Carto*Graphy maps or relocated charts in hand and asked 'Where is the best place to find romance?' or 'Will I be successful here?', as if a move to a Venus line would bring romance or the Jupiter line would bring success. But wherever we go we take ourselves. Character is not changed by place. Place offers character a new outlook and experience of Self. And in that place we have the opportunity to consciously cooperate with a new outlook on inherent archetypal patterns.

12

DREAM

'Wake up, Alice dear!' said her sister.
'Why, what a long sleep you've had!' …

… So Alice got up and ran off, thinking while she ran, as well she might, what a wonderful dream it had been.[226]

Lewis Carroll,
Alice's Adventures in Wonderland

And what an astonishing dreamtime Alice had in the wonderland of Lewis Carroll's imagination. Like epic poets, playwrights, mythmakers and storytellers before him, the dream was the means through which Carroll creatively expressed the irrational and the bizarre: the aspects of life that Alice had found underground.

In the last half of the 19th century, imagination was beginning to stir again. The intellectual enlightenment that glowed during the 18th and 19th centuries had eclipsed much of the interest in imaginative studies. During the period the rationalist paradigm, synchronous with social and political reforms, had little room for subjective wisdom; hence practices like astrology and dreamwork were forced down the rabbit hole. But while both were lingering underground they were baptized once again in the unconscious waters of the collective, awaiting their time for renewal and re-introduction.

At the dawn of the 20th century, Sigmund Freud published his book *The Interpretation of Dreams* and brought the long-forgotten yet ancient tradition of dream interpretation to the foreground of psychoanalysis. Shortly after publishing he complained that his book had little impact; however, in reality, Freud was a seminal vessel for the return of the dream, not only to psychoanalysis but popular culture and literature as well. Alongside the dream, astrology also reawakened. Intertwined with the burgeoning interest in metaphysics, astrology's new era emerged in the late 19th century. Alan Leo personifies the resurrection of astrology and its modernization.[227]

In 1814, almost a century before Freud's *Interpretation of Dreams*, a treatise on dreams by G.H. von Schubert, entitled *The Symbolism of Dreams*, was published. The author described the language of sleep as a 'picture language', a hieroglyphic amalgam of concepts and pictures using a universal language of symbols. These symbols were collective and timeless. The horoscope, like dreams, is also a language of the soul that speaks through images and symbols, yet dreams, unlike the horoscope, are projected onto the inner chambers of the psyche, not the outer arc of the heavens. Yet both are daughters of the night; therefore astrological handicraft has much in common with dreamwork because their symbols and images are neither literal nor quantifiable, yet they reveal unknown and deeper parts of the soul.

In western literature, dreams had already been sung, retold and written down through epic poetry, tragedy and literature for nearly three millennia before Carroll and Freud began work. Homer in *The Odyssey* used dreams to link the dreamer with divine forces and to weave the patterns of fate into the lives of his characters. By the 5th century BCE, Aeschylus portrayed Clytemnestra interpreting her dream of giving birth to and suckling a snake, introducing his audience to the profound impact the dream imprints upon the psyche. This was a foretaste of the dreams that would consistently be woven through inspirational literature of western culture.

During the later Classical period, healing sanctuaries drawing on the restorative powers of sleep and dreams were established. In the sacred precinct of the healing god Asclepius, pilgrims and patients would enter the Abaton, lie down and sleep in preparation for the healing dream. The healing dream rituals envisioned an encounter between the god and the sleeping patient. The dream was considered to be the lifeblood of the soul and ensured contact between the corporeal world of body and the invisible world of soul. Contrary to the informational and interpretive paradigms of the modern world, healing dreams were acknowledged as a visitation from the god and that in itself was the healing. Through the dream, the inner and divine world could be accessed and befriended.

An earlier colleague, Artemidorus, nearly two millennia before Freud, had written the seminal *Interpretation of Dreams*. *Oneirocritia*, an ancient Greek text comprising five books on dream interpretation, is the first known Greek work on the subject. Dreamwork is a long-established sacred tradition that supports and facilitates contact with the soul. Thanks to Sigmund Freud, Carl Jung, James Hillman, Peter O'Connor and other psychotherapists, it has been re-cognized. Working with our dreams restores contact with the ancient ways that promoted communication with the gods, a process akin to astrological work.

When asleep, in the country of dreams, we are far away from the daily corporate and economic pressures of life experienced during the day. In sleep we inhabit the night world on the other side of day. In this world a phantasmagoria of images, shadows, colours, shades, feelings, visions, desires and fantasies congregates on the stage of our inner theatre. In sleep's stillness we are closer to the soul through the dream.

Working with our dreams is an act of soul-making. Reflecting on our dreams in the light of day enables a continuity of psychic life. When we dream, the outer and worldly images experienced in our life are absorbed, processed and converted into felt experiences; hence they become more personal and subjective. This process allows the objective and literal world outside the self to become internalized and private. The outer world becomes more connected to the Self. From this introspective and imaginative perspective, a deeper relationship with our inner life is stimulated.

Through this type of reflection, our experiences, relationships and ambitions become more personalized. For instance, when we dream of our mothers or fathers, brothers or sisters, friends or enemies, lovers or betrayers, the images and feelings they evoke are felt inside the chamber of the soul. Their image is internalized, becoming less literal, allowing the feelings and impressions they evoke to develop and be recognized as part of our self. We relinquish the fixed position they occupy in the outer world to consider their image in our inner world.

Our reactions and impressions encourage us to reflect on how we feel about this part of our self. In a psychological sense we identify with the symbol of our self that the literal person is wearing or characterizing for us. Even though this person is flesh and blood, soul-making is the act of internalizing these images so the world outside us is felt within.

Similarly, working with the astrological horoscope is an act of soul-making. Astrological symbols characterize the people and places of our lives. Even though an individual's qualities may be illustrated through astrological symbols quite accurately, it is not just the actual person who is being illustrated, but similar inner qualities which are revealed through the images of the horoscope.

When we reflect on the image of someone in a dream or horoscope, we confront what that person means to us, what they represent and what parts of ourselves they characterize. Soul-making is facilitated by the astrologer when they consider the outer personifications as reflections of inner qualities. Therefore, we might contemplate the horoscope as though it is a dream and work with it as though it is active imagination. Like a dream, the images in the horoscope not only symbolize the outer world reality but also the individual's internal psychic landscape. As we consider these images more soulfully, our mothers or fathers, brothers or sisters, friends or enemies, lovers or betrayers are no longer exclusively the literal people of our dreams or our horoscope, but part of our internal soul life.[228] Dreams and astrology make connections between the projective environment and the inner world through their evocative imagery. Personal history, biography and factual details are significant to a case history, but these are not the same elements needed for a soul history. It is the feeling content, impressions, images, associations and censored thoughts that contribute to the soul's account.

Both dreams and astrology are divinatory and oracular by nature. Their languages are symbolic and metaphoric, and each process has traditions and tenets which attempt to make their meanings accessible. But divinatory art is never as literate as we would like and its perceptions are usually dispensed through riddles. Like oracles, astrologers and dreamworkers may not fully know the individual's history, associations or feelings. Therefore we need to suspend our logical knowing of these images and symbols to be able to listen in the context of the individual's experience, not from our personal perspective of the symbol. In this way we move from more literal interpretations to more soulful perceptions.

Both systems have a rational and scientific construct for their methodology. Astrology has a rich history in the ancient and medieval sciences, while dreams are continually being investigated scientifically. But by nature both are subjective and therefore their revelatory quality cannot be measured by scientific standards. Ultimately, our word 'astrology' does suggest that it is based on *logos* or reason; however, it is with the reason of the soul, not intellectual analysis, that astrology is primarily concerned. As a means of divination, it defies logical reason. This paradox often rests uncomfortably with some practitioners, yet it is in the fusion of the two that soul-making can occur.

Dreams and astrology have links to healing and well-being in the ancient world. Early Hippocratic writers linked astronomical and weather patterns with well-being, associating disturbances in the natural world with health. Dreams were the healing agencies of the gods practised through incubation rituals in ancient Egypt and Greece. Patients would lie down in the sanctuary in anticipation of the healing dream. During the medieval period, doctors practised the art of decumbiture, linking the horoscope cast for when the patient laid down with the illness to its diagnosis and prognosis. Dream and astrological processes have a history of linking healing and the soul.

Dreams are the microscopic view of the soul's journey, revealing themselves night after night as we descend into the dark of sleep. Astrology is the telescopic view night by night of the starry symbols of the sky. Both are observable at night: the dream is light images projected onto the vault of the psyche, while astrology is light images projected onto the vault of the heavens. The dream occurs in our inner theatre, and astrology is played out on the cosmic stage to reveal the interlocked patterns of our personal relationship with the cosmos. Each natal horoscope captures the moment when the child awakens to live the dream of life; therefore, our natal horoscope might be likened to the dream of our being, while night dreams are the continuous weaving of the fibres of our character that are already interlaced through the birth chart.

While both dreams and astrology can be known in descriptive, literal or interpretative ways to give information about the self, they both stem from traditions that facilitate a deeper understanding of the soul. Their history is often told through kings, generals and laymen seeking answers to their questions, yet ultimately the question being asked is not literal or mundane, but a deeper enquiry about the nature of a soulful life. We often seek answers to the uncertainties in the outer world, as this is the world we see. And even though reading a dream or a horoscope provides some clues to these concerns, by their very nature they question what it is we cannot see and invite us into their night world. As Jung said:

> Dreams provide the most interesting information for those who take the trouble to understand their symbols. The results, it is true, have little to do with such worldly concerns as buying and selling. But the meaning of life is not exhaustingly explained by one's business life, nor is the deep desire of the human heart answered by a bank account.[229]

Dreams and astrology recollect the mysteries of who we are; they are not solutions to a problem.[230] Both astrology and dreams are imaginative and polytheistic, not literal nor factual; therefore they move in retrograde fashion, counter to the dominant paradigm of western culture. And in a culture that prefers solutions to meaning, astrology is prone to being called to the service of problem-solving and supporting the ego. In this line of service, astrology can become a commodity.

Dreams speak the soul's language through images. Astrology speaks the language of the soul through symbols; both facilitate a more imaginative and soulful perspective. We might say that the only equivalent of the universe within is the universe without, the two regions that the two sisters, dreams and astrology, chart.

Astrology and the Dream
One way to think about the two sisters is that astrology is telescopic whereas the dream is microscopic; therefore, the combination of these two ways of seeing the soul can be unusually revealing. Astrologically, these two points of view can be observed through two horoscopes: the natal horoscope and the dream chart. The natal chart might be likened to the dream of our life, the big dream or our personal story of the dreamtime, while the dream chart represents a

record of the soul's voice during the night. Horoscope is the dream of life; dreams are the horoscopes of our nights.

The dream horoscope is cast for the approximate time of the dream; this is generally when the client remembers awakening from the dream or their best estimation of the time of the dream. For an experienced dreamer, the time is logged from their bedside clock or watch and noted in their dream journal. The dream chart is read from the perspective of the dream; therefore, the astrological symbols help to amplify, identify, confirm and give voice to the dream symbols. Since the dream chart represents the transits to the natal chart, cross-referencing this chart to the natal horoscope identifies the areas of concern and interest that the night world is revealing to the day world of consciousness. It is a snapshot of a present concern or something of interest to the soul. Dream charts are nightly horoscopes so their frequency brings the faster-moving angles, points and planets to the foreground.

There are patterns to our dreaming. Dreams may start about 20 minutes after falling asleep and recur through the night in cycles. The first dream may be only 5–10 minutes long, but as the night progresses dreams may last up to 40 minutes. As sleep becomes deeper, so do our dreams; the innermost dreams may occur between 3 a.m. and 4 a.m. Dreams also come to mind on waking; however, the nature of these waking dreams is often closer to consciousness than the earlier, deeper dreams.

Dreams belong to the night; therefore, they mostly occur while the Sun travels below the horizon, the imaginary line that separates sky and underworld. This nocturnal solar journey is the hero's descent into the underworld, which astrology maps though the six houses underfoot. Astrology offers us a way to think about the timing of dreams through its nightly transit of the houses below the horizon.[231] The setting place is the western horizon, the mythological Hesperides of the horoscope.[232] From the time it sets to approximately two hours after sunset, the Sun inhabits the 6th house, where the rituals of life are focused on the change from the day world to the night and the preparation for eventide. From approximately 8 to 10 p.m. the Sun transits the 5th house, where the creativity of the night world can be enjoyed before the descent into sleep. From approximately 10 p.m. to midnight, the Sun resides in the 4th house, anchored in all that is past and familial. At midnight the Sun reaches the nadir of its journey, crossing the meridian that astrologically separates Self and Other. As it enters the 3rd house the Sun turns away from Otherness to face its Self and prepare for its ascent through the shady world of the dreamtime.

Dreams between midnight and 2 a.m. occur while the Sun is in the 3rd house; between 2 and 4 a.m. while the Sun is in the 2nd house, and between roughly 4 a.m. and sunrise while the Sun is in the 1st house. This quadrant of the natal chart focuses on infancy; therefore, the Sun's ascent through this area is likely to connect with phantoms of the past. Waking dreams occur while the Sun is near the Ascendant. Having reached the horizon once again, the Sun rises into view, dispelling the shades of night. As it crosses over the horizon, the night world cedes to the day as Eos, the dawn goddess, brings the first light. As the Sun passes into the 12th, dawning heralds the day world. Stirring from sleep we are more likely to bring to mind our dreams while we linger for a moment on the threshold between these two worlds. The dream stays behind momentarily available to consciousness as the Sun enters the 12th house. While this is only one way of thinking about the solar timing of the dream, it is an interesting image of which environs the solar consciousness is focused on as it journeys below the horizon.

Ancients knew the 12th house as the house of 'undoing', an apt description of the process of disengaging from the night world. As the house that marks the entry to the day out of the night, it is where the planets rise to offer us a mindful and reflective expression of what they have exhumed during their underworld journey. Hence the 12th house is similar to dream recall as it offers excavated images of the night or dream world. It is the house of asylum, where disenfranchised and disconnected images that have been unearthed through our encounter with night seek refuge from the day.

In the 12th house we undo the 'night' experience, whether that is in terms of the dream, the unconscious, the ancestral shadows or past life karma. As the transitional zone between sleeping and waking, this metaphorically suggests a powerful time for seeing through, before the inner negatives become exposed by the sunlight. Dream researchers point out that we spend one-third of our lives sleeping and we dream during one-quarter of this time; therefore one-twelfth of life is spent dreaming. As the 12th house is above the horizon, in the day world, it is the metaphorical environment where we awake from the inner experiences of the dreamscape. Here is where we re-member the dream in conscious life. Since the 12th house is the place where planets surface from their night journeys, astrologers often portray these planetary archetypes as channels for expressing the inner life.

Considering the Sun's passage below the horizon allows us to reflect on the difference between a diurnal and nocturnal Sun in the horoscope. When the Sun is above the horizon it shines, is central to the life force and aligns itself with the waking ego. At night, the Sun is invisible, yet still there. Its essence is the same, yet is no longer directed by the waking ego which has now fallen asleep. A more reflective and subtle solar energy promotes soul consciousness through sleep and dreams. When the Sun descends beneath the horizon it encounters the shades and phantoms of the night world which are ensouled through the dream.

As mentioned in Chapter 4, 'Night', early astrological thought embraced the demarcation between the night and day worlds. From the Hellenistic perspective the distinction between nocturnal and diurnal horoscopes was respected in a tradition called 'sect'. Etymologically, the word has developed to mean a distinctive system of beliefs or observances, such as a religious group. From the Latin *secta*, the word suggests a school of thought. Implied in the technique of sect is that the planetary alliances or archetypal arrangements during the day differ from those of the night; in other words, day and night energies arise from different schools of thought. When the Sun is above the horizon it pursues a different mode of being from when it is below.

Early astrologers *sect*ioned the luminaries and planets into two schools of thought. The Sun, of course, was diurnal, along with Jupiter and Saturn, the social planets. Queen of the night, the Moon, partnered with the faster-moving and personal planets Venus and Mars. Mercury, whose mythological nature had always given him permission to move between the worlds, had both memberships, diurnal when he was the morning star and nocturnal as the evening star, so he connected with both but aligned with neither.

As social planets, Jupiter and Saturn are concerned with the functioning of society; therefore, they are given rulership of the morals, ethics, beliefs, conventions, traditions, ambitions and laws of the group. These are the societal codes of conduct that are upheld and expected. During the day these energies support the solar impulse. But when the Sun is no longer visible, its reflective companion the Moon and its allies, Venus and Mars, become dominant. Here in the night world the more personal feelings, senses, impressions, values, likes, pleasures, desires, drives and urges are made known to the solar self through the dream. As it rises into the day world the Sun brings with it the experience of its night sea journey. Since the dream chart is usually nocturnal, the archetypes of the Moon, Venus and Mars often reveal what they censor during the day. In the night world of the dream I have noticed that astrological points not easily articulated during the day are more readily understood in the night chart of the dream.[233]

Horoscope Dreaming

Dreamwork has been an intimate partner to my astrological work, as both originate from the lands of darkness and use psyche's symbols to reveal their meaning. Clients often tell me dreams in response to something I have said or when a similar image from their dream also arises in their horoscope. Working with dreams on astrological retreats brings the symbols of the horoscope to life in a new way. For students I have always encouraged the exploration of dreams, as so often dream imagery replicates images from their horoscope or transits of the time. Both dreams and astrology inhabit the psychic landscape.

Jo was a graduate student in our Astro*Synthesis Diploma program. As part of the syllabus one of the modules was an astrological dream group, facilitated by Mary Symes.[234] During each weekly class the group would amplify one of the student's dreams and then examine the dream chart along with the natal horoscope. Often the students valued the process so much that they continued in the dream groups that Mary facilitated privately.

When Jo relocated to Melbourne from the UK she immediately joined our classes, and for over a decade was a vibrant and engaged member of our Chiron Centre community. She returned to the UK in 2011 and died on 30 July 2018. We had email contact with each other in the months before her death. In early June, two months before she died, she dreamt:

I was in a cell-like room. It was painted white with white bars at the window. There was a beautiful bright blue butterfly trying to find its way out but it was feeble. I directed it to a space in the bars and it flew away. I had been able to give it a bit more of life.

Jo then said: 'As I lay there, recalling the dream, I asked to see a butterfly as a sign! Honestly, that very day a friend came over and we sat outside in the garden and a blue butterfly appeared and fluttered around us for 15 minutes or so. I don't think I've ever seen a blue butterfly before!'

I could not think of a more profound image for the soul than a butterfly, *a beautiful bright blue butterfly*. The inner image appeared to Jo in the outer world, like a visitation from Psyche herself. Jo ended her email by saying: 'The astrology has been so precise and

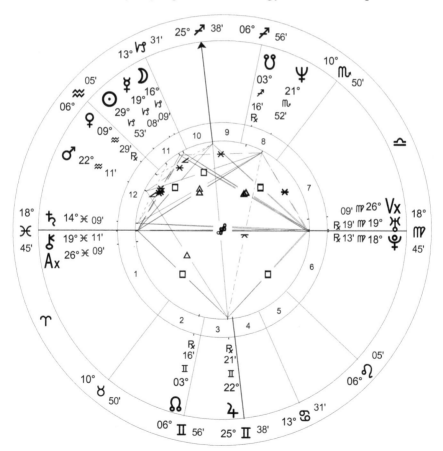

Jo, 20 January 1966, 9.45 a.m., Kingston upon Thames, England

together with the dream, I know there is a bigger story happening and that gives me huge comfort. What a pleasure it was for me to be a part of the dream group for so many years and the gift of understanding and insight that I was left with.'

ASTROLOGY IN SERVICE OF THE SOUL

The stars are mansions built by Nature's hand,
And, haply, there the spirits of the blest
Dwell, clothed in radiance, their immortal vest;
Huge Ocean shows, within his yellow strand,
A habitation marvellously planned,
For life to occupy in love and rest;[235]

William Wordsworth,
'The Stars are Mansions Built by Nature's Hand'

Astrology rests on the coherent patterning of the cosmos, which can be seen as an ordered and balanced construct. But it is metaphoric of human life, not causal. And since astrology is intimately involved with the heavens, it will always be intimately involved with the divine. In this way astrology is divinatory, as it concerns the will of the gods and inspires a knowledge that is beyond our rational control and often outside our own understanding. As we have been discussing, this knowledge is transmitted through astrology's symbols and images, which speak in tongues far removed from our 'mother tongue'. But whatever beliefs we have inherited or inhaled, it is imperative that we fashion our own understanding to become more authentic curators of astrology.

In Jo's last email to me, she shared her experience of the solace that knowing astrology had given her in her life: 'I know there is a bigger story happening and that gives me huge comfort', she said. This is consistent with many clients and students who feel that astrology has opened a window to the soul, a portal to another world, and given them a broader view of life. Astrology's connection to the natural spiritual intelligence of the universe is often felt like a blessing to those who follow its path. Its revelation of signs and symbols and meaningful associations offers a connection to soul. I do not suggest that knowing astrology eases anything on our path;

more that it awakens a reverence for Life and a consciousness, as Jo said, of 'a bigger story'. It invites us to be a part of a larger story by participating in the timeless tides of the cosmos.

The practice of astrology is vocational in that its path is not defined by the 'real' world; that is, the corporate, intellectual, organized, governmental world. Being involved with its abundance of symbols leads to other worlds beyond the one we know. It invites us to stand outside ourselves, to be marginal, individual and sensitive to what remains unseen, engaging the maverick qualities of Chiron. It offers us an encounter with Psyche, a way to explore, recognize, understand and value the depths of the Self. In this way, astrology is a precious instrument in service of the soul.

APPENDIX 1: Birth Data and Sources

Rainer Maria Rilke	3 December 1875, 11.50 p.m. -0.57.44, Prague, Czech Republic	Mother's memory Chapter 4
William Blake	28 November 1757, 7.45 p.m. +0.00.40, London, England	From a personal acquantance Chapter 5
Daniel (client)	5 March 1955, 7.35 p.m., Geelong, Australia	Client's record Chapter 5
Louis Armstrong	4 August 1901, 10.00 p.m., New Orleans, LA, USA	Baptismal certificate; estimated time from news Chapter 5
Helen (client)	3 September 1942, 1.52 a.m., Melbourne, Australia	Client's record Chapter 8
Jude (client)	30 December 1945, 11.50 p.m., Adelaide, Australia	Birth certificate Chapter 8
Jeff (client)	22 August 1965, 5.14 p.m., Geelong, Australia	Birth certificate Chapter 10
Jim Lewis	5 June 1941, 9.30 a.m., New York, NY, USA	From him Chapter 11
Jo (client)	20 January 1966, 9.45 a.m., Kingston upon Thames, England	Client's record Chapter 12
Carl Jung	26 July 1875, 7.32 p.m. -0.29.44, Kesswil, Switzerland	From daughter, Gret Baumann, who calculated the chart using LMT. However, during this time, parts of Switzerland, including Kesswil, were using a time zone set for Bern, called BMT (Bern Mean Time) or -29.44 from Greenwich. Baumann's chart yields the last degrees of Scorpio on the MC. Using BMT, the MC is in Sagittarius.

For the most comprehensive data source consult Astrodatabank, pioneered by Lois Rodden: http://www.astro.com/astro-databank/

APPENDIX 2: Planetary Cycles (Chapter 2)

Astrologically, there are numerous ways to reflect on the cycles of time as well as various techniques that assist in recording time. Astrological techniques such as transits use the actual positions of the planets to measure time, whereas other methods, such as progressions and directions, use symbolic placements to tell time. Ancient techniques brought into contemporary practice use planetary periods based on recurrent synodic cycles with corresponding time lords.

Horoscopes can be drawn for the return of a planet so we can consider its next cycle, while other charts can assist in imagining a particular time period. Yet, with every technique, the crucial data is contextualizing the planetary cycle, whether that is its orbit around the Sun, its synodic cycle with the Sun or its cycle with another planet. Each planetary cycle has a unique timetable, whether that is the fast-moving Moon orbiting the Earth in 27.3 days, or the slow-moving Uranus which takes a lifetime of 84 years to encircle the Sun. Each orbit records one revolution through the zodiac. In 84 years Uranus has made one complete cycle through the zodiac whereas the Moon in the same period has completed well over 1000 orbits.

Opposite is a summary of the time it takes for each planet to complete one zodiacal round. Note that because Mercury and Venus are between the Earth and the Sun, they are always seen close to the Sun. Although they will complete an orbit of the Sun in a shorter time, their path through the zodiac when viewed from Earth is close to the Sun's.

Planet	Approx. cycle through the zodiac	Approx. time transiting 1/12th of the zodiac (or one zodiac sign)	Approx. time transiting one quarter of the zodiac	Approx time transiting half of the zodiac
Moon	27.3 days	2.25 days	1 week	1 fortnight
Sun	365.25 days	29–31 days	3 months	6 months
Mercury	11–13 months	14–45 days	*These time periods are dependent on whether the planet in question is moving direct or retrograde*	
Venus	10–14 months	25–125 days		
Mars	17–23.5 months	1.5–7 months		
Jupiter	12 years	1 year	3 years	6 years
Saturn	29.5 years	2.5 years	7.5 years	15 years
Chiron	50 years	2–7 years	*This time period is dependent on the sign position at birth*	
Uranus	84 years	7 years	21 years	42 years
Neptune	165 years	14 years	41 years	82.5 years
Pluto	248 years	13–30 years	*This time period is dependent on the sign position at birth*	

APPENDIX 3: Dream Preparation and Recall (Chapter 12)

Dreamwork

Soul is down; therefore we descend into a dream. Like all mythic descents, how we approach the underworld and how we journey down into its landscape is critical. In order to prepare for the journey into the dream, reflect on the following points to enhance your ability to recall the dream.[236]

1 Keep a journal of your dreams. Use an attractive journal or diary, one dedicated solely to your dreamwork, although you might also use this journal to record your moods, impressions and feelings during the day.

2 Be receptive to incubating each dream. Hold the intention to recall your dreams inwardly, asking for guidance. Remind yourself that you want to dream and are interested in reflecting on your dreams.

3 Keep a pen, pencil or a voice-activated recorder, as well as your dream journal, near the bed, so when you awaken from a dream and you are recalling it, you can jot down the dream narrative and any thoughts, feelings or associations that come to mind as you are writing.

4 Relax as you awake. Lie still, reflecting. Wait and be receptive to allowing the dream images to return to you.

5 When you write down your dream, suspend your critical faculties. The ego often judges the dream as silly, weird, over the top, horrible, irrelevant or not a good dream. All these judgements are imposed onto the dream; they are not indicative of the psychic quality of the dream, nor are they helpful in any way. The dream itself is image and does not make judgements.

6 If you are having difficulty recalling dreams, try altering your sleep pattern. Go to bed earlier or wake up earlier. Use an alarm clock to wake you one hour before you need

to get up. Note that during busy and hectic periods you may not recall dreams.

7 Going to bed emotionally charged, having drunk alcohol or having eaten heavily hinders the receptivity to dreams and your inner life. Try to relax when going to sleep. Invite the dream to come to you.

8 Read novels, poetry or biography to simulate your imagination.

Receptivity is the key. The first point suggests your intention to dream; therefore I encourage you to purchase or ask for the gift of a dream journal to start to record your dreams. Find your own way of presenting your journal. For instance, the left-hand pages of your journal could be where you record your dreams, while the opposite pages may be for writing down comments and associations. I also encourage you to write the date and time of each dream. Note in your diary both the Moon sign and its phase. It is important to record the time of the dream because later you can construct the dream chart, which is an exceptional tool for amplifying the dream and its psychic images and messages.

Creating your dream journal is an intention to begin a more reflective approach to your inner world and work; it also helps to re-member what has been forgotten, neglected, repressed or overlooked. Dreamwork re-collects aspects of the soul that support a more holistic self. What is recollected is found in the more confronting, emotive and 'negative' aspects of the dream. You will find your own style of recording your dreams but at the beginning you might want to consider:

1 Write your dreams in the first person, transcribing them as fully as you can recall. Try not to judge or edit as you are recording them.

2 Create a title for each dream. You may also want to number the dream; save some pages at the beginning or end of your journal to create an index of your dreams which may be organized by date, title, theme, etc.

3 After recording the dream, write notes on your feelings
   as you awoke, and later when you were reflecting on the
   dream.

4 Write a few sentences about the theme of the dream.

When reflecting on your dreams, be aware of the emotional
properties in the dream and your responses and feelings. Like a
detective, explore the unusual, what is out of place, what does
not fit. Ask many questions about the nature of the characters, the
action and the scenes of the dream. Let yourself be open to all your
associations. And take your time. Rushing towards a conclusion
or a prognosis may be more immediately gratifying, but this will
not be in service of the dream or soul-satisfying. Some points you
might want to consider are:

- What is the setting of the dream?
- Note the characters in the dream.
- Note any dates, times, objects or places in the dream.
- Are there any unusual words, puns, puzzles, etc?
- Note the symbols in the dream and your associations with
  them.
- Note the action that takes place.

Imagine that your dreams take place in the theatre of your inner
world. Some are grand productions with many characters, many
scenes and much action. Some are one-act, sometimes one-syllable,
plays. Do not judge the production of your dreams by their length,
Technicolor qualities or intricate and interesting plots, as they can
be subtle and ambiguous. Generally, it is your feeling response to
the dream and an inner sense of its intensity and importance that
is significant; however, we can also be deceived by this. When
you feel you have explored the dream in this way, add the detail
of the dream and its natal chart to see how the astrological images
continue to open up and confirm your impressions of the dream.
    To begin working with the dream and the horoscope, I listen to
the dream first. I find that the process of dreamwork is enhanced
when the dreamer has recorded the dream because it is often
necessary to have multiple readings of the dream. Even with a

written account, each reading of the dream reveals something new; however, without the written account, each telling of the dream can be unconsciously edited and modified by the dreamer, aligning itself with the day world rather than the night where it originated. Amplifying the dream images, looking for personal associations, honouring spontaneous feelings or memories that arise will all be helpful in amplifying the dream. However, on listening to the dream an astrologer hears the inner images of the dream astrologically.

In working with both the dream and the natal charts, I find it useful to examine the dream chart first for themes and images that are consistent with the images of the dream, as this allows amplification of the dream using astrological imagery. Since the dream belongs to the night world, dreamwork is never as ordered and straightforward as we might like. It invites a lunar approach. Even though dream images are often nonsensical in a literal way, they are embedded with meaning imaginatively; therefore, the intuitive amplification of the dream, along with the dream horoscope symbols, become an awesome team.

I start with the faster-moving planets, especially the Moon, along with the angles that highlight aspects of the natal chart relevant to the dream. The inner planets and angles often repeat themes and direct the astrologer to examine certain environs. In the context of the dream the inner planetary constellation is microcosmic of a larger soulful picture. Inner planetary movements often escape the wakeful eye because they move quickly and are taken for granted. Yet the soul knows their voice and this is confirmed in the dialogue of the dream. I often find the social planets are indicative of the morals and truths that might be stirred during the news of the day. The dream chart gives us an inner view of how the outer life impresses the soul, what it senses and how it feels.

Within the pantheon of the planets, the outer planets' transits may amplify and confirm the context of the dream. Outer planet imagery can be differentiated and therefore, in reference to the dream, can help to confirm the nature of the dream. Since the outer planets in the dream chart are transits to the natal chart, they reveal the larger background context and framework of the dream. The outer planets transit the natal chart for some time, so there is often a series of associated dreams that are related to the particular transit.

Transits to the natal chart of the outer planets are reflected in dreams through analogous symbols and images. Their importance in both the dream and by astrological transit is that their character is trans-Saturnian or beyond the visible boundary of human experience. Symbolically speaking, the outer planets lie outside the orbit of order or the system that is dominated by the ego. This in itself arouses soul. Dane Rudhyar referred to the outer planets in his later work as the 'ambassadors of the galaxy':

> Astrology may add another dimension to our analysis of the dream process by making us differentiate dreams into three basic categories: Uranian, Neptunian and Plutonian.[237]

In contemporary astrology the outer planets are beyond tradition.[238] Invisible to the ancients, they reveal themselves in the modern era and symbolize agents of what is beyond the human capacity to control or civilize. In this way they are agents of the soul and to modern astrologers like Rudhyar they helped to differentiate three ways of being open to energies most unfamiliar to, and at most times at odds with, the ego, because they all represent states beyond its control. For instance, a Pluto transit may be reflected in the dream as giving birth, or it might be a toilet dream or contain symbols of sewers, garbage and pollution. Neptune may correlate to floods, disappearance or diving into the sea, while Uranus could be compared to fractures or fractured images, flying, breaking through or shattering.

– ENDNOTES –

[1] Edna St Vincent Millay, 'Renascence', The Poetry Foundation, available from https://www.poetryfoundation.org/poems/55993/renascence [accessed 14 January 2019].

[2] William Wordsworth, *Ode on Intimations of Immortality from Recollections of Early Childhood from Treasury of Favorite Poems*, edited by Louis Untermeyer, Barnes & Noble (New York: 1996), lines 58-66.

[3] I am using the words 'ensoul' and 'ensouled' to represent the enchantment and animation of an object or place. By the Greek Classical period, the adjective 'ensouled' (*empsuchos*) emerged to signify being alive. See Hendrik Lorenz, 'Ancient Theories of Soul', *Stanford Encyclopaedia of Philosophy*, available from http://plato.stanford.edu/entries/ancient-soul/ [accessed 16 January, 2019].

[4] *An Intermediate Greek-English Lexicon*, 7th Edition, Oxford University Press (Oxford: 1889), p. 903. The entry for ψυχή or psyche lists many definitions including breath, signs of life, spirit, ghost, heart and appetite. See also James Hillman, *Suicide and the Soul*, 2nd Edition, Spring Publications (New York: 2011), p. 44, for his amplification of soul.

[5] Adolf Guggenbühl-Craig, 'Projections: Soul and Money', from *Soul and Money*, Spring Publications (Dallas: 1982), p. 83.

[6] Simon Hornblower and Antony Spawforth (eds.), *The Oxford Companion to Classical Civilization*, Oxford University Press (Oxford: 1998), p. 673.

[7] *An Intermediate Greek-English Lexicon*, p. 903.

[8] Robert K. Barnhart, ed., *The Barnhart Concise Dictionary of Etymology*, Harper Collins (New York: 1995), p. 614.

[9] In contemporary vernacular the words 'psychology', 'psychological' and 'psychologist' are aligned with organizations under governmental regulation and control, far removed from the soulful meaning of the word.

[10] For instance, in *Oedipus Rex* (lines 62–5), Oedipus's soul is sick with what is happening in Thebes and with its inhabitants. Euripides in *Hippolytus* (1008) describes his eponymous male lead as having a 'virgin soul'. The playwrights identified intense emotion, appetite and sexual desire with the soul. Pindar and other poets also referred to the soul, often translated as spirit.

[11] John Keats, *The Letters of John Keats, Volume II*, ed. H. Buxton Forman, Gowars & Gray (Glasgow: 1901), p. 106.

[12] Ibid, p. 53.

[13] Ibid, pp. 53–4.

[14] James Hillman, *Re-Visioning Psychology*, Harper & Row (New York: 1975), p. ix.

[15] Ibid, p. x.

[16] James Hillman, *The Soul's Code*, Random House (New York: 1996), p. 6.

[17] James Hillman, *Insearch*, Hodder and Stoughton (London: 1967), p. 37.

[18] James Hillman in *Myth of Analysis*, Harper Collins (New York: 1992), p. 24 suggests: 'the soul is better imagined, as in earliest Greek times, as a relatively autonomous factor consisting of vaporous substance.'

[19] Ibid, p. 24.

[20] C.G. Jung, *The Red Book, A Reader's Edition*, ed. Sonu Shamdasani, W. W. Norton & Company (New York: 2009). This details Jung's nightly descent into the creative reveries with his own soul.

[21] James Hillman, *Re-Visioning Psychology*, p. x.

[22] *Modern Man in Search of a Soul* is the title of a book of Jung's essays. While the text is a compilation of material originally delivered as lectures, Cary F. Baynes in the translator's preface suggests the book is for those who seek to acknowledge psyche in their lives or for those who 'have experienced the soul as vividly as the body'. C.G. Jung, *Modern Man in Search of a Soul*, translated by W.S. Dell and Cary F. Baynes, Routledge & Kegan Paul (London: 1953).

[23] I have found that this feeling of being seen, held or recognized by the astrological sky, which gives meaning to one's inner and outer life, can be especially profound for those who have suffered early trauma. It is as if a sky full of stars is a nourishing and protecting mother and astrology gives rise to these early feelings. Thanks to Jason Holley for our discussions on this and the reference: Donald Kalsched, *Trauma and the Soul*, Routledge, (New York: 2013).

[24] Emily Jane Brontë, 'To Imagination', from the *Complete Poems of Emily Jane Brontë*, edited by C.W. Hatfield, Columbia University Press (New York: 1995), pp. 205–6.

[25] Dane Rudhyar, *The Astrology of Transformation*, Theosophical Publishing House (Wheaton, Il: 1980), p. 193.

[26] Astrological voices through time, such as those of Valens, Plotinus and Ficino, have highly valued imagination. In modern astrological discourse the role of imagination is rarely discussed. An exception is Geoffrey Cornelius's article 'Astrology, Imagination and the Imaginal', *The Astrological Journal*, Volume

56, # 1, January/February 2014, pp. 12-16. He begins the article with the bold statement: 'Without imagination there is no astrology'.

[27] Dane Rudhyar, *The Astrology of Transformation*, back cover.

[28] When you have reflective time, try active imagination to amplify a planet. First outline the planet's position in your horoscope: its sign, house position, the house/s it rules, its aspects, as well as any other astrological information, i.e. essential dignities, strengths, weaknesses, observations, etc. Note your feelings, impressions or sensations while you summarize this information. Now personify the planet: give it a nickname. Humanize the planet: who does it remind you of, who does it symbolize? Give the planet a human face. What images can you use to represent the planet – what stories, myths, vignettes, anecdotes spring to mind? Begin a conversation with the planet and see where it takes you. For me the craft of astrology has been significantly enriched through imaginative processes.

[29] Carl Jung, from an interview in *Neues Weiner Journal* on 9 November 1932, translated by Ruth Horine. See *C. G. Jung Speaking*, Princeton University Press (Princeton: 1977), p. 58.

[30] Henry Corbin, 'Mundus Imaginalis or the Imaginary and the Imaginal', Spring, 1972, p. 2. Available from: http://www.bahaistudies.net/asma/mundus_imaginalis.pdf [accessed 5 March 2019].

[31] W.B. Yeats, *The Collected Works of W.B. Yeats, Volume I, Early Essays*, edited by Richard J. Finneran and George Burnstein, Simon and Schuster (New York: 2007), p. 119.

[32] Ibid, p. 119.

[33] I highly recommend Lindsay Radermacher's discussion on symbols from her MPhil thesis in Theology and Religious Studies (2011) entitled 'The Role of Dialogue in Astrological Divination', available at: http://www.the9thhouse.org/docs/Lindsay%20

Radermacher%20MPhil%20Thesis%202011.pdf [accessed 15 August 2017].

[34] Henri F. Ellenberger, *The Discovery of the Unconscious*, Basic Books (New York: 1970), p. 205.

[35] Paul Tillich, 'The Nature of Religious Language', *Theology of Culture*, Oxford University Press (Oxford: 1959), pp. 56–7.

[36] C.G. Jung, *Psychological Types*, The Collected Works, Volume 6, translated by R.F.C. Hull, Routledge & Kegan Paul (London: 1971), ¶816.

[37] Dane Rudhyar, *The Astrology of Transformation*, p. 161. By 'every factor', Rudhyar implied the birth chart, transits, progressions and the client's life experience.

[38] Thanks to Darby Costello as she was the first person I heard mention this phrase,

[39] C.G. Jung, *Psychological Types*, The Collected Works, Volume 6: ¶817. Jung said a 'mere sign'.

[40] Dane Rudhyar, *The Astrology of Transformation*, p. 29.

[41] Ibid, pp. 30–1.

[42] James Hillman used this expression in his work – see Thomas Moore (ed.), *The Essential James Hillman, A Blue Fire*, Routledge (London: 1990), p. 75.

[43] Henry Van Dyke, 'Time Is', from The Poem Hunter, https://www.poemhunter.com/poem/time-is/ [accessed 18 January 2019].

[44] Themis was a Titan, the goddess of divine law and order.

[45] When we are anticipating time, we no longer are participating with it. Pulled into the linearity of time and objectivity, we lose access to the cyclicality and subjectivity of the subtle world that

astrology reveals. At this juncture the spontaneity of divination can become literalized. The porous boundaries vital to subjective involvement are eclipsed by literality and objectivity.

[46] An orb is a given allowance of variable zodiacal degrees either side of a planet, point or angle where the influence or receptivity to aspects is considered to operate. There are no agreed-upon standards in astrology regarding the allowance of orbs, but a general rule for natal aspects suggests that faster-moving planets should have wider orbs – with this directive the Moon could have an orb of up to 10 degrees. Major aspects are often granted wider orbs than the minor aspects. Astrologers also vary considerably on the orb of influence for transiting planets. The usage of orbs in classical astrology is also confusing and unarticulated.

[47] Edward S. Casey, *Spirit and Soul Essays in Philosophical Psychology*, Spring Publications, Inc. (Putnam, CT: 2004), pp. 279–80.

[48] The lecture by James Hillman was originally given at the 1997 Return of Soul to the Cosmos conference and repeated at the Alchemical Sky conference in Bath, UK, in May 2005. James Hillman, 'Heaven Retains Within Its Sphere Half of All Bodies and Maladies', at http://www.springpub.com/astro.html [accessed 15 January 2004 – no longer available].

[49] Geoffrey Cornelius, *The Moment of Astrology*, Penguin Arkana (London: 1994), p. 190: 'the Ptolemaic model of astrology has obscured the foundation in participatory significance by treating symbolism as an expression of causes, or as an expression of some objective cosmic order.'

[50] The ancient Greeks saw the planets as wanderers, unlike the fixed stars. Embedded in our word 'planet' is this Greek notion of wandering. While Edward S. Casey does not refer to astrology, he does associate the planets' patterns with soul, which to me is inspiring: see *Spirit and Soul Essays in Philosophical Psychology*, p. 279.

[51] For a discussion on the development of thought around Chronus and time see John Cohen, 'Subjective Time' from *The Voices of Time*, edited by J.T. Fraser, George Braziller (New York: 1966), pp. 274–5.

[52] Hesiod describes the Golden Age in his *Works and Days*. This quote is from the translation by Hugh G. Evelyn-White, Harvard University Press (Cambridge: 2002), p. 11.

[53] James Hillman, 'Notes on Opportunism'; in *Puer Papers*, edited by James Hillman, Spring (Dallas: 1994), p. 153.

[54] For a discussion on symbols of time, including time's arrow, see Joost A.M. Meerloo, 'The Time Sense in Psychiatry' from *The Voices of Time*, pp. 246–52.

[55] James Hillman, 'Notes on Opportunism'; in *Puer Papers*, p. 153.

[56] Dane Rudhyar, *The Astrology of Personality*, Servire/ Wassenaaar (Netherlands: 1936), p. 52.

[57] Anyone who has a pet knows they have an internal clock. My dog Winnie knew when I was due home, when it was time to go out before bedtime and rambunctiously knew when it was mealtime. This is a pet's circadian rhythms and not necessarily an awareness of time as we know it.

[58] For instance, a synchronistic phenomenon is not bound by the mundane but is psychic in nature. Synchronicity is four-dimensional, engaging in the world of psyche that defies reason.

[59] Alfred, Lord Tennyson, 'Tithonus', The Poetry Foundation, https://www.poetryfoundation.org/poems/45389/tithonus [accessed 15 January 2019].

[60] Homer, *The Iliad of Homer*, translated by Richmond Lattimore, The University of Chicago Press (Chicago: 1961), Book 11: 1–2. The same lines are repeated in Homer's *The*

Odyssey, translated by Richmond Lattimore, Harper Perennial (New York: 1991), Book 5, pp. 1–2.

[61] See Ginette Paris, *Pagan Grace*, Spring (Woodstock: 1995), p. 121.

[62] 'The Homeric Hymn to Hermes', *The Homeric Hymns*, translated by Michael Crudden, Oxford University Press (Oxford: 2001), lines 429–30, p. 58.

[63] Edward S. Casey, *Spirit and Soul Essays in Philosophical Psychology*, p. 157.

[64] The underlying theme of Geoffrey Cornelius's *The Moment of Astrology* amplifies and addresses this essential question.

[65] C. G. Jung, *The Visions Seminars, Book One*, Spring (Zurich: 1976), p. 44.

[66] *Astronomy or Astrology*, as Plutarch called it, as well as Hesiod's *Works and Days* were early Greek epics that related the constellations to timing. See *Hesiod Homeric Hymns Homerica*, translated by Hugh G. Evelyn-White, The Loeb Classical Library, Harvard University Press (Cambridge: 2002), p. xix.

[67] Gregory Szanto, *Perfect Timing*, The Aquarian Press (Wellingborough, UK: 1989), p. 46.

[68] What is used as the time of the question is subject to debate, but medieval horary astrologer William Lilly suggested that the time of the horary chart is cast for when the astrologer is committed to the question – see William Lilly, *Christian Astrology*, Astrology Center of America (Bel Air, MD: 2004), p. 167. A modern scholar of horary astrology echoes a similar belief: 'To my mind it makes sense to cast it [the horary chart] for the time when you commit to the question and sit down to answer it.' See *The Book of the Nine Judges*, translated by B. Dykes, Cazimi Press (Minneapolis: 2001), p. 23. This confirms the necessity for the astrologer to not only be engaged in the question but to participate with it.

[69] *Dictionary of Etymology*, edited by Robert K. Barnhart, Harper Collins (New York: 1995), p. 154.

[70] See Geoffrey Cornelius, *The Moment of Astrology*, Chapters 6–8, for a valuable discussion on Katarche, and its astrological offshoots of horary and electional astrology.

[71] Synchronicity is another aspect of time that is important in any astrological discourse. This has already been widely explored and I would point to three outstanding astrological references for this: Michael Harding, *Hymns to Ancient Gods*, Penguin Arkana (London: 1992), pp. 23–41; Richard Tarnas, *Cosmos and Psyche*, Penguin (New York: 2006), p. 3 and pp. 50–60; and Maggie Hyde, *Jung and Astrology*, Aquarian (London: 1992). *Jung and Astrology* contains a skilful examination of synchronicity that includes Jung's experiment.

[72] Manoj Thulasidas, The Nature of Time, www. theunrealuniverse.com/2-nature-of-time [accessed 16 July 2013].

[73] Edward S. Casey, *Spirit and Soul Essays in Philosophical Psychology*, p. 273.

[74] Emily Dickinson, '"Hope" is the thing with feathers', The Poetry Foundation, https://www.poetryfoundation.org/ poems/42889/hope-is-the-thing-with-feathers-314 [accessed 16 January 2019].

[75] Leonard Shlain, *The Alphabet versus the Goddess*, Penguin (London: 1998), p. 20.

[76] See Robert Schmidt, 'The System of Hermes: A Report from Project Hindsight', *The Mountain Astrologer*, June/July 2004.

[77] The dates for Thales of Miletus, often referred to as the first philosopher, are 624–546 BCE. Aristotle's dates are 384–322 BCE. During this time there was enough evidence to suggest the rational and imaginative paradigms co-existed and created a cultural blossoming in architecture, medicine, theatre, art, etc. The rise

of rational thought seems to have fostered binary thinking and compromised imaginative and symbolic ways of being.

[78] George Kakoff and Mark Johnson, *Metaphors We Live By*, University of Chicago Press (Chicago: 1980), p. 186.

[79] Originally a clinic was a metaphor for being receptive to the divine – from the Greek *cline* or the 'couch' on which patients laid down in the temple of Asclepius. Two millennia later, Freud reclaimed the image in his psychotherapy work. See C.A. Meier, *Ancient Incubation and Modern Psychotherapy*, Northwestern University Press (Evanston, Il: 1967), p. 56.

[80] C.G. Jung, *Archetypes and the Collective Unconscious*, The Collected Works, Volume 9(1), translated by R.F.C. Hull, Routledge & Kegan Paul (London:1959), ¶267.

[81] See Dane Rudhyar, *The Astrology of Transformation*, pp. 24–45, for a valuable discussion on discerning signs and symbols in astrology and distinguishing information from meaning.

[82] Saturnian can also imply 'prosperous and happy' from the Roman myth of Saturn's rule over the Golden Age.

[83] John Keats in a letter to George and Thomas Keats, Hampstead 28 December 1817, from H. Buxton Forman (ed.), *The Complete Works of John Keats Volume IV*, Gowars & Gray (Glasgow: 1901), p. 50.

[84] James Hillman, *Suicide and the Soul*, p. 24.

[85] James Hillman, 'Oedipus Revisited', from *Oedipus Variations*, Spring (Dallas, TX: 1991), p. 98.

[86] C.G. Jung, *Alchemical Studies*, The Collected Works, Volume 13, translated by R.F.C. Hull, Routledge & Kegan Paul (London: 1967), ¶285.

[87] In Sanskrit, 'star' is Tara and her origins have been traced to the Mesopotamian goddesses Ishtar and Astarte. Our modern 'star' and 'Tara' are perhaps linked via the Persian *sitara*, the Greek *aster* and the Latin *stella*.

[88] See Michael Attyah Flower, *The Seer in Ancient Greece*, University of California (Berkley: 2008), p. 214.

[89] Aeschylus, *The Eumenides*, translated by Philip Vellacott, Penguin Books (London: 1959), pp. 4–9.

[90] Zeus named the small rocky outcrop Ortygia after the quail. However, the land mass was also known as Asteria, but its most common name in the classical period was Delos.

[91] Hesiod, *Theogony*, translated by Dorothea Wender, Penguin (London: 1973), lines 748–57.

[92] C.G. Jung, *Alchemical Studies*, The Collected Works, Volume 13, ¶285.

[93] Rainer Maria Rilke, 'The Night', Daily Poetry, https://dailypoetry.me/rilke/the-night/ [accessed 15 January 2019].

[94] See source notes on Astro-Databank: https://www.astro.com/astro-databank/Rilke,_Rainer_Maria [accessed 28 November 2018].

[95] Parmenides, *Proem*, Fragment 1, lines 8–11: https://en.wikisource.org/wiki/Fragments_of_Parmenides [accessed 13 December 2018].

[96] E.R. Dodds, *The Greeks and the Irrational*, University of California Press (Berkeley: 1951), p. 102. Dodds challenged the widely held notion of the time that the Greeks seemed to be immune from primal and magical ways of thinking.

[97] C.G. Jung, *Memories, Dreams, Reflections*, translated by Richard and Clara Winston, Pantheon Books (New York: 1973), p. 45, and C.G. Jung, *The Red Book, A Reader's Edition*, pp. 12–30.

[98] William McGuire, ed. *The Freud/Jung Letters*, translated by Ralph Manheim and R.F.C. Hull, Princeton University Press (Princeton: 1974), p. 427.

[99] C.G. Jung, *Memories, Dreams, Reflections*, p. 199.

[100] C.G. Jung, *The Red Book, A Reader's Edition*, p. 138.

[101] Carl Jung was a Leo! He was fond of saying he was born when the last rays of the setting sun lit the room, born at the gate between day and night.

[102] C.G. Jung, *Dream Analysis, Notes of the Seminar Given in 1928–1920*, edited by William C. McGuire, Routledge & Kegan Paul (London: 1984), November 1929, pp. 392–393.

[103] Gaia will mate with Ouranus to produce the Titans, the first generation of gods. Hyperion and Theia, the Titans associated with light, give birth to Helios the Sun, Selene the Moon and Eos the Dawn.

[104] See Jules Cashford, *Imagination as a Mode of Knowing*, Kingfisher Art Productions (Somerset, UK: 2015), pp. 9–10. Cashford writes insightfully about these two ways of knowing.

[105] James Hillman, *The Dream and the Underworld*, Harper & Row (New York: 1979), p. 34.

[106] For further amplification see Brian Clark, 'The Muses of Heaven', *The Astrological Journal*, January/February 2014, Volume 56, No. 1.

[107] James Hillman in *The Dream and the Underworld*, pp. 39–40, describes this process as food for the soul.

[108] William Blake, 'Auguries of Innocence', The Poetry Foundation, https://www.poetryfoundation.org/poems/43650/auguries-of-innocence [accessed 15 January 2019].

[109] William Blake, from a letter to Rev. Dr Trusler, dated 23 August 1799, *Blake: Complete Poetry and Prose*, edited by Geoffrey Keynes, Nonesuch Press (London: 1961), p. 835.

[110] C.G. Jung, *Structure and Dynamics of the Psyche*, The Collected Works, Volume 8, translated by R.F.C. Hull, Routledge & Kegan Paul (London: 1960), ¶244.

[111] D.W. Winnicott, *Playing and Reality*, Routledge Classics (New York: 2005).

[112] Laurence J. Peter, *Peter's Quotations: Ideas for Our Time*, Bantam Books (New York: 1979), p. 25.

[113] Sigmund Freud, 'Creative Writers and Daydreaming', published in 1908 from a talk the previous year, available at: http://www.kleal.com/AP12%20member%20area%20pd2%20 2013/Freud%20and%20Frye.pdf [accessed 22 June 2018].

[114] Astro-Databank lists the data as 'A': Louis Armstrong, 4 August 1901, 10 p.m., New Orleans, LA. See https://www.astro. com/astro-databank/Armstrong,_Louis [accessed 14 January 2019].

[115] Samuel Taylor Coleridge, 'Prefatory note to Kubla Khan', *The Creative Process*, edited by B. Ghiselin, University of California (Berkeley: 1954), pp. 83–4.

[116] Sigmund Freud, 'Creative Writers and Daydreaming'.

[117] Dane Rudhyar, *The Astrology of Transformation*, p.193.

[118] *The Letters of John Keats*, edited by H.E. Rollins, 2 volumes, Cambridge University Press (Cambridge: 1958), pp. 386–7. 'Camelion' is Middle English spelling of 'chameleon'.

[119] The 12th house is also cited in the context of creativity, being linked to the domain of artistry, the dreamtime and spirituality. It is an environment where imagination stirs and energy and imagery are aligned with creativity.

[120] For an exhaustive exploration of the *daimon* in astrology, see Dorian Greenbaum, *The Daimon in Hellenistic Astrology: Origins and Influence*, Brill (Leiden: 2016).

[121] For an insightful commentary on creativity, see Rosemary Gordon, *Dying and Creating: A Search for Meaning*, Karnac Books (London: 2000), Part III.

[122] R.J. Hallman, 'The Necessary and Sufficient Conditions of Creativity', *Journal of Humanistic Psychology*, (1963). 3 (1), pp. 14–27.

[123] Joyce McDougall, *The Many Faces of Eros*, W.W. Norton & Co. (New York: 1995), p. 56. McDougall identifies the highly productive nature of artists and inventors such as Mozart, Rubens, van Gogh, Euripides, Edison and Picasso.

[124] D.H. Lawrence, 'Healing' – see http://springsnowpublications.com/healing/ [accessed 13 January 2019].

[125] Eric J. Cassell, *The Healer's Art*, Penguin (London, 1978), p. 48.

[126] Approximate dates for these periods would be:
    Mycenaean period: Mid 2nd millennium BCE
    Homeric epic: 8th century BCE
    Late Archaic and early Classical period: 6th–5th century BCE.

[127] For evidence and discussion of the transmission of medical knowledge, see: Robert Arnott, 'Healing and Medicine in the Aegean Bronze Age', *Journal of the Royal Society of Medicine*, London, Volume 89, May, 1996; Walter Burkert, *Greek Religion*, translated by John Raffan, Basil Blackwell (London: 1985); Walter Addison Jayne, *The Healing Gods of Ancient Civilizations*,

University Books, Inc., 1962; and C. Kerenyi, *Asklepios: Archetypal Image of the Physician's Existence*, Thames and Hudson (London: 1960).

[128] Euripides, *Iphigenia at Aulis*, translated by W.S. Merwin and George E. Dimock, Jr., Oxford University Press (Oxford: 1978), p. 961.

[129] Jody Rubin Pinault, *Hippocratic Lives and Legends*, Brill (Leiden: 1992), p. 7. Other ancient sources, including Eratosthenes, Apollodorus and Pherecydes, also mention this lineage.

[130] Paracelsus, *Selected Writings*, translated by Norbert Guterman, edited by Jolande Jacobi, Routledge & Kegan Paul Ltd. (London, 1955).

[131] James Hillman, 'Puer Wounds and Ulysses' Scar'; in *Puer Papers*.

[132] James Hillman, *Suicide and the Soul*, p. 121.

[133] C.G. Jung, *Alchemical Studies*, The Collected Works, Volume 13, ¶54.

[134] I have found that astrological images of the 12th house (the cusp, planets in this house, the ruler of the house and aspects) are very helpful in imagining trans-generational repression that might lead to illness. As the 4th and 8th houses are ancestral storehouses, I have found these houses often reveal inherited pain and wounding.

[135] For instance, inner planets strongly aspected to Uranus might suggest that personal urges have become disassociated or fragmented due to early trauma, a lack of attachment, disengaged feeling, trans-generational dislocation, abandonment or severance from parental figures. Neptune's challenging aspects to inner planets suggest that unexplained and mystifying symptoms could underpin unacceptable feelings that find their outlet in

fantasy, idealized rather than authentic feelings or the sacrifice of individuality for the collective, being a result of the trans-generational renunciation of the self and its creative process. When dealing with demanding aspects to inner planets, Pluto's response may be denial and dismemberment. Beneath the symptoms may be family secrets and taboos, emotional control, repressed sexual fantasies or trans-generational abuse too shameful to reveal. Chiron's aspects to inner planets highlight wounds being symptomatic of inherited and experienced feelings of marginalization, disenfranchisement and displacement trauma.

[136] From a private conversation with psychotherapist Dr Peter O'Connor.

[137] Ella Wheeler Wilcox, 'To an Astrologer'; in *Custer and Other Poems*, W.B. Conkey Company (Chicago: 1896).

[138] Fate has been identified and personified in different ways, such as Heimarmene, Tyche, Necessity, Nemesis, Fortune and Providence.

[139] C.G. Jung, *Psychology and Alchemy*, The Collected Works, Volume 12, translated by R.F.C. Hull, Routledge & Kegan Paul (London: 1953), n. 16, p. 30.

[140] Ralph Waldo Emerson, *The Complete Works of Ralph Waldo Emerson: Poems Volume 9*. For a digital edition of the complete works of Ralph Waldo Emerson, see https://quod.lib.umich.edu/e/emerson/4957107.0009.001/1:10.5?rgn=div2;view=fulltext [accessed 8 December 2018]

[141] *The Barnhart Concise Dictionary of Etymology*, edited by Robert K. Barnhart, p. 200.

[142] Hesiod, *Theogony*, line 218 says: 'She [Night] bore the Destinies and the ruthless Fates.'

[143] Hesiod, *Theogony*, lines 211–30. Often associated with Death, the Keres were female death-spirits. Sometimes the term is used in the sense of fate or having a choice.

[144] Hesiod, *Theogony*, lines 902–6.

[145] Herodotus, *The Histories*, from Robert B. Strassler (ed.), *The Landmark Herodotus*, translated by Andrea L. Purvis, Quercus (London: 2007), 1.91. Herodotus prefaces this with the Pythia saying 'Fated destiny is impossible to avoid even for a god.' Aeschylus, *Prometheus Bound*, translated by Philip Vellacott, Penguin (London: 1961), line 518.

[146] E.R. Dodds, *The Greeks and the Irrational*, p. 20, endnote 21.

[147] Heimarmene was amplified by the Stoics into a form of astral fate. See Robert Hand, 'Fate and Astrology, Some Ancient Insights', *The Mountain Astrologer*, February/March 2006 and Liz Greene, *Jung's Studies in Astrology*, Routledge (London: 2018), pp. 117–50.

[148] C.G. Jung, *Symbols of Transformation*, The Collected Works, Volume 5, translated by R.F.C. Hull, Routledge & Kegan Paul (London: 1956), ¶102 and p. 67 footnote 51.

[149] Ibid, ¶644.

[150] Erich Neumann, *The Great Mother*, Princeton University Press (Princeton, NJ: 1955), p. 230.

[151] Pausanias, *Guide to Greece*, Volume 2, translated by Peter Levi, Penguin Books (London: 1979), p. 242; Book 5: 15.5.

[152] *The Odyssey*, translated by Richmond Lattimore, Book 1, pp. 32–4.

[153] Robert Eisner, *The Road to Daulis: Psychoanalysis, Psychology, and Classical Mythology*, Syracuse University Press (Syracuse: 1987), p. 12.

[154] Liz Greene, *The Astrology of Fate*, George Allen & Unwin (London: 1984), p. 6.

[155] Sigmund Freud, 'Leonardo Da Vinci and a Memory of His Childhood' from *Standard Edition*, Volume XI, translated by James Strachey, The Hogarth Press (London: 1957), p. 125.

[156] Aeschylus, *Prometheus Bound*, p. 35, lines 511–6.

[157] This is told in the last book of the Republic I; see *The Essential Plato*, translated by Benjamin Jowett, The Softback Preview, 1999, p. 410–1.

[158] Marsilio Ficino, *The Letters of Marsilio Ficino*, translated by the Language Department of the School of Economic Science, Fellowship of the School of Economic Science (London: 1975), p. 95.

[159] Ibid.

[160] Ibid.

[161] James Hillman, *The Force of Character*, Random House (Sydney: 1999), p. 198.

[162] C.G. Jung, *The Symbolic Life*, The Collected Works, Volume 18, translated by R.F.C. Hull, Routledge & Kegan Paul (London: 1976), ¶523.

[163] Liz Greene, *The Astrology of Fate*, pp. 25–6.

[164] C.G. Jung, *Structure and Dynamics of the Psyche*, The Collected Works, Volume 8, ¶270 & ¶325.

[165] Ibid, p. 133, footnotes 7.

[166] C.G. Jung, *Two Essays on Analytical Psychology*, The Collected Works, Volume 7, translated by R.F.C. Hull, Routledge & Kegan Paul (London: 1953), ¶183.

[167] James Hillman, *The Soul's Code*, p. 6.

[168] Ibid, p. 8.

[169] C.G. Jung, *Psychology and Religion: West and East*, The Collected Works, Volume 11, translated by R.F.C. Hull, Routledge & Kegan Paul (London: 1958), ¶143.

[170] I borrow this phrase from Tom Moore; see Thomas Moore, *A Religion of One's Own*, Gotham Books (New York, NY: 2014). In his life's work Tom Moore has written profoundly about soul through his insightful books such as *Care of the Soul*, *Soul Mates* and *The Dark Night of the Soul*.

[171] James Shirley, 'Death the Leveller', The Poem Hunter, https://www.poemhunter.com/best-poems/james-shirley/death-the-leveller/ [accessed 19 January 2019].

[172] Simone de Beauvoir, *A Very Easy Death*, translated from the French by Patrick O'Brian, Pantheon Books (New York: 1965); David Rieff, *Swimming in a Sea of Death, A Son's Memoir*, Melbourne University Press (Melbourne: 2008). Both Simone de Beauvoir and Susan Sontag were philosophical writers, perhaps best known for their feminist literature and thinking. Both are buried in Montparnasse Cemetery in Paris.

[173] James Hillman explored the relationship with soul and death in many of his writings. In *Revisioning Psychology*, p. x, he said: 'The significance that soul makes possible in relationships or religious concerns derives from its special *relation with death*.'

[174] Helen gave me permission to tell her story; we had discussed this before she died. I also used her genogram in our astrological program on family as an example while she was alive, but changed the name and some details. Her genogram example

is also used in my book *The Family Legacy*, Astro*Synthesis (Stanley, Australia: 2016), using the name Alice. As a very private person in life, in death she felt her story was no longer hers.

[175] Helen's chart details are:
  First appointment: 10 November 1986, 12.30 p.m., Kew, Victoria, Australia
  First breath, natal chart: 3 September 1942, 1.52 a.m., Melbourne, Victoria, Australia
  Last breath, death chart: 10 December 2013, 5.45 a.m., Prahran, Victoria, Australia
  Kew and Prahran are inner suburbs of Melbourne.

[176] As I was writing this (November 2017), the state government of Victoria, Australia, passed legislation to allow assisted suicide in the state.

[177] William Wordsworth, *Ode on Intimations of Immortality from Recollections of Early Childhood.*

[178] Early psychoanalysis also drew the parallel between mythic accounts and childhood experiences. Freud suggested myths were 'the age-long dreams of young humanity', while Jung argued that 'myth is certainly not an infantile phantasm, but one of the most important prerequisites of primitive life.' Karl Abraham suggested myth as a 'fragment of the superseded infantile psychic life of the race' – see C.G. Jung, *Symbols of Transformation*, The Collected Works, Volume 5, ¶28–9. In *Introduction to a Science of Mythology* Carl Jung and Carl Kerenyi focused on the archetype of the child – see C.G. Jung and C. Kerenyi, *Introduction to a Science of Mythology*, translated by R.F.C. Hull, Routledge & Kegan Paul (London: 1951), pp.10–11

[179] In anatomy this closure is akin to the fontanelles on a baby's head closing up between 18–24 months, near the first Mars Return.

[180] James Hillman (ed.), *Facing the Gods*, Spring Publications, University of Dallas (Dallas: 1980), p. iv.

[181] C.G. Jung, *Archetypes and the Collective Unconscious*, The Collected Works, Volume 9(1), ¶8.

[182] Mircea Eliade, 'Time and Eternity in Indian Thought', in: *Man and Time*, edited by Joseph Campbell, Princeton University Press (Princeton: 1983), p. 174.

[183] I use the Greek *mythos* as a reminder of the wider dimensions of myth. By definition *mythos* suggests a story, generally delivered orally, therefore placing us in a time before philosophy and writing, and the split of logos into debate and logic and *mythos* into poetry and fiction. Inherent in the word is a recurrent narrative, theme or plot which is valuable in amplifying archetypal patterns as well as astrological ones.

[184] C.G. Jung, *Symbols of Transformation*, The Collected Works, Volume 5, ¶466.

[185] C. G. Jung, *Structure and Dynamics of the Psyche*, The Collected Works, Volume 8, ¶325.

[186] Otto Rank used this expression in *The Birth of the Hero* – see C. G. Jung, *Symbols of Transformation*, The Collected Works, Volume 5, ¶28.

[187] We might say dis-mythed.

[188] Dr Devdutt Pattanaik, *A Handbook of Hindu Mythology*, Penguin Books (India: 2006), p. xiii.

[189] C.G. Jung, *Archetypes and the Collective Unconscious*, The Collected Works, Volume 9i, ¶7.

[190] Sigmund Freud, *The Interpretation of Dreams*, translated by Dr. A.A. Brill, The Modern Library (New York: 1994), pp. 159–61.

[191] For a detailed account see Brian Clark, Freud and Oedipus https://www.astrosynthesis.com.au/wp-content/uploads/2017/11/freud-oedipus-myth-brian-clark.pdf [accessed 16 January 2019].

[192] Sophocles's drama *Oedipus the King* was produced around 429 BCE.

[193] Christine Downing, *Psyche's Sisters*, Continuum Publishing Company (New York: 1990).

[194] For an insightful differentiation between astrological symbolism and myth, see Liz Greene, *The Astrology of Fate*, pp. 172–5.

[195] The Greek Classical period was between the Archaic and Hellenistic periods, from approximately 479–323 BCE including the flourishing golden 5th century in Athens.

[196] See Nicholas Campion, *The Dawn of Astrology, A Cultural History of Western Astrology*, Continuum (London: 2008), pp. 173–84.

[197] See Brian Clark, *The Zodiacal Imagination*, Astro*Synthesis (Melbourne: 2000), available at https://www.astrosynthesis.com.au/astrology-e-booklets/

[198] The word comes from the roots *zoe* (life) and *diaklos* (wheel). The zodiac as the wheel of life is an ancient symbol for the eternal round, the circle of life.

[199] Robert Schmidt, 'Translator's Preface' from Vettius Valens, *The Anthology: Book I*, Project Hindsight's Greek Track IV, Golden Hind Press (Berkeley Springs, WV: 1993), pp. vvi –xvii.

[200] See Thomas Moore, *The Planets Within*, Lindisfarrne Press (Great Barrington, ME: 1990).

[201] C. G. Jung, *Psychology and Religion: West and East*, The Collected Works, Volume 11, ¶242.

[202] Mark Morford and Robert Lenardon, *Classical Mythology*, 5th Edition, Longman (White Plains: 1995), p. 562.

[203] James Hillman, *The Dream and the Underworld*, p. 23.

[204] See Dane Rudhyar, *From Humanistic to Transpersonal Astrology*, The Seed Centre (Palo Alto: 1975) and *The Astrology of Transformation*, Quest.

[205] Dane Rudhyar, *The Astrology of Transformation*, Quest, p. xiii.

[206] Liz Greene's book Saturn, *A New Look at an Old Devil* was released in 1976. Her next book, *Relating*, was released the following year. Both volumes amplified myth and psychological concepts.

[207] Demetra George used the myths of the four Olympian goddesses to intensify the meaning of the first asteroids that were discovered – see Demetra George, *Asteroid Goddesses*, ACS Publications, Inc. (San Diego: 1986). Her work not only brought the asteroids into astrological consciousness but encouraged others to become literate with myths that underpinned astrological images.

The discovery and naming of the first four asteroids not only brought these Olympian goddesses into astrological view but also paralleled Hesiod's creation myth. After Metis gives Cronus (Saturn) the emetic, his first five children who were swallowed are released from his belly: Hestia (Vesta), Demeter (Ceres), Hera (Juno), Poseidon (Neptune) and Hades (Pluto). None of these deities was named as a planet by the ancients. Zeus (Jupiter) was the only sibling not swallowed, and was named as one of the five traditional planets. Ceres, Juno and Vesta were discovered and named in the first decade of the 19th century, then Neptune was discovered in 1846 and Pluto in 1930. After the discovery (or release) of the asteroids, the brothers Neptune and Pluto were discovered, thereby reinstating all six children of Cronus to the starry heavens. During the time of the asteroids' discovery, astrology was in a hiatus. While traditional astrology would be altered by these discoveries, it would take another century and a half before they would emerge in their own right.

[208] Jules Cashford, *Symbolism as the Language of the Imagination*, Kingfisher Art Productions (Somerset: 2015), p. 7.

[209] In the latter years of his vocation, James Hillman wrote *The Soul's Code*, which echoed astrological thinking. His acorn theory could be likened to the horoscope; in fact it was an image previously proposed by astrologers, including Dane Rudhyar.

[210] 'The Road Not Taken' by Robert Frost from *The Poetry of Robert Frost*, Holt, Rinehart and Winston (New York: 1969), p. 105.

[211] For a thorough astrological examination of vocation, see Brian Clark, *Vocation, the Astrology of Career, Creativity and Calling*, Astro*Synthesis (Stanley, Australia: 2016).

[212] Quotes are from C.G. Jung, *Development of Personality*, The Collected Works, Volume 17, translated by R.F.C. Hull, Routledge & Kegan Paul (London: 1954), ¶ 299–305.

[213] Thomas Moore, *A Life at Work*, Broadway Books (New York: 2008), p. 132.

[214] Ibid, p.132.

[215] James Hillman, *The Essential James Hillman A Blue Fire*, edited by Thomas Moore, Routledge (London: 1990), p. 172.

[216] Thomas Moore, *Care of the Soul*, Harper Perennial (New York: 1992), p.182.

[217] 'Desert Places' by Robert Frost from *The Poetry of Robert Frost*, p. 296.

[218] Max Jammer, 'The Concept of Space in Antiquity' in: *Problems of Space and Time*, edited by J.J.C. Smart, Macmillan Publishing (New York: 1976).

[219] Robert Sardello, *Facing the World with Soul*, Harper Collins (New York: 1994), p. 35.

[220] Clerestory, or clear storey, from which the term originates, is the upper section of a temple, basilica or church that contains a series of windows that flood it with light.

[221] Gaston Bachelard, *The Poetics of Space*, translated by Maria Jolas, Beacon Press (Boston: 1969), p. 5: 'All really inhabited space bears the essence of the notion of home.'

[222] For instance, the Moon in the 1st house may suggest that the emotional nature is near the surface but it also suggests a deeper attachment to one's surroundings and how the body and personality respond when the soul's needs are unmet. Pluto in the 2nd might suggest a fear of loss of money, yet it also implies deeper values and transforming talents. Saturn in the 3rd may characterize an older and controlling sibling; however, it also invites a respect for solitude and being alone. Uranus in the 4th might be your parent's divorce or family schisms, yet it is also signifies the soul task of finding one's unique sense of self in the experience of kinship and familiarity. Planets in the houses are archetypal resonances on many levels with many forms of expression.

[223] Edward S. Casey, *Spirit and Soul*, p. 322.

[224] From my experience I have often seen this pattern in connection with Chiron and/or Uranus in difficult aspect to the Moon or in the 4th or 12th houses. I have also witnessed 12th house planets and/or planets near the Ascendant synchronizing with traumatic relocations. When there are difficult aspects to the inner planets, especially the Moon, I am often alert to themes of dislocation.

[225] See Jim Lewis with Kenneth Irving, *The Psychology of Astro*Carto*Graphy*, Penguin (London: 1997).

[226] Lewis Carroll, *Alice's Adventures in Wonderland* from *The Annotated Alice*, Bramhall House (New York), p. 162.

[227] For a thorough biography and commentary on Alan Leo see *A Brief Biography of Alan Leo* by Kim Farnell on http://www. skyscript.co.uk/Alan_Leo.html [accessed 5 April 2019].

[228] James Hillman in *The Dream and the Underworld*, p. 96: 'The more I dream of my mother and father, brother and sister, son and daughter, the less these actual persons are as I perceive them in my naïve and literal naturalism and the more they become psychic inhabitants of the underworld. As they rise into the vision of my nights and I mull and digest their comings and goings, the family becomes *familaris*, internal accomplishments, no longer quite the literal people I engage with daily.'

[229] C.G. Jung is quoted in *The Way of the Dream*, Windrose Films (Toronto, 1988), p. 3.

[230] Thomas Moore succinctly states this idea: 'My dream is an intimation of my mystery, not the solution to my problems.' See Thomas Moore, *The Re-enchantment of Everyday Life*, Harper Collins (New York: 1996), p. 175.

[231] Hours of the day represent the Sun's approximate movement through the houses, which, on average, is the same at the equator. As we move north or south of the equator this timing is only approximate. Seasons also affect this as the Sun sets later in the summer than the winter. Astrology offers us a way of thinking about the archetypal journey of the Sun through the houses below the horizon and what dream images may arise as its passes through this area.

[232] In Greek mythology, the Hesperides were the guardians of the tree of the golden apples that Gaia gave to Hera on her wedding day. They were known as the daughters of the evening

or the nymphs of the West, aligned with the golden light of the setting sun.

[233] For instance, I have noted that the Vertex, often equated with fate or unconscious compulsion, is highlighted in a dream chart, as is the Lot of Fortune or other lots. It is as if the dream chart articulates what is not as coherent or communicable during the day.

[234] See Mary Symes, *Grief and Dreams*, Rene Gordon (Melbourne: 1987), available at maryjsymes@yahoo.com.au/. Dreamwork is Mary Symes' lifeblood. Called to her vocation through a personal tragedy, Mary has worked with dreams for over 37 years, and for much of this time in tandem with the astrological horoscope and the dream chart. Mary's weekly astrological dream group was an integral part of the Astro*Synthesis *Diploma in Applied Astrology* program.

[235] William Wordsworth, 'The Stars are Mansions Built by Nature's Hand', The Poem Hunter, https://www.poemhunter.com/best-poems/william-wordsworth/the-stars-are-mansions-built-by-nature-s-hand/ [accessed 20 January 2019].

[236] These suggestions have been taken from Peter O'Connor's book *Dreams and the Search for Meaning*, Methuen, (Melbourne: 1986), pp. 227–31. Dr O'Connor is a practitioner whose life's work has been focused on working with dreams individually and in groups; therefore, his book is highly recommended.

[237] Dane Rudhyar, *Astrology and the Modern Psyche*, CRCS Publications (Vancouver, WA: 1976), p. 155.

[238] Some traditional astrologers do not use the outer planets as they are not part of the tradition of astrology. Uranus was discovered in 1784 during astrology's hiatus while Neptune was discovered in 1846 as spirituality and imagination began to stir again in the collective.

Astro*Synthesis

Astro*Synthesis was founded in Melbourne in 1986 as an astrological education programme. Since that time Astro*Synthesis has consistently offered an in-depth training programme into the application of astrology from a psychological perspective. The foundation of the course has been constructed to utilize astrology as a tool for greater awareness of the self, others and the world at large.

From 1986 to 2010, Astro*Synthesis offered its dynamic four-year teaching program in the classroom. Astro*Synthesis now offers the complete program of 12 modules through distance learning.

For a detailed syllabus or more information on Astro*Synthesis E-Workbooks, E- Booklets or reports please visit our website:

www.astrosynthesis.com.au